Technology Infrastructure

Technology infrastructure supports the design, deployment and use of both individual technology-based components and the systems of such components that form the knowledge-based economy. As such, it plays a central role in the innovation process and in the promotion of the diffusion of technologies. Thus, it is an important element contributing to the operation of innovation systems and innovation performance in any modern economy.

Technology infrastructure, either in the narrow or broad sense, is not well understood as an element of a sector's technology platform or of a national innovation system. Similarly misunderstood are the processes by which such infrastructure is embodied in standards or diffused through various institutional frameworks. In fact, because of the public and quasi-public good nature of technology infrastructure, firms as well as public-sector agencies under invest in it, thus inhibiting long-term technological advancement and economic growth.

This book brings together a collection of papers from eminent scholars on all of the various dimensions of technology infrastructure mentioned above. To our knowledge, it is the first such collection of papers and we expect this scholarship to become the foundation for future research in this area.

This book was published as a special issue of *Economics of Innovation and New Technology*.

Cristiano Antonelli is Professor of Economics at the University of Torino (Italy) and managing editor of *Economics of Innovation and New Technology*.

Albert N. Link is Professor of Economics at the University of North Carolina, Greensboro, USA.

Stan Metcalfe is Emeritus Professor at University of Manchester, Visiting Professor at the Curtin University of Technology and University of Queensland, and Visiting Fellow in the Centre for Business Research at Cambridge University.

Technology Infrastructure

Edited by Cristiano Antonelli, Albert N. Link
and Stan Metcalfe

Routledge
Taylor & Francis Group
LONDON AND NEW YORK

First published 2009 by Routledge
2 Park Square, Milton Park, Abingdon, Oxon, OX14 4RN

Simultaneously published in the USA and Canada
by Routledge
270 Madison Avenue, New York, NY 10016

Routledge is an imprint of the Taylor & Francis Group, an informa business

Transferred to Digital Printing 2010

© 2009 Edited by Cristiano Antonelli, Albert N. Link and Stan Metcalfe

Typeset in Times by Value Chain, India

British Library Cataloguing in Publication Data
A catalogue record for this book is available from the British Library

ISBN10: 0-415-47266-0
ISBN13: 978-0-415-47266-1

Contents

TECHNOLOGY INFRASTRUCTURE: INTRODUCTION

CRISTIANO ANTONELLI,[a] ALBERT N. LINK[b] and STAN METCALFE[c]

[a] Department of Economics, University of Torino, Italy; [b] Department of Economics, University of North Carolina at Greensboro, USA; [c] Manchester Institute of Innovation Research, University of Manchester, UK

Technology infrastructure supports the design, deployment and use of both individual technology-based components and the systems of such components that form the knowledge-based economy. As such, it plays a central role in the innovation process and in the promotion of the diffusion of technologies. Thus, it is an important element contributing to the formation and operation of innovation systems and innovation performance in any modern economy. It is a characteristic of the innovation process in such economies that it depends not only upon the internal innovative efforts of firms but additionally on their links with a wider framework of innovation supporting activities, that is to say, as Alfred Marshall once expressed it, it depends on the internal and the external organization of the firm. It is to the formation of the external organization of innovation processes that technology infrastructure makes its vital contribution.

Technology infrastructures have many dimensions. They can be classified first, and typically, by the set of physical and virtual tools, methods, and data that enable all three stages of technology-based economic activity: the conduct research and development R&D, the control of production processes to achieve target quality and yield, and the consummation of market place transactions at minimum time and cost. The underlying 'infratechnologies' – including measurement and test methods, process and quality control techniques, evaluated scientific and engineering data, and the technical dimensions of product interfaces – are ubiquitous in the typical technology-based industry. The collective economic benefits of such infrastructure are therefore considerable, as are the consequences of not having it in place at critical points in a technology's life cycle.

Characterization of technology infrastructure can also include organizational or institutional forms that leverage knowledge creation and knowledge flows in technology developers and users, including research/science parks, incubators, university research centers, and focused public–private partnerships. The efficiency of these institutions in providing infratechnologies and related infrastructure services are essential to an efficiently functioning national innovation 'ecology' and to the capacity of that ecology to form and reform innovation systems around innovation problems.

Technology infrastructure, either in the narrow or broad sense, is not well understood as an element of a sector's technology platform or of a national innovation system. Similarly misunderstood are the processes by which such infrastructure is embodied in standards or diffused through various institutional frameworks. In fact, because of the public and quasi-public good nature of technology infrastructure, firms as well as public-sector agencies underinvest in it, thus inhibiting long-term technological advancement and economic growth.

This book brings together a collection of papers from eminent scholars on all of the various dimensions of technology infrastructure mentioned above. To our knowledge, it is the first such collection of papers and we expect this scholarship to become the foundation for future research in this area.

Greg Tassey argues that designing and managing an economy's technology infrastructure requires both accurate economic models and data to drive them. Previous models treat technology as a homogeneous entity, thereby precluding assessing investment barriers affecting infrastructure elements. The model he presents overcomes this deficiency by disaggregating the knowledge production function into key elements of the typical industrial technology based on the distinctly different investment incentives associated with each element. Without such a model, the economist's and the policy analyst's ability to assess important market failures associated with investment in the major technology elements, including those with infrastructure (i.e., public-good) characteristics, is compromised. Unfortunately, even with the correct knowledge production function, the required data are difficult to collect. This forces government agencies, which fund a majority of technology infrastructure research, to use second-best approaches for economic and policy analyses. The second half of his paper therefore presents an analytical framework that can be driven by more accessible data and provide reasonable impact assessments until better data become available.

Adams, Marcu, and Wang define public technology infrastructure to mean public resources that bring new R&D into existence. Examples are public research that yields knowledge spillovers and government contracts that broker new research. Using this definition they explore the role of public infrastructure on cooperative R&D, especially R&D sourcing and research joint ventures (RJVs). Their findings strongly suggest that public infrastructure promotes cooperative R&D. The author's evidence comes from two different sources. First, they study the role of federal laboratories in R&D sourcing by private laboratories as a whole. Even controlling for simultaneity bias they find that private sourcing increases as a result of federal laboratories. Second, they examine patents that arise from individual projects within private laboratories. These are RJVs sponsored by the Advanced Technology Program (ATP). They find that R&D subsidies as well as difficulty and novelty increase patents produced by the RJVs. Oversight by ATP has no direct effect, but an indirect governance effect seems to exist, since firms value oversight more in the case of more difficult and novel projects, which produce more patents.

O'Connor and Rowe present a quantitative case analysis of one US ATP public–private partnership that advanced the technology infrastructure of molecular diagnostics, resulting in substantial downstream economic and public health benefits. Biotechnology R&D, they argue, is generally characterized by technologies requiring substantial investments in time, money, and energy to develop and sustain concepts through long incubation times. Public sponsorship made possible a partnership between two firms that would have not otherwise collaborated. Affymetrix and Molecular Dynamics accelerated the development of DNA analysis technologies and induced innovation at competitor firms. The research conducted by these firms accelerated the completion of the human genome project and improved both the quality and speed with which the biotechnology industry and medical science could acquire genetic information. The authors rely on counterfactual scenarios to quantify net public benefits by estimating the hypothetical costs of achieving the same outcomes as using the processes and technologies the ATP-cofunded innovations leveraged.

Cassi, Corrocher, Malerba, and Vonortas examine the role of research network infrastructure in fostering the dissemination of innovation-related knowledge. They emphasize the structure of collaborative networks and of knowledge transfer between research, innovation and deployment activities in the field of information and communication technology (ICT) for the European Union as a whole, and for several European regions. Research networks complement diffusion networks by providing additional links and by increasing the number of organizations involved in sharing and exchanging knowledge. Two types of actors, they argue, are key players in these networks: hubs and gatekeepers. Hubs maintain the bulk of ties in the networks, also helping the smaller and more isolated members remain connected. Gatekeepers bridge research and diffusion networks. Such organizations naturally offer greater policy leverage in establishing a European knowledge infrastructure. Moreover, they conclude, strengthening inter-network connectivity among research and diffusion activities (deployment) would raise the effectiveness of European research in terms of accelerating innovation.

Leech and Scott provide preliminary estimates of the productivity impact of intelligent machine technology (IMT) and the rate of return to IMT R&D over the next two decades. They argue that IMT is, in part, enabling technology in that it will allow new machine-intensive and labor-saving production techniques across a wide range of industries; and it is, in part, infrastructure technology in that it ideally will conform to standards ensuring it will provide access across industries to human performance-like, machine-based, generic technology that is necessary for the development of innovative labor-saving processes. Their paper adapts the economists' traditional, residual productivity growth model to enable the use of industrial experts' forecasts of a few key parameters of the model to form the estimates of productivity growth and rate of return. Respondents – from a sample of firms operating in IMT development and applications in the automotive, aerospace, and capital construction industries – anticipate that IMT will generate substantial productivity growth over the next two decades, and the estimated social rates of return to IMT R&D are substantial.

Layson, Leyden, and Neufeld offer a theoretical model to explore the determinants of the optimum size of a private research/science park and the effect of university affiliation on that optimum size. Parks provide a venue for research firms and organizations to operate in close proximity, thus enabling easier communication among professionals in different organizations, enhancing the research productivity of all of them. Parks also enable communities to leverage economic development through technology-based investments, and they facilitate advancement through the stages of technology-based economic activity by reducing relevant market transactions especially with respect to technical labor. In their model, parks are assumed to operate as cooperatives where costs are equally shared among the member firms, and optimality occurs when the firms' average net benefits are maximized. To achieve this, existing members of a park will limit the park's size, denying entry to firms who wish to join and are willing to share the costs. University affiliation may either increase or decrease the optimum size of a park.

Consoli and Patrucco view innovation as a collective process that entails the coordination of distributed knowledge across diverse organizations. Technology infrastructures, within their framework, provide innovation systems with governance mechanisms to create and sustain complementarities across otherwise dispersed competences. Innovation platforms are discussed as a specific case of technology infrastructure. Operating strategically at the interface between the public and the private sectors, platforms enable capacity- and capability-building for individuals, teams and organizations. Illustrative evidence on innovation platforms in the United Kingdom and Italy confirms the importance of institutional strategies to stimulate variety and ensure coordination in the context of collective innovation processes.

Siegel, Wright, Chapple, and Lockett examine an institutional technology infrastructure, namely university technology transfer offices (henceforth, TTOs). TTOs play a critical role in the diffusion of innovation and the development of new technology infrastructure. Studies of the relative efficiency of TTOs have been based on licensing output measures and data from a single country. In contrast, the authors present the first cross-country comparison of the relative performance of TTOs, based on stochastic multiple output distance functions. The additional dimension of output considered is the university's propensity to generate start-up companies, based on technologies developed at these institutions. They find that US universities are more efficient than UK universities and that the production process is characterized by either decreasing or constant returns to scale. Universities with a medical school and an incubator are closer to the frontier.

Auerswald and Kulkarni utilize a novel approach to measuring innovation in order to identify emergent technology clusters. They illustrate their approach by using US patent counts to compare established technology regions within the country with emerging ones and to describe how technologies migrate as they develop and mature over time.

Finally, Bozeman, Hardin, and Link provide the first empirical information about barriers related to the diffusion of nanotechnology – a general purpose technology and a key element of technology infrastructure that is the foundation to the design, development, deployment, and use of other technologies and technology-based products and processes that are or could be central to the innovation process. Their empirical analysis is based on the findings from a state-wide survey of companies in North Carolina, USA. The primary diffusion barrier is lack of access to early-stage capital, and the extent of this barrier is greater when the company contributes to the value chain for nanotechnology through R&D as opposed to through products or services. Another barrier is lack of access to university equipment and facilities, a problem greater in companies involved in nanotechnology research. From a policy perspective, their analysis suggests that state governments could act as venture capitalists to overcome market failure in the capital market, and that states could provide incentives to universities through public/private centers of excellence for sharing capital equipment and facilities with nanotechnology companies.

From this rich set of findings, we may expect new studies of technology infrastructure to be developed especially ones engaging in international comparative work and the particular problems of creating and sustaining technology structures in developing economies. More work is needed too on the conceptual foundations of technology infrastructures in relation to the formation of innovation systems and in relation to the way they shape the emergence of particular sequences of innovations. What we have before us is surely a major step along this road.

MODELING AND MEASURING THE ECONOMIC ROLES OF TECHNOLOGY INFRASTRUCTURE

GREGORY TASSEY

National Institute of Standards and Technology, Gaithersburg, MD, USA

The first part of this paper presents a disaggregated or 'multi-element' model of technological change. Such a model allows examination of the roles and impacts of the major elements of technology, each of which is distinguished by a different degree and type of public-good content. This distinction implies unique investment behavior with respect to each element with consequent public-policy implications. The second part draws upon the considerable experience of the US National Institute of Standards and Technology in designing and conducting practical approaches to estimate the economic benefits from public and private investment in these quasi-public-good technology elements.

1 DISAGGREGATING THE KNOWLEDGE PRODUCTION FUNCTION

The typical industrial technology is composed of three elements: the generic technology base (also, technology platform); supporting infratechnologies; and proprietary market applications (innovations and subsequent improvements). The first two have public-good content and there-fore, embody infrastructure characteristics. These critical quasi-public technology goods are supplied by a combination of firm-specific assets and sources external to the innovating unit of the firm, such as central corporate research labs, government labs, and increasingly, univer-sities. The fundamental relationships among these elements require a technology production function that captures the interactive nature of the two quasi-public-good elements with each other and with private-sector investments in the third element, proprietary technologies. Most important, each element responds to different sets of investment incentives (Tassey, 2005a).

The failure to disaggregate the technology variable based on the distinctly different char-acter of each element and its associated unique investment incentives has limited economists' ability to explain R&D investment behavior and the subsequent relationships with economic growth. Both macroeconomic and microeconomic growth models have made technology an endogenous explanatory variable. However, the vast majority of this literature has treated technology and the process that creates it, R&D, as homogeneous entities. Only a few efforts have attempted even a partial disaggregation, and those have been limited to separating sci-entific research from technology research. In other words, the *technology* variable remains aggregated.

This failure has also inhibited government technology investment policies by prohibiting assessments of the distinctly different incentives associated with each of these three elements. This policy analysis problem is becoming more severe for several reasons: (1) corporate laboratories have reduced their share of national spending on the quasi-public elements, in particular, early-phase research on new, radical technologies; (2) in many countries, such as the USA, government spending on such research has been erratic and skewed toward a few technologies tied to specific social objectives; and (3) universities in many economies are assuming a larger role in such early-phase technology research, with implications for intellectual property (IP) and research portfolio management.

1.1   The Three Elements of Industrial Technology

The enabling role of generic technologies for the development of market applications (inno-vations) has been discussed qualitatively (Link and Tassey, 1987; Nelson, 1992; Tassey, 1997, 2007).[1] Dosi (1982, 1988) defines a 'technology paradigm' as a 'pattern' of solutions to selected techno-economic problems based on highly selected principles derived from the nat-ural sciences. Such 'highly selected principles' form a generic technology base from which market applications are drawn. A generic technology provides in essence a 'proof of concept' that reduces technical risk sufficiently to enable applied R&D investments to be rationalized.[2]

Infratechnologies are the other quasi-public technology element. They include research tools (measurement and test methods), scientific and engineering data, the technical basis for interface standards, quality control techniques, etc. Collectively, they constitute a diverse

---

[1] A generic technology is not the same thing as a 'general purpose technology' as defined by Bresnahan and Trajtenberg (1995). The latter refers to a technology with multiple market applications (i.e., market economies of scope exist), a distinctly different concept from the generic base from which a particular set of technology applications is developed.

[2] The classic example of a generic *product* technology is Bell labs' proof in the late 1940s and early 1950s of the concept that the principles of solid state physics can be used to construct a semiconductor switch or amplifier, resulting in the creation of the transistor (Nelson, 1962). One of the best examples of a generic *systems* technology is the Internet. As a system (the communications network), technological advances were first required in its major underlying network technologies, such as queuing theory, packet switching, and routing. Demonstration of such in the 1960s led to prototype networks in the 1970s (ARPANET) and 1980s (NSFNET), which eventually led to the Internet (National Research Council, 1999). Occasionally, a generic technology can take the form of a 'method of inventing'. Examples are methods for manufacturing hybrid corn seeds and research methods for developing nanotechnologies (Darby and Zucker, 2003).

technical infrastructure, various types of which are applied at each stage of economic activity. Infratechnologies often are implemented as industry standards (Tassey, 1997, 2000).[3]

Both generic technology and infratechnology elements are drawn upon by competing firms to create proprietary technology. However, although attainment of partial property rights is possible, spillovers and other sources of market failure are prominent. In fact, widespread use of generic technologies is desirable from a public-policy perspective because the more firms draw upon a technology platform, the larger the number and variety of innovations produced. When infratechnologies are adopted as the technical basis for standards, uniform as well as widespread use is mandatory. These characteristics result in various degrees of underinvestment across technologies and over each technology's life cycle. Consequently, every industrialized nation provides funds to leverage generic technology and infratechnology research and subsequent assimilation by domestic industries. Such funding policies constitute recognition of the public-good content, even though identifying and measuring this content remains difficult conceptually and empirically.

1.2 The Multi-element Knowledge Production Function

The microeconomics literature has partially recognized the need for a disaggregated technology framework to address these phenomena but has not progressed beyond a dichotomous model in which technology is separated into scientific and technological stocks of knowledge. In such models, scientific information is appropriately characterized as a pure public good (Nelson, 1959) with external (to the industry) sources of supply. However, in such models, technological knowledge is implicitly assumed to be a purely private good, even while acknowledging the existence of spillovers.[4]

The following disaggregated knowledge production function separately specifies the key public and private technology elements and thereby allows the explicit representation of the critical elements of an industrial technology, specifically generic technologies and infratechnologies. Such an investment-based model of innovation allows assessment of the productivity of private-sector applied R&D, as determined by both private and public-sector expenditures that precede or concurrently support it.[5]

As a point of departure for explicitly separating the proprietary technology element from the quasi-public-good elements, the following generalized model is used:

$$Q_i = S \cdot F(KN_j, KE_i, \phi_j, X) \tag{1}$$

where Q is a firm's output of technology-based goods and services. KN represents the non-excludable (and hence public-good) portion of the industry's generic technology and is assumed equally available to all firms in the industry. X is a set of factors that affect output/performance in addition to the public and private technology elements. ϕ represents the innovation infrastructure of the industry, which consists of a set of infratechnologies and associated standards, as well as other infrastructure elements such as the availability of risk capital, IP laws, technical support for entrepreneurs, etc. This infrastructure affects the efficiency of production and commercialization. S is the science upon which the industry's generic

---

[3] Note that infratechnologies are part of an industry's technology base in contrast to what are referred to as 'infrastructure technologies.' The latter are produced by industries whose primary role is to provide an economic infrastructure function for other industries (electricity, transportation, and communications).

[4] A number of studies have attempted to empirically test this general specification by separately including basic research and applied R&D variables in a modified production framework (Mansfield, 1980, 1991; Link, 1981; Griliches, 1986; Jaffe, 1989; Leyden and Link, 1991; Toole, 1999).

[5] See Tassey (2005b) for a comprehensive treatment of this model, including comparisons with endogenous growth theory and alternative output/performance functions.

technology is based. Because, the vast majority of science is developed outside the industry by universities and government research institutes and because major breakthroughs in science occur infrequently, the science base is considered to be externally determined and constant and therefore is entered in the model as a shift parameter.

KE_i is a firm's stock of excludable (proprietary) knowledge that is used to create new products and services, i.e., innovations. At any point in time, a firm's proprietary technical knowledge creation is equivalent to the growth in KE_i, represented by

$$\Delta KE_i = \delta_i RE_i^{\lambda}, \tag{2}$$

where RE is applied R&D expenditures targeted at developing innovations, λ is a scale parameter, and δ is a firm's R&D productivity factor.[6]

The productivity factor is represented by

$$\delta_i = \eta_j e^{-KN_j/RE_i} \tag{3}$$

An important point from a policy perspective is the negative sign on KN. It implies a hurdle for investment in innovations, specifically an initial technical-risk barrier that must be overcome before substantial private investment in RE will be forthcoming. The negative sign may seem to be counter intuitive because generic technology does in fact enable the conduct of applied R&D, which in turn produces innovations. However, it is a barrier to applied R&D in the sense that: (1) it must be available for innovation effort to occur; and (2) on average, the greater the potential of a new technology, the greater the required advance in early-phase proof-of-concept research, i.e., the greater the initial barrier to innovative effort posed by the needed investment in the generic technology.

η_j is an efficiency parameter that represents the portion of an industry's technical infrastructure that supports knowledge production. This infrastructure is the collective effect of an industry's (or supply chain's) infratechnologies and associated standards that affect R&D efficiency. For example, the development and characterization of biomarkers and the ability to detect and interpret them in the human body greatly increases the productivity of biotechnology R&D. Similarly, the ability to accurately image biological activity and transmit the results for analysis also increases R&D efficiency. In general, the availability of such techniques increases potential economic benefits from inventive activity and thereby provides incentives to create proprietary technical knowledge. Such technical infrastructure only changes occasionally (i.e., slower than proprietary technologies). Moreover, because of their large public-good content, they often become industry standards, which themselves are only changed periodically. They, therefore, can be considered constant relative to the firm's R&D investment aimed at invention and then innovation (RE in Eq. (3)).[7] Thus, η_j is assumed to be a process constant over a technology life cycle in industry j.

The above model implies that industries based on radically new technologies require larger initial generic technology research expenditures. They will therefore experience lower rates of technical knowledge production for a given level of private R&D expenditures for some time. This phenomenon helps explain the S-shaped growth curve that characterizes the typical

---

[6] KE is assumed to be largely determined by KN, so the rate of growth is d/dt(KE). To the extent the existing stock of proprietary knowledge influences the growth of KE over the technology's life cycle, the rate of growth is more appropriately 1/KE d/dt (KE). Further, some models assume that the rate of growth of KE is equivalent to the rate of innovation. However, Eq. (1) shows that this is not the case, which further complicates public policy.

[7] Critical measurement methods, interface specifications, etc. are typically required to be in place before substantial R&D can be conducted efficiently, but once adopted as standards, they tend to remain unchanged for extended periods of time.

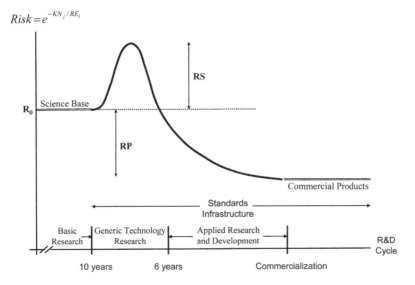

$$Risk = e^{-KN_j / RE_i}$$

Source: Tassey (2005a, b, 2007)

FIGURE 1   Risk reduction in the R&D cycle.

technology life cycle. In particular, a 'risk spike' is created by the need for investment early in the R&D cycle in a technology platform (generic technology) that enables subsequent innovation; that is, its existence blocks private investment in innovation early in the life cycle (Tassey, 2005a, b, 2007).[8] In this early phase of the technology life cycle when the generic technology is immature, initial attempts at innovation through applied R&D typically fail miserably.

The exponential function in Eq. (3) is, in effect, a measure of the risk faced by investors at different points in the R&D cycle. When the targeted technological advance is large, as is the case for a radically new technology, the risk is also high that expenditures for developing innovations (through expanding KE) will fail. That is, the hump or risk spike in Figure 1 will be larger than for investment in new but less advanced technologies (for example, a next-generation generic technology, as opposed to one based on new scientific principles).

In all cases, investment in expanding the generic technology base is required to overcome the risk spike, RS, and allow private investments in KE to proceed. Such a risk profile explains why rates of innovation based on emerging technologies can languish for years, even decades. However, once the risk spike is overcome, private investment in R&D can reduce private risk, RP, to levels that permit commercialization.[9]

The extreme case is no generic technology (KN = 0). Under this condition, applied R&D has very low productivity and will likely not be attempted. Growth in the stock of technical knowledge and hence the rate of innovation is then determined by $\delta = \eta$. This case could be called the 'natural rate of innovation' because it is driven solely by the general economic environment included in η. Such inventions fall into 'Pasteur's quadrant'; that is, inventions

---

[8] The large size of total risk and subsequent investment barrier created at this point also has been referred to as the 'valley of death.'

[9] More radical technologies present higher risk spikes. However, once such spikes are overcome, commercialization risk actually can be reduced to a greater extent than is the case for less radical technologies because the superior performance attributes enhance market penetration (Tassey, 2005b; 2007).

that occur through trial-and-error or 'inspiration' processes.[10] This source of invention is increasingly rare for today's science-driven and complex technologies.

Substituting Eq. (3) into (2) gives the technology production function:

$$\Delta KE_i = \eta_j e^{-KN_j/RE_i} RE_i^\lambda. \tag{4}$$

Equation (4) shows that the growth rate of technical knowledge is negatively related to the magnitude of initial technical and market risk associated with prospective investments in 'killer apps'. Thus, the efficiency parameter, η_j, is a critical factor in knowledge production because it can help to compensate for the risks that companies face when deciding to commit to new technologies and/or markets.

1.3   Investment Implications of the Model

For corporate R&D decision making, the amount of generic technology, KN, and the quality of the infratechnologies and standards available to an industry directly determine the adequacy of an industry's technical infrastructure. The efficacy of this infrastructure directly affects the technical and market risk associated with R&D project selection, i.e, with RE expenditures.

The requirement for firms to estimate both technical risk associated with market-driven attributes and market risk associated with variations in expected market demand is especially critical in the early phases of the R&D cycle. The impact is to retard private investment in the generic technology research that produces KN. Similarly, the unavailability of sufficient technical efficiency, η, contributes to this risk spike and, in fact, risk over the entire R&D cycle. Increasing η through better and more timely standardization improves the efficiency of research by defining and measuring interactions of specific performance attributes with the overall product technology and with complementary products in a technology system (Tassey, 2005a, b).

Because both KN and η are widely and commonly used, their inadequacy in effect creates 'public risk'. Thus, all technology-based economies subsidize generic technology and infratechnology research (the latter providing the technical basis for standards).[11] If the risk spike is overcome by subsidizing KN and η, then private investment, RE, can sufficiently reduce aggregate (technical and market) risk to enable commercialization of new technology.

Note that the i firms in industry j draw upon the same industry-level infratechnology endowment. This is particularly the case the greater the extent of standardization. To an extent, the non-excludable generic technology endowment KN_j available to each firm in an industry is also assumed to be approximately identical to the industry endowment because, by definition, the non-excludable character of this technology element and its role as a platform for innovations within the industry leads to both approximately equal access and common use by all firms in the industry.

1.4   Qualifications to the Model

The model is complicated by the quasi-public-good nature of generic technologies (and infratechnologies to a lesser extent), which means that some degree of property rights can

---

[10] See Stokes (1997). The term 'Pasteur's quadrant' refers to Louis Pasteur's invention of the vaccine, which preceded subsequent discovery of some new principles of microbiology. More recently, packet switching – the basis for computer networks including the Internet – evolved to a significant degree ahead of network theory (National Research Council, 1999).

[11] With respect to support of generic technology research, DoD/DARPA, NIH, and NIST/ATP are examples in the USA, while the framework program is the major example in the European Union. Infratechnology research is supported by national research institutes, such as the NIST.

be attained and maintained by individual firms. Thus, both government and industry fund generic technology research and both private firms and universities patent generic technologies. Companies also develop infratechnologies to varying degrees (some of which contribute to industry standards). Thus, at the R&D stage, KN and η represent the non-proprietary segments of these two technology elements, with the proprietary portions embodied in KE.[12]

Therefore, the quasi-public-good character of these two technology elements and the consequent need to assimilate them from external sources means that endowments may not be identical across firms, especially in the early portion of a technology's life cycle. This situation can lead to at least temporary competitive advantages both among firms within domestic industries and across competing industries in the global economy. Beyond the early phase of the technology life cycle (i.e., movement up the S-shaped performance/cost curve), competitive advantage is increasingly influenced, not only by efficiency in producing KE, but also by various infratechnologies that affect the production and market development stages of economic growth (Tassey, 2007).

2 THE RATIONALE FOR GOVERNMENT SUPPORT OF TECHNOLOGY INFRASTRUCTURE

Policy analysis requires a framework to identify and characterize R&D underinvestment phenomena. If industrial technologies were homogeneous entities (i.e., the so-called 'black box' model prevails), the traditional knowledge production function and output/performance models would be sufficient to inform policy makers. However for the reasons stated here and in previous papers, the typical industrial technology must be disaggregated into the several major elements implied by Eq. (4). The existence of distinctly different investment barriers is the key construct in determining government R&D support roles and is the rationale for the disaggregated model. Two of the elements have significant public-good content and hence have the characteristics of technical infrastructure.

Following the model developed in the previous section, this disaggregation is shown in Figure 2. The shading indicates the degree of public good content in each of the major elements of the typical industrial technology. The technology box is derived from an underlying science base (a pure public good). The existence of the three distinct elements comprising industrial technologies defies the notion that technologies are 'black boxes'. Instead, the three technology elements shown arise from different sources in response to distinctly different investment incentives and research processes. It is the differences in investment incentives that create the need for disaggregation that then drives policy analysis.

Specifically, an industrial technology is based on a set of fundamental or generic concepts. Although examples can be found of technologies emerging before significant proof of concept, an industry's generic technology increasingly must evolve (basic concepts demonstrated, prototypes developed and tested) before industry is willing to commit significant funds to the more applied R&D required for market applications of the technology. This linearity in the R&D cycle occurs for two reasons. First, modern technologies are increasingly dependent on prior scientific advances. Second, the associated increase in technological complexity means that proving the overall technology concept is essential to enable the much larger subsequent applied R&D that results in a stream of innovations.

Generic technologies are not widely recognized as an important element of industrial technology and they are not perceived as a type of technical infrastructure. However, such

---

[12] As indicated in footnote 6, KE could be included as an explanatory variable in the knowledge production function and would include any proprietary segments of KN and η.

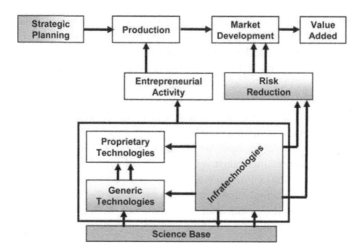

FIGURE 2   Technology-based industry model.

technology platforms have definite infrastructure characteristics. First, they are subject to substantial spillovers due to the tacit character of the knowledge created. Second, they also typically exhibit economies of scope, frequently well beyond the strategic scope of most firms. Both factors lead to underinvestment (Tassey, 2005a).

In Figure 2, the arrows convey the linear character of progressive knowledge application from basic science to generic technology development to proprietary products, processes, and services. Further, the diagram indicates that this evolutionary process (which is more complicated than shown because of feedback loops) is facilitated and in many cases made possible by a set of infratechnologies (included in η in Eq. (4)). As previously indicated, these tools include measurement methods for R&D and production control, technical support for interfaces between components of systems technologies, scientific and engineering databases, techniques such as quality assurance procedures, and test methods for facilitating marketplace transactions of complex technology-based products. They are ubiquitous in technology-based industries and often exert their impacts the form of industry standards. This technology element suffers from extensive spillovers. In fact, spillovers in the form of widespread use of standards are actually essential if this form of technical infrastructure is to be effective.

Which quasi-public-good technology element is the target of the government research program/project determines the analytical and data collection approaches to strategic planning and retrospective impact assessment. Assuming the target has been determined by underinvestment analysis (i.e., the policy rationale has been determined), the analyst will choose an analytical framework with the appropriate set of metrics. Doing so will allow accurate determination of the nature of the prospective/retrospective technical outputs from the research, the specific outcome (economic impact) metrics to be estimated/measured, the relevant types of qualitative analyses of the impact, and summary economic role assessments that will provide feedback/justification to government managers and other stakeholders (in particular, industry and government).

3   ALTERNATIVE METHODS FOR ECONOMIC IMPACT ASSESSMENT

Pressures to conduct systematic strategic planning for and retrospective impact assessments of research projects and programs are of relatively recent vintage, so most government agencies have not acquired the internal capability to select appropriate models and impact metrics and then to develop the necessary data sources or to find contractor support with the appropriate economic assessment skills. Moreover, R&D agencies are for the most part managed by technically trained people who are unfamiliar with economic assessment tools and have difficulty in understanding the imperative for such analysis or who are uncomfortable with the use and interpretation of information produced by a distinctly different discipline. And, while some universities have curricula that include impact assessment techniques, little of it is designed for government research program evaluation.

Thus, without an understanding and acceptance of the appropriate economic models, inadequate and inappropriate data are collected. Ideally, economists and policy analysts would like to estimate a fully specified performance function of the form represented by Eq. (1). Doing so requires the estimation of a number of functions, including a technology production function such as Eq. (4). The latter is the focus for R&D policy analysis because it shows the relationships among potential investment targets (KN, η, and RE) and the subsequent output of technical knowledge with innovation potential, KE.[13] Unfortunately, the quantity and quality of data required to drive the multi-element technology production function are not yet available.

The implication is that the policy analyst must look for a second best approach until better data are made available. An alternative frequently used by many government policy groups is to simply collect descriptive statistics through surveys. Examples would be the number of companies that: (1) changed their investment behavior (say, increased generic technology research) in response to an R&D subsidy; (2) adopted an infratechnology from a government laboratory and experienced a production productivity improvement; or (3) achieved a commercialization objective in a shorter period of time due to increased R&D efficiency resulting from some combination of government-supported generic technology and infratechnology research and an integrated innovation infrastructure. Unfortunately, descriptive statistics only provide general qualitative indicators of impact and therefore do not provide rankings or cause-and-effect information. Moreover, because of their lack of specificity, the results are frequently misinterpreted. That is, the efficiency or relative effectiveness of the specific applications of a policy instrument (direct funding of R&D, tax incentives, etc.) and ultimately the general effectiveness of each instrument for different types of market failures cannot be determined with reasonable accuracy.

A second alternative is to use metrics that provide quantitative measures of an S&T policy's economic impact but for which data are more easily obtained than is the case for the parametric statistics associated with production and performance functions. Such 'compromise' metrics are found in corporate finance and, while not as potentially robust as parametric statistics, they are compatible with the project or program orientation of government R&D subsidies. If used properly and combined with qualitative assessments, they can provide policy makers with substantial information useful for managing such programs.

4   ANALYTICAL TOOLS

The following describes a set of policy analysis tools that National Institute of Standards and Technology (NIST) has developed, which: (1) enable practical qualitative and quantitative

---

[13] Economists have focused on production functions that combine labor and capital inputs with technology assumed either to be determined outside the industry being studied or sufficiently constant to allow inclusion in the function as a shift parameter. Totally ignored is the fact that a marketing function exists, the output of which combines with the technology created to determine performance in technology-based markets (Tassey, 2005b).

assessments of the economic impacts of ongoing or completed technology infrastructure programs (retrospective studies); and (2) enable identification of new technologies and economic sectors that may potentially be targeted for support in the future (strategic planning studies). The NIST studies have focused on the two quasi-public-good technology elements: infratechnology research conducted in NIST's laboratories and generic technology research supported by the Institute's advanced technology program (ATP).[14]

Selection of a framework for economic analysis of R&D projects and programs is confounded by the fact that the output of this investment does not have an explicit market (in contrast to a good or service). Moreover, the results of R&D are neither comparable across projects nor countable (Griliches, 1977). Because of such constraints, it is generally not feasible to directly estimate a knowledge production function. Therefore, selection of an analytical framework for assessing impacts of specific R&D projects frequently is determined by data availability, which results in one of the two above alternative approaches being chosen to approximate Eq. (1).

In applying the second methodology, the analyst would like to construct a time series of costs and economic outcomes for the affected industries that include a period before government intervention. At some point in the time series, a government-funded project (R&D and technology transfer or technical information dissemination) occurs and the subsequent portion of the time series reflects the technical and economic impacts of the intervention which affect one or more of the three stages of economic activity (R&D, production, commercialization).

The ability to effectively apply this approach depends significantly on the nature of the R&D project, as well as available data. Generic technologies are typically developed early in a technology's life cycle and hence little technology investment data are generated prior to government intervention. That is, frequently no historical time series exists to allow specification of the intervention. In fact, a major government role in most industrialized nations is to promote early life-cycle (generic) technology research through support policies such as NIST's ATP or Europe's framework program. In contrast, because certain types of infratechnologies are needed in the middle of a technology life cycle, an increased potential exists for obtaining data on economic activity prior to the government intervention.

However, data on economic activity 'before' the intervention is frequently unattainable for either type of government project. Obviously, these data are generated farther back in time than subsequent post-intervention data. Therefore, unless a real-time data collection program is implemented, sources of data degenerate and eventually disappear over time. Consequently, the longer the optimal time series the lower the quality of data obtainable in the 'before' period, if it is obtainable at all. Even when an intervention can be clearly defined in the middle of a technology life cycle, the feasibility of collecting accurate data farther back in time than about 6 years is low in most technology-based industries.[15]

Because of availability of data and other difficulties frequently preclude the construction of a time series of economic trends before government intervention, the analyst must often use a 'counterfactual' technique to estimate the differential impacts of the government R&D project.[16] In the application of such a technique, industry respondents are asked a series of 'what if' questions focusing on the implications of additional costs incurred by industry if the government project did not exist. This approach works well when the government project

---

[14] The economic impact assessment methodology described below is discussed in greater detail in Tassey (2003).

[15] In fact, discussions with managers in some industries put a limit of 3 years on collections of some types of data due to the dynamic character of their industries (mergers, acquisitions, exits, labor mobility).

[16] A frequently cited early application of the counterfactual technique is Fogel's [1962] study of 'social savings' from the emergence of railroads in the USA. Although much social research involves implicit counterfactuals, Fogel is recognized by economic historians as the first researcher to explicitly state a counterfactual as the basis for analysis.

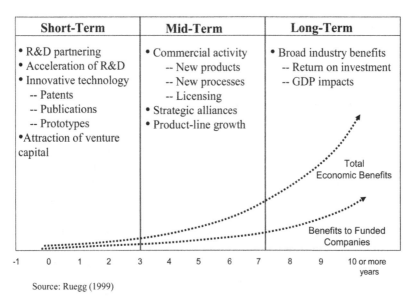

Short-Term	Mid-Term	Long-Term

• R&D partnering
• Acceleration of R&D
• Innovative technology
  -- Patents
  -- Publications
  -- Prototypes
•Attraction of venture
capital
	• Commercial activity
	  -- New products
	  -- New processes
	  -- Licensing
	• Strategic alliances
	• Product-line growth
		• Broad industry benefits
		  -- Return on investment
		  -- GDP impacts

Total Economic Benefits

Benefits to Funded Companies

-1 0 1 2 3 4 5 6 7 8 9 10 or more years

Source: Ruegg (1999)

FIGURE 3   Organization of metrics by technology life cycle: NIST's ATP.

either is initiated beyond the early phases of the current technology life cycle so that some experience without the government contribution exists, or the project is an intervention in a life cycle that has similarities with related technologies, thereby allowing the respondents to extrapolate from prior experience.

The counterfactual approach has been used extensively by NIST in assessing the economic impacts of its infratechnology research programs. In many cases, a new infratechnology replaces less efficient forms used in the current or previous technology life cycles. Experience with the less efficient infrastructure being replaced or knowledge of similar infrastructure from past life cycles provides industry respondents with an ability to estimate the increased costs that would be incurred if the new infrastructure were not available.

While this approach may sound similar to the time series intervention, the counterfactual approach is a 'second best' solution to characterizing costs in the period before interventions because annual cost data cannot be estimated or data collection is judged to be too difficult. As a substitute, the counterfactual approach obtains a rough estimate of annual costs in the pre-intervention period.[17]

NIST's ATP has also used the counterfactual approach to assess the impacts of its generic technology funding on corporate R&D investment decisions. ATP economic studies use the same counterfactual technique described above for a sample of funded projects. The program also collects descriptive statistics for all projects together through broad surveys of all grant applicants as well as grant awardees. Here counterfactuals would be no R&D project, a smaller or less ambitious project, or a time delay in funding the same project. Whatever metrics are chosen, they must be changed over the course of the technology life cycle, as indicated in Figure 3.

In effect, such impact estimation techniques do not explicitly measure ΔKE, ΔKN or η. Instead, inputs (investments in these variables) are related to outcomes (Q in Eq. (1)).

---

[17] If the impact of a single project is being assessed, an unambiguous time series of costs may be available from budget records. However, program-level impact assessment typically entails several projects, some of which may have multiple objectives. Moreover, industry assimilation costs, if significant, must also be estimated. Thus, retrospective time series specification will usually be less than ideal.

5   SELECTION OF METRICS

This step is critical because it drives survey design and eventual impact estimates. Unfortunately, it is frequently mishandled. The general approach requires decisions about the scope and heterogeneity of the technology to be studied, what to include with respect to subsequent categories of investment necessary to achieve commercialization, and how to account for the 'cost' of scrapping the existing technology.

Historically, government-funded R&D and subsequent government procurement in areas with social objectives such as national defense and energy independence have jump-started new industries or at least significantly expanded embryonic ones. Digital computers and network communications are examples. The degree to which government R&D programs facilitate the formation of new companies and an effective industry structure will determine the efficiency with which a social objective (such as better health care) is attained. Thus, useful impact assessment in virtually all cases will require economic impact metrics, which must be modified over the technology life cycle if ultimate economic impacts are to be estimated (see Figure 3).

In selecting such metrics, the structure and coverage of benefits and costs is particularly important for the ultimate estimation procedure. One of the initial decisions focuses on the desirability of establishing and including a baseline of net benefits from an existing technology. For example, in studies of social rates of return from private-sector innovations, Mansfield *et al.* (1977) argued that benefits (profits) to imitators should be added to benefits accruing to the innovating firm and that benefits lost to competitors supplying the old technology should be subtracted. Further, unsuccessful R&D by competing firms should be added to total costs.

These issues are mitigated somewhat for quasi-public-goods such as infratechnologies. In many (but not all) cases, infratechnologies and associated industry standards are introduced at points in the technology life cycle where markets already exist. In such cases, the existing product structure is not replaced; rather, measurement of the performance of some attribute of the product or an attribute that provides an interface with other products is standardized. The resulting productivity increase can be measured as an incremental gain in an existing production process, which is, in effect, equivalent to Mansfield *et al.*'s requirement to net out the residual value of obsolete technology.[18]

For new generic technologies that replace older generations as technology platforms for innovation efforts, the issue of subtracting benefits lost requires more attention. Even here, for prospective studies, at least a capital budgeting approach would only require estimating rates of return over the study period for both the new and defender technologies from the point in time of the analysis and making an investment decision accordingly (that is, R&D and other initial investments associated with the defender technology are regarded as sunk costs and ignored in the calculation). For retrospective studies, one also can rationalize ignoring the defender technology. What really counts is the rate of return realized by the technology under study relative to an appropriate hurdle rate.

5.1   Input (Cost) Metrics

All costs, private and public, should be included. Some cost data may have to be disaggregated and a portion assigned to the project under study. Specific cost categories are:

- *Direct and indirect government research program costs.* Research labor, production labor (for prototypes and other transfer artifacts such as standard reference materials), overhead, equipment, and technology transfer/outreach.

---

[18] If assimilating the new infratechnology results in the purchase of new equipment, for example, writing off the old equipment could be viewed as constituting a 'cost'.

- *Industry research program costs.* Research labor, equipment and overhead (for independent or joint research projects), 'pull' (technology assimilation) costs, including fees paid to government or universities for technology transfer, and related services.
- *Industry commercialization costs.* Applied R&D investment, IP acquisition, production scale-up, market research, and workforce training costs.

5.2 Output (Technical Knowledge) Metrics

Conducting economic impact studies of government research requires the selection of performance variables that can be directly attributed to the government funded or conducted research project and that can be related to subsequent economic impacts (outcomes). Examples of output measures frequently identified are:

- contributions to underlying science;
- generic technology or infratechnologies developed; and
- IP produced and its dissemination resulting from the research project, including patents or licenses in the case of generic technology and the technical basis for and adoption of standards in the case of infratechnologies.

5.3 Outcome (Economic Impact) Metrics

Selection of specific outcome metrics depends on a number of factors, including the type of R&D targeted by the project being studied (in particular, generic technology *vs.* infratechnology) and the objectives of the broader research program of which the project is a part (which may include industry structure and industry growth objectives). Categories of outcome metrics frequently estimated include impacts on

- post-project assimilation/use by industry of generic technology or infratechnology;
- post-project applied R&D investment by industry;
- post-project increase in venture capital;
- market access created and subsequent market entry decisions;
- reductions in industry R&D cycle times (time to commercialization);
- productivity increases (R&D or production process);
- market penetration of new technology (sales and/or profits generated);
- product quality;
- increase in product and system reliability; and
- reduction in transaction costs (equity in trade, performance verification).

Effective use of these metrics in assessments of the economic impact of technology infrastructure projects requires the selection of quantitative measures. Because of the demanding data requirements for estimating Eqs. (3) and (4), the analyst will have to rely on corporate finance measures: net present value, benefit-cost ratio, and internal (social) rate of return. Adequate data typically can be collected from government project records (costs) and industry surveys (benefits) to enable estimation of these measures, but each has a unique set of strengths and weaknesses. The analyst should therefore estimate all three measures.[19]

---

[19] See Tassey (2003) for a detailed discussion of the use of each measure and their collective utility for economic impact assessment.

6 SUMMARY

Technology infrastructure is a multifaceted and complex part of every industrial technology. Its two basic elements, generic technologies and infratechnologies, have different but profound impacts on the technology life cycle, and therefore on innovation and technology-based economic growth. The model presented disaggregates the traditional knowledge production function, thereby allowing analysis of the two categories of technology infrastructure and their combined effect on private-sector investments in applied R&D.

The quasi-public-good character of generic technologies and infratechnologies means that both industry and government will fund portions the R&D for these technology elements, which means that the assessment of private-sector investment behavior is complex. For policy analysis purposes, data and impact assessment methods must be adapted to both the appropriate economic models and the feasibility of data collection. Unfortunately, both prospective studies for strategic planning and retrospective studies for program impact evaluation must make compromises with respect to the metrics selected because of data quality issues. Nevertheless, empirical analyses to date indicate that technology infrastructure has a substantial enabling effect on private-sector R&D investment decisions and performance.

Acknowledgements

The author is indebted to Gary Anderson, Daniel Josell and an anonymous referee for constructive comments regarding characterization of several elements of the model.

References

Bresnahan, T. and Trajtenberg, M. (1995) General Purpose Technologies: 'Engines of Growth'? *Journal of Econometrics*, **65**(1), 83–108.
Darby, M. and Zucker, L. (2003) Grilichesian Breakthroughs: Inventions of Methods of Inventing and Firm Entry in Nanotechnology. NBER Working Paper No. 9825. Cambridge, MA: National Bureau of Economic Research (July).
Dosi, G. (1982) Technological Paradigms and Technological Trajectories. *Research Policy*, **11**, 147–162.
Dosi, G. (1988) Source, Procedures, and Microeconomic Effects of Innovation. *Journal of Economic Literature*, **26**(3), 1120–71.
Fogel, R.W. (1962) A Quantitative Approach to the Study of Railroads in American Ecnomic Growth: A Report of Some Preliminary Findings. *Journal of Economic History*, **22**(2), 163–197.
Griliches, Z. (1977) Economic Problems of Measuring Returns on Research. In Elkana, V. (ed.) *Towards a Metric of Science: The Advent of Science Indicators*. New York: John Wiley & Sons.
Griliches, Z. (1986) Productivity, R&D, and Basic Research at the Firm Level in the 1970's. *American Economic Review*, **77**(1), 141–154.
Griliches, Z. (1995) R&D and Productivity: Econometric Results and Measurement Issues. In Stoneman, P. (ed.) *Handbook of the Economics of Innovation and Technological Change*. Cambridge, MA: Blackwell.
Leyden, D. and Link, A. (1991) Why are Government and Private R&D Complements? *Applied Economics*, **23**(4), 1673–1681.
Link, A. (1981) Basic Research and Productivity Increase in Manufacturing: Additional Evidence. *American Economic Review*, **71**(4), 1111–1112.
Link, A, and Tassey, G. (1987) *Strategies for Technology-based Competition*. Lexington, MA: Lexington Books.
Link, A. and Tassey, G. (1993) The Technology Infrastructure of Firms: Investments in Infratechnology. *IEEE Transactions on Engineering Management*, **40**(3), 312–315.
Mansfield, E., Rapport, J., Romeo, A., Wagner, S. and Beardsley, G. (1977) Social and Private Rates of Return from Industrial Innovations. *Quarterly Journal of Economics*, **91**(2), 221–240.
Mansfield, E. (1980) Basic Research and Productivity Increase in Manufacturing. *American Economic Review*, **70**(3), 863–873.
Mansfield, E. (1991) Academic Research and Industrial Innovation. *Research Policy*, **20**(1), 1–12.
National Research Council (1999) *Funding a Revolution: Government Support for Computing Research*. Washington, DC: National Academy Press.
Nelson, R. (1959) The Simple Economics of Basic Scientific Research. *Journal of Political Economy*, **49**(2), 297–306.

Nelson, R. (1962) The Link Between Science and Invention: The Case of the Transistor in National Bureau of Economic Research. In *The Rate and Direction of Inventive Activity*. Princeton: Princeton University Press, pp. 549–583.

Nelson, R. (1992) What is 'Commercial' and What is 'Public' about Technology, and What Should Be? In Rosenberg, N., Landau, R. and Mowery, D. (eds.) *Technology and the Wealth of Nations*. Stanford, CA: Stanford University Press, pp. 57–71.

Ruegg, R. (1999) Advanced Technology Program's Approach to Technology Diffusion. NISTR 6385. Gaithersburg, MD: National Institute of Standards and Technology (September).

Stokes, D. (1997) *Pasteur's Quadrant: Basic Science and Technological Innovation*. Washington, DC: Brookings Institution.

Tassey, G. (1997) *The Economics of R&D Policy*. Westport, CT: Greenwood Publishing Group (Quorum Books).

Tassey, G. (2000) Standardization in Technology-Based Markets. In Link, A. and Roessner, D. (eds.) *The Economics of Technology Policy*. Special issue of *Research Policy* **20**, 587–602.

Tassey, G. (2003) Methods for Assessing the Economic Impacts of Government R&D. NIST Planning Report 03-1. Gaithersburg, MD: National Institute of Standards and Technology (September). Available online at: www.nist.gov/director/prog-ofc/report03-1.pdf.

Tassey, G. (2005a) Underinvestment in Public Good Technologies. *Journal of Technology Transfer*, **30**(1), 89–113. Special issue in honor of Edwin Mansfield.

Tassey, G. (2005b) The Disaggregated Technology Production Function: A New Model of University and Corporate Research. In Link, A.N. and Siegel, D. (eds.) *University-Based Technology Initiatives*. Special issue of *Research Policy*, **34**, 287–303.

Tassey, G. (2007) *The Technology Imperative*. Cheltenham, UK and Northhampton, MA, USA: Edward Elgar.

Toole, A.A. (1999) Public Research, Public Regulation, and Expected Profitability: The Determinants of Pharmaceutical Research and Development Investment. Stanford Institute for Economic Policy Research Working Paper, Stanford University.

PUBLIC TECHNOLOGY INFRASTRUCTURE, R&D SOURCING, AND RESEARCH JOINT VENTURES

J. D. ADAMS[a], M. MARCU[b] and A. J. WANG[c]

[a]Department of Economics, Rensselaer Polytechnic Institute and NBER, Troy, NY, USA; [b]Department of Economics, University of Florida, Gainesville, FL, USA; [c]National Institute of Standards and Technology, Gaithersburg, MD, USA

1 INTRODUCTORY REMARKS

In this paper, we define public technology infrastructure to mean public resources that bring new R&D into existence. This renders the idea testable, in that public infrastructure expands private R&D. Examples are research support of a type that the private sector does not supply; knowledge spillovers from public research; and government contracts whose incentives successfully broker new kinds of joint research.[1] Cooperative Research and Development Agreements (CRADAs), Small Business Innovation Research (SBIR) awards, or publicly sponsored Research Joint Ventures (RJVs) are cases in point. These arrangements contain incentives amounting to forfeiture of matching federal funds if a project fails.

This paper explores the particular role of public technology infrastructure in R&D alliances involving R&D sourcing and RJVs.[2] Like infrastructure, the term R&D alliance is fraught with ambiguity. It can refer to public–private or purely private sector alliances. It can consist

---

[1] Griliches (1991) discusses different types of spillovers and Jones (2002, Ch. 4) discusses fixed costs of knowledge creation as a source of spillovers and increasing returns.

[2] Hagedoorn *et al.* (2000) offer an overview of the reasons behind R&D alliances.

of R&D sourcing, in which agencies or firms seek to lower the cost of R&D by contracting with other firms to perform it.[3] In turn, sourcing can be transitory or permanent. Then again, R&D alliances may consist of RJVs in which firms share research. We consider all these cases. In the process we uncover evidence for a positive effect of public technology infrastructure on R&D alliances.

The rest of the paper consists of three sections.[4] Section 2 examines R&D sourcing and its interactions with public technology infrastructure using a sample of R&D laboratories or research groups within firms.[5] Public sector agents in Section 2 are federal laboratories. Private sector agents are research laboratories in R&D-performing firms. They are the source of the data and the level at which the analysis is conducted. Indicators in this section combine different aspects of public infrastructure: knowledge transfer, contractual incentives, and R&D subsidies. The results suggest that federal laboratories increase R&D sourcing. Section 3 explores the role of public infrastructure in RJVs sponsored by the Advanced Technology Program (ATP).[6] In Section 3, the public sector agents are ATP managers, and private sector agents are laboratories in R&D-performing firms. But now the analysis is conducted at the level of individual RJV projects. Using these data we find that ATP financial support directly increases patents from RJVs. ATP contractual structure, while it does not directly increase patents, does so indirectly, through the favoring of more productive projects. Section 4 concludes.

2 PUBLIC TECHNOLOGY INFRASTRUCTURE AND R&D SOURCING

Below we report findings on the determinants of R&D sourcing, otherwise known as contract R&D. The indicators of public technology infrastructure that could drive sourcing behavior specifically relate to federal laboratories.[7] But to understand the findings it is first necessary to explain the policy background in the United States that leads up to them.

Starting in 1980 several pieces of legislation altered the role played by federal laboratories in public–private partnerships. The Stevenson–Wydler Act of 1980 made technology transfer an objective of federal laboratories. The Bayh–Dole Act of 1980 not only provided incentives for universities to commercialize their R&D, but it did the same for federal laboratories, by helping to make Stevenson–Wydler operational. Thus, under Bayh–Dole contractors operating federal laboratories could patent federally-funded inventions. This is consistent with the avowed purpose of the legislation, to increase commercialization of federal R&D.

Then, in 1982, Congress passed the SBIR Act. Its purpose was to support R&D by small firms and to attract venture capital to the firms. SBIR required agencies to set aside 0.2% of R&D budget for this purpose. By encouraging federal laboratories to support small firms, the SBIR program probably increased R&D sourcing. Under SBIR small firms could insource R&D from customers such as federal laboratories or firms, and likewise the customers could outsource R&D to SBIR firms.

---

[3] By sourcing we mean both insourcing, in which firms are hired to perform R&D for other firms, and outsourcing, in which one firm hires another firm to perform R&D for it.

[4] This paper is related to a vast literature on the limits of the firm and the limits of the firm in R&D. Representative examples are Teece (1977), Monteverde and Teece (1982), Von Hippel (1988), Pisano (1990), Mowery (1992), Aghion and Tirole (1994), Mowery (1995), Mowery *et al.* (1998), Holmstrom and Roberts (1998), and Azoulay (2004). A full list is too extensive to go into within the limits of this paper.

[5] Adams (2006) discusses the data in Section 2 at length, which were collected by the Survey of Industrial Laboratory Technologies 1996, conducted in 1997–1998. The financial data in this section originates in Standard and Poor's Compustat (various years); the geographic data derives from U.S. Bureau of the Census (1998).

[6] The Survey of ATP Joint Ventures, conducted in 2004, yielded the data in Section 3.

[7] Adams and Marcu (2004) includes a more extensive version of Section 2.

TABLE I   Research laboratories in R&D-performing firms: descriptive statistics for a study of R&D sourcing.

Variable	Mean	S.D.
R&D sourcing Indicators		
Percent of engineering hours on new products contributed by customers[a]	4.84	7.93
Percent of engineering hours on new products contributed by suppliers[a]	7.19	8.65
Percent of laboratory R&D budget outsourced[a,b]	1.57	3.95
Percent of laboratory R&D budget insourced[a,b]	1.67	7.42
Determinants of R&D sourcing		
RJVs important to the laboratory (1 if yes, 0 if no)	0.69	0.47
M&A important to the laboratory (1 if yes, 0 if no)	0.50	0.50
RJVs–M&A important to the laboratory (1 if yes, 0 if no)	0.81	0.40
Number of important technologies in the laboratory	9.15	5.41
Laboratory R&D budget (in $'92 million)[b]	14.01	41.75
Fraction of lab scientists and engineers with the PhD or MD[b]	0.13	0.17
Number of closely affiliated government laboratories	1.17	2.90
SBIR program or CRADAs important (1 if yes, 0 if no)[c]	0.33	0.47
Standard deviation of the logarithm of parent firm sales	0.20	0.18
Growth rate of parent firm sales	0.06	0.09
Overlap of firm's industry with important Technologies in the lab	0.25	0.25
Diversity of employment in the laboratory's metro area	0.94	0.03
Employment in the laboratory's metro area (in millions)	1.27	1.32

Notes: Data sources are the *Survey of Industrial Laboratory Technologies 1996*, Standard and Poor's Compustat, and the U.S. Bureau of the Census. Survey data were collected in 1997–1998.
[a]The midpoint of each interval has been assigned to the variable.
[b]Data refer to 1991 and 1996 and hence are time-varying.
[c]SBIR stands for the Small Business Innovation Research program, which sets aside a portion of the budget of federal agencies to support small businesses. CRADA stands for Cooperative Research and Development Agreements, which result from another set-aside. In this case part of federal laboratory budget is earmarked for research conducted jointly with firms.

Separate laws governed the intellectual property derived from public–private collaborative R&D. These affected federal laboratories from yet a different direction. The Federal Technology Transfer Act of 1986 created CRADAs for government-owned and operated laboratories, while the National Competitiveness Technology Transfer Act of 1989 did the same for government-owned, contractor-operated laboratories.[8] CRADAs provide matching support in return for firm effort, which is one reason why the projects might represent new research. And if a CRADA supports several firms, it seems likely that this would encourage sharing and sourcing of R&D. All of this serves to explain why public technology infrastructure could have promoted cooperative R&D in the United States in recent years.

2.1 Principal Variables in the R&D Sourcing Study

With this as background, Table I summarizes the data. We begin with the sourcing indicators, which are the dependent variables in the analysis. These are first of all, percents of engineering hours contributed by customers and suppliers, or engineering hours outsourced. They are second of all, indicators of percents of R&D budget that are insourced and outsourced. There is reason to think that the two indicators capture different aspects of sourcing, with engineering hours larger and longer-term than sourcing from laboratory budget. To see this note that in Table I customer and supplier percents of engineering hours outsourced are 4.8 and 7.2%, or 12% in total. Suppose that engineering is representative of other R&D that is outsourced to customers and suppliers. If this is true then the fact that outsourced engineering is 12% suggests that total outsourcing of this type is 12% of R&D budget.[9]

---

[8] See Adams *et al.* (2003) for an analysis of CRADAs.

[9] Jankowski (1993) finds that labor costs are 42% of R&D cost, and that 25% of R&D cost consists of engineering wages. While we lack information on the other 75% of outsourced R&D, it seems likely that other expenditures

Direct sourcing from R&D budget is far less. On average 1.6% of budget is outsourced and 1.7% is insourced. Since engineering hours outsourced are off-budget the two measures are distinct, with sourcing from budget the smaller of the two. Add to this the suspicion that customers and suppliers are lasting partners and one might think that engineering hours outsourced are larger and longer-term than direct sourcing.

Notice that sourcing of either kind could be an information gathering device, prior to a joint venture, which provides an option to merge and acquire.[10] Reflecting this 69% of the laboratories view RJVs as important, 50% view mergers and acquisition (M&A) as important, and a combined 81% view both RJV and M&A activity as important.

Next consider the determinants of R&D sourcing summarized in the lower half of Table I. The number of important technologies suggests complexity, which could increase demand for sourcing. Its mean is 9.2 (out of 102) with a standard deviation of 5.4. Size is captured by R&D budget, which could increase sourcing if larger laboratories require a wider range of skills and equipment. Mean R&D budget is 14 million dollars of 1987. Its standard deviation is 41.8 million and indicates the skew of R&D. Thirteen percent of the laboratory workforce consists of PhDs or MDs. Its effect on sourcing is two-sided. If skill substitutes for outside R&D this reduces outsourcing. But PhDs or MDs offer a range of skills to potential clients. This would increase insourcing.

Two indicators of public technology infrastructure follow next. We expect that they increase sourcing through subsidization or governance of inter-firm alliances. The number of closely affiliated federal laboratories has a mean of 1.2 with a standard deviation of 2.9. Fully a third of the laboratories regard the indicator of CRADAs or SBIR grants as important.

Three variables describe the parent firm. Growth of deflated firm sales is likely to increase outsourcing, because at least some growth is unanticipated. Its mean is 6%.[11] A second measure, the standard deviation of the logarithm of firm sales, captures volatility of firm demand. Its mean equals 20%. This will affect sourcing if the buffer motive is operative. A third measure, overlap, gets at the availability of technologies elsewhere in the firm and suggests replacement of outsourcing by inter-divisional contract work. The mean of overlap is 25%: a fourth of technologies in the laboratory coincide with parent firm technologies.

We conclude this description with a measure of diversity of employment in the laboratory's locality. This is the complement to employment concentration in the laboratory's Standard Metropolitan Statistical Area (SMSA).[12] Its mean equals 0.94, with a standard deviation of 0.03. We expect this measure to matter more for transitory sourcing, which is more likely to characterize the minor amount of sourcing from R&D budget in our data.

2.2   Determinants of Engineering Hours Outsourced

The dependent variables in Table II are engineering hours outsourced to customers and suppliers, which form a two-equation system that we estimate using bivariate ordered probit.[13] This method is useful because the observed sourcing indicators are measured in increasing

---

would move in tandem with engineering hours and wages. The reason is that the R&D production process is similar in different firms, especially those in the same industry.

[10] See Kogut (1991).

[11] The sales data derive from Standard and Poor Corporation's Compustat (various years). Overlap compares the industries of important technologies in the laboratory with industries in which the firm is classified in Compustat.

[12] Diversity of SMSA employment equals one minus the Herfindahl index of employment concentration among industries in an SMSA in 1992. This and total SMSA employment are contained in U.S. Bureau of the Census (1998).

[13] Greene (2000), Chapter 19, Section 19.8 discusses the single equation ordered probit likelihood function. Adams (2006) derives the bivariate ordered probit likelihood.

TABLE II   Research laboratories in R&D-performing firms: Engineering hours contributed to new products by customers and suppliers (asymptotic standard errors in parentheses).

Variable or statistic	System A		System B	
	Customers II.1	Suppliers II.2	Customers II.3	Suppliers II.4
Parent firm in motor vehicles (1 if yes, 0 if no)		0.77* (0.27)		0.72* (0.26)
RJV–M&A important to the laboratory (1 if yes, 0 if no)	0.77* (0.28)	0.39 (0.26)	0.71* (0.28)	0.37 (0.26)
Log (number of important technologies)	−0.16 (0.15)	0.01 (0.15)	−0.20 (0.16)	−0.01 (0.15)
Log (laboratory R&D budget)	−0.02 (0.06)	−0.06 (0.06)	−0.04 (0.06)	−0.07 (0.06)
Fraction of lab scientists and engineers with the PhD or MD	−2.69* (0.68)	−1.92* (0.58)	−2.88* (0.69)	−1.97* (0.59)
Direct contact with customers important (1 if yes, 0 if no)	0.93** (0.42)		0.94** (0.43)	
Direct contact/problem solving with suppliers important (1 if yes, 0 if no)		2.03* (0.75)		1.96* (0.75)
Log (number of closely affiliated government laboratories)	0.10* (0.03)	0.01 (0.03)		
SBIR or CRADAs important (1 if yes, 0 if no)			0.88* (0.22)	0.26 (0.22)
Number of closely affiliated firms	−0.04 (0.06)	0.09 (0.06)	−0.01 (0.06)	0.08 (0.06)
Lower cut point	0.02	1.12	0.59	1.06
Upper cut point	1.72	3.07	2.32	3.02
Cross-equation correlation coefficient	0.38* (0.10)		0.36* (0.10)	
Log likelihood	−255.8		−253.8	
χ^2	34.5*		37.8*	

Notes: Principal data source is the *Survey of Industrial Laboratory Technologies 1996*. The estimation method is bivariate ordered probit. The data are a cross-section that spans the period 1991–1996, since percent engineering hours variables are time-invariant. The number of observations is $N = 158$.
*Parameter or statistic is significantly different from zero at the 1% level.
**Parameter or statistic is significantly different from zero at the 5% level.

intervals and are positively correlated.[14]. Since the percents are time-invariant the data form a cross-section of 158 laboratories after missing values are removed. The system takes the cross-equation correlation of the errors into account; these are positive and significant. The equations take the form,

$$\text{Outsource Engineering}_C^* = X_C'\beta_C + u_C$$
$$\text{Outsource Engineering}_S^* = X_S'\beta_S + u_S$$

(1)

In which subscript C stands for customers, subscript S stands for suppliers, the asterisk refers to latent indicators of outsourcing, and the error terms are, respectively, u_C and u_S. Notice that the right-hand side variables, discussed in Section 2.1 and below, can differ for outsourcing of engineering hours to both downstream customers (X_C) and upstream suppliers (X_S). For the likelihood function for the exact case studied in this paper see the appendix to Adams (2006).

System A in Table II consists of II.1 and II.2. The χ^2 statistics show that the independent variables are highly significant as a group. The supplier equation includes a dummy indicator if the main industry of the parent firm is motor vehicles. This is significant and suggestive of the importance of suppliers in this industry. Coefficients of other industry dummies are insignificant and for this reason are omitted.

---

[14] Engineering hours contributed by customers and suppliers are coded as follows: if engineering hours equal 0%, then the variable equals 1; if engineering lies between 0 and 10%, then the variable equals 2; and if engineering hours equal 11% or more, then the variable equals 3. These categories are chosen to avoid small numbers of observations in the different cells.

The RJV–M&A indicator significantly increases customer engineering hours outsourcing, suggesting that this could be a step toward full integration (Kogut, 1991). Its effect on supplier engineering is the same but the coefficient is insignificant. The fraction of workforce holding the PhD (or MD) reduces engineering hours and suggests that skill substitutes for outsourcing.

The dependent variables reflect customer and supplier research effort. We test for internal consistency by introducing measures of the importance of customers and suppliers. Equation II.1 includes the importance of direct contact with customers. Customers do in fact contribute more engineering when direct contact with them is seen as important. Equation II.2 includes indicators of the importance of direct contact with suppliers, supplier problem solving, and long term supplier relations. Consistent with this, supplier outsourcing rises when these contributions are seen as important. Number of federal laboratories is significant in the customer Equation II.1 but not II.2. Along with other results this implies that supplier laboratories dominate the sample.

System B consists of II.3 and II.4. In this system, we replace the logarithm of number of government laboratories with a combined indicator of the importance of SBIR grants and CRADAs. This is again significant in the customer Equation II.3 but not II.4. In both systems the RJV–M&A indicator is positively associated with customer sourcing. The indicators imply sourcing to customers because in this sample laboratories are predominantly suppliers of R&D.

2.3 Customer Outsourcing and the Influence of Federal R&D

We have seen that the number of closely affiliated federal laboratories, as well as an indicator of the importance of SBIR and CRADA grants, both increase engineering hours outsourced to customers. We explore this connection in more detail in Table III, which allows for the endogeneity of the importance of federal R&D. A convenient way to approach this is to employ discrete indicators of federal R&D, which are then determined within a bivariate ordered probit–probit system. The model is,

$$
\begin{aligned}
y_C^* &\equiv \text{Outsource Engineering}_C^* = \gamma y_F + X_C' \beta_C + u_C \\
y_F^* &\equiv \text{Federal R\&D}^* = X_F' \beta_F + u_F
\end{aligned}
\tag{2}
$$

We have employed short hand notation for outsourcing of engineering hours to customers on the left of the top equation (y_C^*), and the same for the latent indicator of the importance of federal R&D (y_F^*). Here y_F is the observed 0–1 indicator of the importance of federal R&D, and latent values are shown by asterisks. The first equation is ordered probit, while the second, for the importance of federal R&D, is probit. The two are jointly estimated. The method is discussed in Adams et al. (2003), but the Appendix derives the likelihood function for the exact case studied in this article.

We employ two measures of the importance of federal R&D. Instead of the logarithm of the number of closely affiliated federal laboratories, we set an indicator of their importance equal to 1 if the number exceeds zero and 0 otherwise. Estimates of the system involving this indicator appear in III.1 and III.2. The second system uses the importance of CRADA or SBIR, which equals 1 if true and 0 otherwise as we have seen. Estimates are shown in III.3 and III.4. In each system the indicator of the importance of federal R&D in the probit equation is treated as a function of the logarithm of laboratory R&D budget and an indicator of whether the laboratory is five years old or less.[15] Also in the probit equations are dummy

---

[15] We affectionately call this indicator BABYLAB in the computer programs that produce the results.

TABLE III Research laboratories in R&D-performing firms: Engineering hours contributed to new products by customers, jointly estimated with importance of government laboratories, SBIR or CRADA (asymptotic standard errors in parentheses).

Variable or statistic	System A		System B	
	Engineering hours, customers III.1	Government laboratory Important[a] III.2	Engineering hours customers III.3	SBIR or CRADA Important[a] III.4
RJV-M&A important to the laboratory (1 if yes, 0 if no)	0.70* (0.27)		0.46 (0.27)	
Log (number of important technologies)	−0.19 (0.15)		−0.21 (0.15)	
Log (laboratory R&D budget)	−0.04 (0.06)	0.20* (0.07)	−0.11 (0.06)	0.28* (0.07)
Fraction of lab scientists and engineers with the PhD or MD	−2.63* (0.67)		−2.43* (0.63)	
Laboratory is under five years old (1 if yes, 0 if no)		0.96** (0.41)		0.70** (0.32)
Direct contact with customers important (1 if yes, 0 if no)	1.04** (0.43)		0.91** (0.38)	
Direct contact/problem solving with suppliers important (1 if yes, 0 if no)				
Government laboratory important (1 if yes, 0 if no)	1.29* (0.37)			
SBIR or CRADAs important (1 if yes, 0 if no)			1.91* (0.25)	
Number of closely affiliated firms	−0.01 (0.06)		0.03 (0.05)	
Lower cut point	0.85		0.74	
Upper cut point	2.51		2.23	
Cross-equation correlation coefficient	−0.46 (0.28)		−0.85* (0.15)	
Log likelihood	−200.1		−200.2	
χ^2	45.8*		102.7*	

Notes: Principal data source is the *Survey of Industrial Laboratory Technologies 1996*. Estimation method is bivariate probit-ordered probit. Data are a cross-section that spans the period 1991–1996, since percent engineering hours variables are time-invariant. Number of observations is $N = 158$.
[a] Equation includes vector of 16 technology dummies.
*Parameter or statistic differs significantly from zero at the 1% level.
**Parameter or statistic differs significantly from zero at the 5% level.

indicators of 16 different technologies, which we treat as predetermined.[16] The cross-equation correlations of the error terms are negative and sometimes significant. The chi-square statistics at the bottom show that the right hand side variables are highly significant as a group.

The equations for outsourcing of engineering to customers (III.1 and III.3) are similar to the single equation results (II.1 and II.3). The government laboratory and SBIR/CRADA indicators are significantly greater than zero, implying that public technology infrastructure stimulates cooperative R&D even after endogeneity is taken into account. In the probit Equations III.2 and III.4 larger laboratories are more likely to view public technology infrastructure as important, consistent with Adams *et al.* (2003). Especially intriguing is the finding that very young laboratories view public infrastructure as more important, suggesting that SBIR or CRADA arrangements target young firms. However, Table V below suggests that CRADA is more important than SBIR in this respect.

---

[16] The 16 technologies range from automobiles and biotechnology, through telecommunications and other transportation. The significant technologies that predict the importance of federal R&D are biotechnology, defense, energy, and advanced materials. We omit these results for brevity's sake.

2.4 Determinants of Sourcing from R&D Budget

We turn next to Table IV, where the dependent variables are percents of R&D budget outsourced and insourced.[17] The data form a panel that covers the years 1991 and 1996. After removing missing values the table includes 227 observations or 114 laboratories per year.

Both systems are estimated using bivariate ordered probit, and the estimated cross-equation correlations are highly significant. The equation system is:

$$\text{Insource R\& D}^* = Z_I' \gamma_I + v_I$$
$$\text{Outsource R\& D}^* = Z_O' \gamma_O + v_O$$

(3)

Subscript I stands for insourcing as a proportion of R&D, subscript O stands for outsourcing, the asterisk refers to latent indicators, and the error terms are, respectively, v_I and v_O. Notice that the right hand side variables can differ for insourcing (Z_I) and outsourcing (Z_O) of R&D. For an explanation of the methodology again see the appendix to Adams (2006).

The χ^2 statistics at the bottom of Table IV show that the independent variables are highly significant as a whole. In all equations we include a dummy variable that equals 1 if the year is 1996 and 0 otherwise to capture changes in sourcing propensities. However, the year dummy is insignificant. Industry dummies are entirely insignificant and are omitted.

System A consists of IV.1 and IV.2. Joint housing with manufacturing is positive and significant in the insourcing equation. This may proxy for development work, indicating that an applied research group is able to engage in contract research and is more likely to insource.

The RJV–M&A indicator increases sourcing throughout. The number of important technologies has no effect on outsourcing but instead captures technical scope of insourcing laboratories. As expected laboratory R&D budget increases outsourcing. The fraction of the workforce comprised of PhDs increases insourcing but not outsourcing, implying that insourcing laboratories are more skill intensive than average.

We observe that PhD-intensive laboratories using many technologies are more likely to insource. In contrast, larger laboratories outsource a larger fraction of their R&D. All of this suggests a division of labor in which larger laboratories outsource to highly skilled laboratories that span a wide range of technologies.

The discussion of IV.1 and IV.2 concludes with firm growth, volatility, and overlap of laboratory technologies. Growth of the parent firm increases sourcing, while volatility discourages it. This last result refutes the idea that outsourcing buffers the firm's R&D from uncertainty. Instead it suggests that volatility permits reassignment in off-peak times and reduces outsourcing.[18] Overlap reduces outsourcing, implying that within-firm technologies substitute for technologies outside the firm.

System B is shown in IV.3 and IV.4. This adds to IV.1 and IV.2 the public infrastructure indicator consisting of the logarithm of the number of closely affiliated government laboratories. Insourcing rises sharply with the number of government laboratories. In addition the system adds the number of influential firms. Outside firms are influential in part because of outsourcing. IV.3 and IV.4 also include characteristics of the laboratory's SMSA. Diversity of employment increases outsourcing, consistent with the specialized services view of sourcing.

---

[17] Percentages of R&D budget sourced are coded as follows: if the proportion sourced equals 0%, then the variable equals 1; if the proportion sourced lies between 0 and 1% then the variable equals 2; if the proportion lies between 2 and 3% then the variable equals 3; and if the proportion is 4+% then the variable equals 4. The categories are chosen to avoid small numbers of observations in the different cells.

[18] These findings on volatility of sales are similar to those in Abraham and Taylor (1996) for labor outsourcing. In their paper industry seasonality and cyclicality discourage outsourcing.

TABLE IV　Research laboratories in R&D-performing firms: Determinants of percent of R&D budget outsourced and insourced (asymptotic standard errors in parentheses).

	System A		System B	
Variable or statistic	Insourced IV.1	Outsourced IV.2	Insourced IV.3	Outsourced IV.4
Year Dummy	−0.07 (0.17)	−0.08 (0.16)	−0.08 (0.18)	−0.08 (0.16)
Laboratory is jointly housed with manufacturing (1 if yes, 0 if no)	0.68* (0.20)	0.30 (0.17)	0.58* (0.22)	0.21 (0.18)
RJV–M&A is important to the laboratory (1 if yes, 0 if no)	0.84* (0.30)	0.64* (0.25)	0.95* (0.32)	0.68* (0.25)
Log (number of important technologies)	0.51* (0.16)	0.15 (0.13)	0.48* (0.18)	0.07 (0.14)
Log (laboratory R&D budget)	−0.02 (0.06)	0.16* (0.05)	−0.08 (0.06)	0.15* (0.05)
Fraction of laboratory scientists and engineers with the PhD or MD	2.22* (0.56)	0.41 (0.51)	1.96* (0.59)	0.18 (0.54)
Log (number of closely affiliated government laboratories)			0.08* (0.03)	0.03 (0.02)
Log (number of closely affiliated outside firms)			0.07 (0.05)	0.12** (0.05)
Rate of growth in firm sales	1.93 (1.06)	1.78 (1.01)	2.64** (1.10)	2.07** (1.04)
Standard deviation of the logarithm of firm sales	−1.29 (0.67)	−0.99 (0.55)	−1.77** (0.69)	−1.30** (0.57)
Overlap of firm technologies with important technologies to the laboratory	−0.03 (0.38)	−0.90* (0.35)	0.21 (0.44)	−1.09* (0.40)
Diversity of employment in laboratory's SMSA			10.21** (4.34)	8.57* (3.55)
Log (employment in laboratory's SMSA)			0.17** (0.08)	0.03 (0.07)
Lower cut point	2.83	0.71	14.4	8.9
Upper cut point	3.56	1.59	15.3	9.9
Cross-equation correlation coefficient	0.41* (0.09)		0.33* (0.10)	
Log likelihood	−383.3		−366.6	
χ^2	41.8*		55.8*	

Notes: Principal data source is the *Survey of Industrial Laboratory Technologies 1996*. Estimation method is bivariate ordered probit. The data are a panel covering the years 1991 and 1996 since sourcing indicators are time varying. Number of observations is $N = 227$.
*Parameter or statistic is significantly different from zero at the 1% level.
**Parameter or statistic is significantly different from zero at the 5% level.

Table V presents variations on IV.3 and IV.4. The table replaces the number of federal laboratories with indicators of importance of CRADAs and SBIR grants. The only significant effect is on insourcing: see Equations V.4 to V.6. While the combined SBIR–CRADA effect is positive in the V.5 as well as V.6, only CRADA comes in strongly when SBIR is entered separately, as it does in V.4. CRADA is the stronger influence.

2.5　Comparative Sourcing of Engineering and R&D

Let us take stock. Table II reports bivariate ordered probit estimates of engineering hours outsourced, while Tables IV and V do the same for R&D outsourced (as well as insourced). Clearly there are important differences among the results. The number of government laboratories and the SBIR–CRADA indicator significantly increase customer engineering outsourced in Table II, but not R&D outsourced in Tables IV and V. We attribute this difference to the nature of sourcing in Table II, which involves contracts with government laboratories and other firms over the long run. While the outsourcing results vary, there is an important sense in which

TABLE V   Research laboratories in R&D-performing firms: Determinants of R&D budget sourced: SBIR and CRADA effects (asymptotic standard errors in parentheses).

Variable or statistic	Percent of R&D budget outsourced			Percent of R&D budget insourced		
	V.1	V.2	V.3	V.4	V.5	V.6
SBIR program important (1 if yes, 0 if no)	0.09 (0.3)			−0.24 (−0.27)		
CRADAs important (1 if yes, 0 if no)	0.11 (0.18)			0.70* (0.22)		
SBIR or CRADAs important (1 if yes, 0 if no)		0.23 (0.18)			0.57* (0.20)	
SBIR + CRADAs Important (range 0 to 2)			0.11 (0.12)			0.31* (0.12)

Notes: Principal data source is the *Survey of Industrial Laboratory Technologies 1996*. Estimation method is bivariate ordered probit. The data are a panel covering the years 1991 and 1996, since the sourcing indicators are time varying. Number of observations is $N = 227$. Besides the government policy interactions shown, the equations are specified as in Equations IV.3 and IV.4 of Table IV. *Parameter is significantly different from zero at the 1% level.

they agree. The public infrastructure indicators sometimes significantly increase sourcing but they never decrease it. In addition, the small sample size means that given more data we cannot rule out significant effects of public infrastructure on outsourcing of supplier hours and R&D. One way to formally sum up the results is to apply a binomial test. Across Tables II, IV, and V there are 14 coefficients on the federal laboratory and SBIR–CRADA variables, of which 13 are positive. On the null hypothesis that the chance of a positive sign is 50–50, the P-value is 0.002 that 13 out of 14 signs would be positive. Thus the null hypothesis is rejected in favor of the alternative, that positive signs are more likely, at more than the 1% level.[19]

In addition, PhD intensity decreases engineering hours outsourced but not R&D outsourced. The influence of PhD intensity on engineering suggests long term substitution of inside for outside skills. The transience of R&D outsourced probably explains why PhD intensity has no effect on it in Table IV.

Other differences are that firm growth, sales volatility, and overlap of laboratory technologies have no effect on engineering hours, though they do affect R&D outsourced. Likewise employment and diversity of the SMSA have little relevance to engineering outsourced, but again they affect R&D sourcing. It is for this reason that we exclude growth, volatility, overlap, and diversity from Table II. Clearly, engineering outsourced is distinct from R&D outsourced. Besides being larger engineering probably represents long-term relationships with customers and suppliers. This would explain why engineering is less tied to the SMSA and to trend and volatility of firm sales, and why it tends to be replaced by within-firm technologies. In contrast R&D outsourcing seems transitory and designed to expedite the flow of R&D projects, which is the 'specialized equipment' view of sourcing (Hagedoorn *et al.*, 2000). What the results for engineering outsourced show is that this is *not* the motivation for longer term and larger scale sourcing. That is driven by permanent differences in the comparative advantage of doing R&D.

3   PUBLIC TECHNOLOGY INFRASTRUCTURE AND RJVs

We turn now to a study of the relationship between public technology infrastructure and RJVs. RJVs in the sample are supported and regulated by the ATP. ATP was created by the Omnibus

---

[19] Using the normal approximation to the binomial (Brownlee, 1965, Ch. 3, Sections 3.1 to 3.2), the unit normal variate is $u_{1-P} = (13 - 0.5 - 14 \times 0.5)/\sqrt{14 \times (0.5)^2} = 2.9399$. Solving for the P-value we find that $P = 0.002$.

Trade and Competitiveness Act of 1988. Its purpose is to fund high-risk R&D that creates knowledge spillovers, of a kind that firms would not undertake on their own. The objective of ATP is not merely to subsidize, but to encourage new forms of research, especially joint research, and then to govern projects to ensure their successful completion. In this section, we identify contractual ATP infrastructure indicators, as well as pecuniary benefits of ATP. We also include some spillover indicators that pertain to universities.

ATP funds between 38 and 50% of project costs and this is the gross pecuniary benefit of program participation, before costs of participation are netted out. Since the mean subsidy rate is 48% and since its standard deviation is 2% the ATP contribution is nearly a constant proportion of project budget and it cannot be identified apart from total budget.

In return for support firms agree to a schedule of work. This is accompanied by milestones that require satisfactory completion in order to receive payment and to progress to the next step. This sequence of steps contributes to monitoring and to verification of progress on the RJVs. ATP support is not free, but instead requires matching effort by firms. In this sense, ATP–RJVs resemble CRADAs, where support by federal laboratories is in principle tied to progress of the research. In the empirical work we employ indicators of the effectiveness of ATP program structure, which are idiosyncratic across projects, to identify an ATP contractual effect, while holding budget and the ATP financial contribution constant.

Table VI reports descriptive statistics for the key variables. The top panel reports patents applied for and granted per project and firm, as well as the budget for the RJV project and the R&D budget of each firm-location that hosts the project. The projects yield an average of two patents applied for and one patent granted per firm. Patent applications are the preferred measure for this study because many projects are in progress or only recently concluded. Therefore, many patents granted are yet to be observed.

TABLE VI Projects of research laboratories in R&D-performing firms: Descriptive statistics for a study of RJVs sponsored by the ATP.

Variable	Mean	S.D.
RJV patent outcomes and budgetary variables		
Number of patent applications[a]	2.15	4.54
Number of patent grants[a]	0.92	2.35
Project R&D budget (in $'92 millions)	13.14	9.92
Number of firms per project	4.10	2.82
Project R&D budget per firm (in $'92 millions)	4.58	5.10
ATP share of project R&D budget	0.48	0.02
R&D budget of a firm (in $'92 millions)[b]	71.03	281.67
RJV project characteristics		
Project in information technology (1 if yes, 0 if no)	0.10	0.29
Firm initiates JV project (1 if yes, 0 if no)	0.71	0.45
RJV goals more ambitious than usual (1 if yes, 0 if no)	0.65	0.48
RJV represents a new direction for the firm (1 if yes, 0 if no)	0.76	0.43
Probability that RJV technical goals will be reached	0.55	0.25
Public technology infrastructure indicators		
ATP ensures stability of company funding (1 if yes, 0 if no)	0.80	0.40
ATP fosters cooperation among partners (1 if yes, 0 if no)	0.63	0.48
University collaboration important (1 if yes, 0 if no)	0.63	0.48
University technology licensing important (1 if yes, 0 if no)	0.11	0.31

Notes: Data source is the *Survey of ATP Joint Ventures*. The data were collected in 2004. They refer to projects that begin in the years from 1991 to 2001. The survey contains as many as 397 firm-participant observations that cover 142 RJVs. By firms in these data we mean branches of firms at specific locations.
[a] Patent applications and grants are at the firm and project level.
[b] R&D budget is at the firm level.

Average project budget amounts to 13.1 million dollars of 1992 for projects starting in years that range from 1991 to 2001. Because ATP's contribution is almost a constant proportion, we cannot identify a separate ATP effect even though ATP funding is half the budget. Notice that in the survey data four firms participate in an average project. If we divide each project budget by the number of firms we obtain an average budget per firm of 4.6 million dollars. The average firm-location spends 71 million dollars on R&D. Thus an average ATP project amounts to one out of 15 projects that comprise the R&D portfolios of the firm-locations.

The second panel of Table VI describes project characteristics that are important in the empirical work. We find that a dummy indicator of whether the project is in information technology (10% of observations) is sometimes significant in the patent equations.[20] Whether the firm initiates the RJV (71% of observations) is highly significant. One way to view this is as a correction for the fact that we know only the average budget per firm. The true allocation within an RJV likely favors initiating firms, which contribute an above average share of overall project budget.

In the analysis we use three indicators of project difficulty and novelty. These concern whether the RJV is more ambitious than a typical project for the firm; whether the RJV represents a new direction for the firm; and the probability that the JV technical goals will be reached. The first two are dummy variables with means of 0.65 and 0.76, respectively. The last is a continuous probability that is bounded between 0 and 1.0. In some of the empirical work we recode the probability in intervals and examine the grouped variable using ordered probit.

The third panel of Table VI contains indicators of contractual public technology infrastructure. These assess whether ATP ensures stability of company funding (mean 0.80); and whether ATP fosters cooperation among partners (mean 0.63). Besides these we have indicators of whether university collaboration is important and whether university licensing is important, whose means are, respectively, 0.63 and 0.11.[21] We turn now to the empirical work on RJVs.

3.1 Patenting at the Firm and Project Level

Table VII contains the results of fitting patent production functions to the firm and project data. The estimation method is negative binomial regression, which generalizes Poisson regression by introducing a Gamma-distributed random effect in the rate of arrival of the patents.[22] Certainly a Poisson model is suggested by the count nature of the data, which includes many zeroes, but in addition the variance exceeds the mean, which Poisson regression does not handle. Negative binomial regression is one way to take this into account.

A central issue is whether public technology infrastructure improves patent productivity or not. Accordingly, we organize the table around the inclusion of the infrastructure variables that we have discussed. Equations VII.1 to VII.4 report findings with patent applications as the dependent variable while VII.5 and VII.6 use patents granted.

In VII.1 and throughout we include an indicator for whether the project is in information technology. Projects in information technology yield significantly fewer patents than other technical areas.[23] We include the logarithm of average project budget and the indicator for

---

[20] Indicators of whether the project is in biotechnology, electronics, and photonics, or manufacturing are never significant and are dropped from the analysis.

[21] Hall *et al.* (2003) use an indicator of university involvement in a sample of 54 ATP projects, to show that this involvement lowers the chance of early project termination. They also demonstrate a positive correlation of university involvement with the difficulty of acquiring basic knowledge on a project.

[22] Hausman *et al.* (1984) is the fundamental paper on the econometrics of count data. See also Cameron and Trivedi (2005), Chapter 20, for an overview and a discussion of recent developments.

[23] Since the arrival rate of the patents is scaled in logarithms, the coefficient on the logarithm of project R&D budget per firm, about 0.7, is the elasticity of patents with respect to budget. This elasticity is usually found to be less than 1.0, either because larger R&D is less productive or aims at larger but fewer inventions.

initiation of the RJV. Both are positive and highly significant, with the initiation variable, as we have noted, likely correcting for errors in project budget.

Equation VII.2 adds indicators of whether the project is more ambitious or difficult than usual; and novelty – whether the project is a new direction for the firm. Difficulty tends to trump new direction. And yet both variables increase patent applications. Evidently, taking on a project that is more ambitious and original amounts to taking on risk. As compensation the project offers more technological opportunity and yields more patents.

VII.3 drops ambition but retains new direction, and it adds the probability that RJV technical goals will be reached, a measure of ease of the project. Because of this new direction absorbs some of the effect of ambition. The sign of the probability of reaching technical goals is negative, both here and elsewhere. One interpretation is that projects that are more likely to be completed are more incremental and yield fewer patents. VII.4 adds to VII.3 the two public infrastructure indicators for ATP (ensures stability; fosters cooperation) as well as the two for universities (collaboration and licensing). None of these indicators have any effect on patents holding constant R&D budget and other project characteristics. This is true jointly as well as individually: a χ^2 test of all four is insignificant ($\chi^2(4) = 5.18$, P-value ≈ 0.827).

VII.5 and VII.6 repeat VII.3 and VII.4 using patents granted as the dependent variable. The results are similar. Again the public infrastructure indicators are individually and jointly insignificant. The test of joint significance is $\chi^2(4) = 2.34$, P-value ≈ 0.327. With the exception of the subsidy provided by ATP, one has to conclude that public technology infrastructure has no effect on patents. To understand other, contractual-incentive effects of public technology infrastructure requires us to take a different approach.

3.2   Characteristics of Projects and Public Technology Infrastructure

It is possible that the effects of infrastructure are indirect and take place through project characteristics. In making this assumption we are in effect postulating a recursive system. Project characteristics consisting of difficulty and novelty drive patents, but prior to that public technology infrastructure may drive difficulty and novelty. This is precisely the intent of the ATP: to promote riskier R&D projects.

Table VIII follows this indirect approach. Equations VIII.1 and VIII.2 explore determinants of RJVs whose goals are more ambitious than usual. Since this is a 0–1 indicator we use probit analysis. In VIII.1 size of R&D budget of the firm-location encourages selection of more challenging projects.[24] Number of firms in the RJV makes projects less ambitious for the individual firm-participant, perhaps because of the substitution of outside resources for the firm's internal capacities. Both roles of ATP, in ensuring company funding as well as in fostering cooperation, are significantly more important for more ambitious projects. VIII.2 adds the importance of university collaboration and licensing. Only university collaboration is significant.

VIII.3 and VIII.4 explore determinants of whether the RJV project represents a new direction for the firm. Since this is a 0–1 indicator we again use probit analysis. Number of firms and size of R&D budget are insignificant but ATP's role in ensuring company funding and in fostering cooperation increase novelty. This pattern persists in VIII.4, which introduces university collaboration and technology licensing. Only collaboration is significant, suggesting that informal research with universities is more important than formal license agreements in the selection of more ambitious and novel projects.

---

[24] The R&D budget of the firm-location is not the project budget, as Table V explains. It captures size rather than causality, since it dates from 2004, after all the projects have started and many have ended.

TABLE VII Projects of research laboratories in R&D-performing firms: Patent Production Functions of RJVs (Asymptotic standard errors in parentheses).

Variable or statistic	Patents applied for				Patents granted	
	VII.1	VII.2	VII.3	VII.4	VII.5	VII.6
Project in information technology (1 if yes, 0 if no)	-1.12* (0.38)	-0.83** (0.40)	-0.97* (0.38)	-0.89** (0.38)	-1.62* (0.49)	-1.65* (0.50)
Log (project R&D budget per firm) (in $'92 millions)	0.71* (0.13)	0.70* (0.13)	0.67* (0.12)	0.65* (0.12)	0.83* (0.15)	0.85* (0.15)
Firm initiates RJV project (1 if yes, 0 if no)	1.99* (0.29)	1.80* (0.30)	1.72* (0.30)	1.56* (0.31)	1.45* (0.35)	1.39* (0.36)
RJV goals more ambitious than usual (1 if yes, 0 if no)		0.68* (0.24)				
RJV represents a new direction for the firm (1 if yes, 0 if no)		0.32 (0.30)	0.64** (0.28)	0.51 (0.29)	0.57 (0.34)	0.51 (0.35)
Probability that RJV technical goals will be reached			-2.29* (0.45)	-2.25** (0.46)	-2.05* (0.51)	-1.93* (0.53)
ATP ensures stability of company funding (1 if yes, 0 if no)				0.24 (0.34)		0.27 (0.39)
ATP fosters cooperation among partners (1 if yes, 0 if no)				0.20 (0.24)		0.07 (0.28)
University collaboration important (1 if yes, 0 if no)				0.41 (0.25)		0.13 (0.28)
University technology licensing important (1 if yes, 0 if no)				-0.30 (0.34)		-0.55 (0.43)
N	381	381	381	381	378	378
Log likelihood	-593.45	-588.12	-578.34	-575.75	-384.22	-383.05
χ^2	96.72*	107.37*	126.92*	132.12*	95.30*	97.64*

Notes: Data source is the Survey of ATP Joint Ventures. Estimation method is negative binomial regression. All equations include dummies for the expected year of project completion.
*Parameter or statistic is significantly different from zero at the 1% level.
**Parameter or statistic is significantly different from zero at the 5% level.

TABLE VIII   Projects of research laboratories in R&D-performing firms ambition of goals, new direction, and probability of success RJVs characteristics (asymptotic standard errors in parentheses).

Variable or statistic	RJV goals more ambitious than usual (1 if yes, 0 if no)		RJV represents a new direction for the firm (1 if yes, 0 if no)		Probability that RJV technical goals will be Reached[a]	
	VIII.1	VIII.2	VIII.3	VIII.4	VIII.5	VIII.6
Estimation method	Probit				Ordered Probit	
Project in information technology (1 if yes, 0 if no)					0.40** (0.19)	0.40** (0.19)
ATP ensures stability of company funding (1 if yes, 0 if no)	0.46* (0.18)	0.41** (0.18)	0.59* (0.18)	0.54* (0.18)	−0.40* (0.15)	−0.39* (0.15)
ATP fosters cooperation among partners (1 if yes, 0 if no)	0.39* (0.15)	0.34** (0.15)	0.41* (0.16)	0.37** (0.16)	0.14 (0.12)	0.16 (0.13)
University collaboration important (1 if yes, 0 if no)		0.36* (0.15)		0.33* (0.16)	−0.07 (0.12)	−0.07 (0.12)
University technology licensing important (1 if yes, 0 if no)		−0.01 (0.23)		−0.11 (0.24)	−0.03 (0.18)	−0.03 (0.18)
Number of firms	−0.04 (0.02)	−0.05* (0.02)	−0.02 (0.03)	−0.03 (0.03)	0.02 (0.02)	0.018 (0.020)
Log (R&D budget of a firm-location) (in $ 1992 millions)	0.044* (0.017)	0.042* (0.017)	0.032 (0.018)	0.030 (0.018)	−0.067* (0.014)	−0.066* (0.014)
Lower cut point					−0.872	−0.897
Middle cut point					−0.054	−0.079
Upper cut point					0.663	0.639
Log likelihood	−237.48	−234.25	−198.12	−195.88	−527.85	−527.62
χ^2	40.39*	46.87*	38.34*	42.82*	40.72*	41.19*

Notes: Data source is the *Survey of ATP Joint Ventures*. The number of observations is $N = 397$. [a] Dependent variable is a recode of the Probability that JV technical goals will be reached into the following intervals: 0–0.4, 0.4–0.6, 0.6–0.8, and 0.8–1.0.
*Parameter or statistic is significantly different from zero at the 1% level.
**Parameter or statistic is significantly different from zero at the 5% level.

Both Table VIII and the empirical work conclude with a study of the probability of RJV success. We group the probability of success into intervals ranging from 0 to 0.4, 0.4 to 0.6, 0.6 to 0.8, and 0.8 to 1.0. Then we apply ordered probit to the grouped variable. The results are shown in VIII.5 and VIII.6. We find that IT-related projects are more likely to attain their goals. Their relative ease may explain why IT was associated with fewer patents in Table II.

The arrangement of VIII.5 and VIII.6 is otherwise the same. Overall R&D budget predicts a lower probability that project goals will be reached, so that larger laboratories select harder projects. The role of ATP in ensuring stability of funding shifts the outcome towards a lower probability of completion. This result is consistent with VIII.1 and VIII.2, which found that ensuring stability selected for more ambitious projects. Together these results suggest that ATP plays a larger role in more difficult and risky projects. The role of ATP in fostering cooperation has no effect on the probability that technical goals will be reached. Likewise, the university collaboration indicator is insignificant in VIII.6.

In summary, contractual-incentive features of ATP projects appear to favor the choice of more difficult and novel projects in Table VIII. These projects are the same ones that produce more patents in Table VII. Besides this, university collaboration also selects for harder projects, as does size of R&D budget of the firm, perhaps because size mitigates risk.

4 CONCLUDING COMMENTS

In this article, public, technology infrastructure consists of resources, such as research subsidies, knowledge spillovers, and contractual incentives that bring new forms of R&D into existence. Such infrastructure seems to increase R&D sourcing and the productivity of RJVs according to our findings. Thus, public technology infrastructure, as well as the legislation that enables it, appears to stimulate R&D alliances in industry.

There are of course, many questions that are left unanswered by these findings. The results do not address the appropriate balance of subsidies and incentives. In particular they do not consider questions as to the appropriate design of the incentives, and for a given design, the minimal subsidy required to attract R&D alliances. Little is known about the cost-benefit analysis of public technology infrastructure, including the social cost of administering the programs as well as the social benefits that flow from them. The design of public programs that can usefully promote R&D alliances in industry is an art that has just recently been born. One might say with some justification that it is not yet in its full infancy.

Acknowledgements

This research was supported by NSF Grant SBR-9502968 and NIST Contract SB1341-03-C-0059. We thank the editors and referees for their comments, as well as seminar participants at the State University of New York at Albany, Union College, Rensselaer Polytechnic Institute, and Boston University School of Management. G.S. Maddala and Chunrong Ai were effective teachers of the econometrics used in this paper.

References

Abraham, K.G. and Taylor, S.K. (1996) Firms' Use of Outside Contractors: Theory and Evidence. *Journal of Labor Economics*, **14**(2), 394–424.

Adams, J.D., Chiang, E.P. and Jensen, J.L. (2003) The Influence of Federal Laboratory R&D on Industrial Research. *Review of Economics and Statistics*, **85**(4), 1003–1020.

Adams, J.D. and Marcu, M. (2004) R&D Sourcing, Joint Ventures and Innovation: A Multiple Indicators Approach. NBER Working Paper No. 10474, Cambridge, Massachusetts.

Adams, J.D. (2006) Learning, Internal Research, and Spillovers. *Economics of Innovation and New Technology*, **15**(1), 5–36.

Aghion, P. and Tirole, J. (1994) The Management of Innovation. *Quarterly Journal of Economics*, **109**(4), 1185–1210.

Azoulay, P. (2004) Capturing Knowledge within and across Firm Boundaries: Evidence from Clinical Development. *American Economic Review*, **94**(4), 1591–1612.

Brownlee, K.A. (1965) *Statistical Theory and Methodology in Science and Engineering*, 2nd edn. New York: John Wiley and Sons.

Cameron, A.C. and Trivedi, P.K. (2005) *Microeconometrics*, 1st edn. New York: Cambridge University Press.

Greene, W.H. (2000) *Econometric Analysis*, 4th edn. Upper Saddle River, NJ: Prentice-Hall.

Griliches, Z. (1991) The Search for R&D Spillovers. *Scandinavian Journal of Economics*, **94**(Suppl.), 29–47.

Hagedoorn, J., Link, A.N. and Vonortas, N.S. (2000) Research Partnerships. *Research Policy*, **29**(4–5), 567–586.

Hall, B.H., Link, A.N. and Scott, J.T. (2003) Universities as Research Partners. *Review of Economics and Statistics*, **85**(2), 485–491.

Hausman, J., Hall, B.H. and Griliches, Z. (1984) Econometric Models for Count Data, with an Application to the Patents–R&D Relationship. *Econometrica*, **52**(4), 909–938.

Holmstrom, B. and Roberts, J. (1998) The Boundaries of the Firm Revisited. *Journal of Economic Perspectives*, **12**(4), 73–94.

Jankowski, J.E. (1993) Do We Need a Price Index for Industrial R&D? *Research Policy*, **22**(2), 195–205.

Jones, C.I. (2002) *Introduction to Modern Economic Growth*, 2nd edn. New York: W.W. Norton and Company.

Kogut, B. (1991) Joint Ventures and the Option to Expand and Acquire. *Management Science*, **37**(1), 19–33.

Monteverde, K. and Teece, D.J. (1982) Supplier Switching Costs and Vertical Integration. *Bell Journal of Economics*, **13**(2), 206–213.

Mowery, D.C. (1992) International Collaborative Ventures and the Commercialization of New Technologies. In Rosenberg, N., Landau, R. and Mowery, D. (eds.) *Technology and the Wealth of Nations*. Stanford, CA: Stanford University Press.

Mowery, D.C. (1995) The Boundaries of the U.S. Firm in R&D. In Lamoreaux, N. and Raff, D. (eds.) *Coordination and Information: Historical Perspectives on the Organization of Enterprise*. Chicago: University of Chicago Press for NBER.

Mowery, D.C., Oxley, J.E. and Silverman, B.S. (1998) Technological Overlap and Inter-Firm Cooperation: Implications for the Resource-Based View of the Firm. *Research Policy*, **27**(2), 507–523.

Pisano, G.P. (1990) The R&D Boundaries of the Firm: An Empirical Analysis. *Administrative Sciences Quarterly*, **35**(1), 153–176.

Standard and Poor Corporation (various years) *Compustat*. New York: McGraw-Hill.

Teece, D.J. (1977) Technology Transfer by Multi-National Firms: The Resource Cost of Transferring Technological Know-How. *The Economic Journal*, **87**(346), 242–261.

U.S. Bureau of the Census (1998) *1992 Economic Census CD-ROM 1J, C1-E92-EC1J-07-US1*. Washington, DC.

Von Hippel, E. (1988) *The Sources of Innovation*. New York: Oxford University Press.

APPENDIX

Bivariate Ordered Probit–Probit Likelihood

The equation system in Section 2.3 is

$$y_C^* \equiv \text{Outsource Engineering}_C^* = \gamma y_F + X_C' \beta_C + u_C$$
$$y_F^* \equiv \text{Federal R\&D}^* = X_F' \beta_F + u_F \tag{A1}$$

For the example in this paper the sample space is divided into six parts. This is because observed values of the ordered probit variable (y_F) are 1, 2, or 3 and by convention the Probit variable (y_F) assumes values of 0 or 1. We arrange these outcomes in a matrix:

$$\begin{pmatrix} 1,0 & 1,1 \\ 2,0 & 2,1 \\ 3,0 & 3,1 \end{pmatrix} \tag{A2}$$

Given (A1) and (A2), the joint probability that outsourcing engineering (to customers) falls in interval j and that federal R&D *is not* important is,

$$\Pr(y_C = j, y_F = 0) = P\left(a_j > y_C^* > a_{j-1}, y_F^* < 0\right) = P\left(a_j > y_C^*, y_F^* < 0\right) -$$
$$P\left(a_{j-1} > y_C^*, y_F^* < 0\right) = F\left(a_j - X_C'\beta_C, -X_F'\beta_F, \rho\right) - F\left(a_{j-1} - X_C'\beta_C, -X_F'\beta_F, \rho\right)$$
(A3)

In (A3) a_j and a_{j-1} are the 'cut' points and $F(\bullet)$ is the standard bivariate normal cumulative distribution function (CDF). We use the standardized normal distribution because probit analysis does not identify variances.

The joint probability that outsourcing engineering (to customers) falls in interval j and that federal R&D *is* important is,

$$\Pr(y_C = j, y_F = 1) = P\left(a_j > y_C^* > a_{j-1}, y_F^* > 0\right)$$
$$= P\left(a_j > y_C^* > a_{j-1}\right) - P\left(a_j > y_C^* > a_{j-1}, y_F^* < 0\right)$$
$$= \left[P\left(a_j > y_C^*\right) - P\left(a_{j-1} > y_C^*\right)\right] - \left[P\left(a_j > y_C^*, y_F^* < 0\right) - P\left(a_{j-1} > y_C^*, y_F^* < 0\right)\right]$$
$$= \left[\Phi\left(a_j - \gamma - X_C'\beta_C\right) - F\left(a_j - \gamma - X_C'\beta_C, -X_F'\beta_F, \rho\right)\right]$$
$$- \left[\Phi\left(a_{j-1} - \gamma - X_C'\beta_C\right) - F\left(a_{j-1} - \gamma - X_C'\beta_C, -X_F'\beta_F, \rho\right)\right]$$
(A4)

Here the function $\Phi(\bullet)$ is the standard univariate normal CDF and $F(\bullet)$ is defined as before.

For (A2), where the ordered probit variable takes on values of 1, 2, and 3, the 'cut points' are: $a_0 \equiv -\infty < a_1 < a_2 < a_3 \equiv +\infty$. Applying this to the probabilities (A3) and (A4) subject to (A2) we reach:

$$\Pr(1, 0) = F\left(a_1 - X_C'\beta_C, -X_F'\beta_F, \rho\right)$$
(A5)

$$\Pr(1, 1) = \Phi\left(a_1 - \gamma - X_C'\beta_C\right) - F\left(a_1 - \gamma - X_C'\beta_C, -X_F'\beta_F, \rho\right)$$
(A6)

$$\Pr(2, 0) = F\left(a_2 - \gamma - X_C'\beta_C, -X_F'\beta_F, \rho\right) - F\left(a_1 - \gamma - X_C'\beta_C, -X_F'\beta_F, \rho\right)$$
(A7)

$$\Pr(2, 1) = \left[\Phi\left(a_2 - \gamma - X_C'\beta_C\right) - F\left(a_2 - \gamma - X_C'\beta_C, -X_F'\beta_F, \rho\right)\right]$$
$$- \left[\Phi\left(a_1 - \gamma - X_C'\beta_C\right) - F\left(a_1 - \gamma - X_C'\beta_C, -X_F'\beta_F, \rho\right)\right]$$
(A8)

$$\Pr(3, 0) = \Phi\left(-X_F'\beta_F\right) - F\left(a_2 - X_C'\beta_C, -X_F'\beta_F, \rho\right)$$
(A9)

$$\Pr(3, 1) = \left[1 - \Phi\left(a_2 - \gamma - X_C'\beta_C\right)\right] - \left[\Phi\left(-X_F'\beta_F\right) - F\left(a_2 - \gamma - X_C'\beta_C, -X_F'\beta_F, \rho\right)\right]$$
(A10)

It can easily be shown that (A5) to (A10) sum to 1.0 so that this is a proper definition of the joint distribution. The likelihood function is

$$L = \prod_{i=1,\ldots,N} \prod_{j=1,2,3} \prod_{k=0,1} \Pr(y_C = j, y_F = k)^{M_{ij}N_{ik}}$$
(A11)

In (A11) i represents the observation, $M_{ij} = 1$ if the observation falls in interval j and 0 otherwise, and $N_{ik} = 1$ if the observation falls in interval k and 0 otherwise. We estimate the likelihood (A11) using STATA ML version 8.1.

PUBLIC–PRIVATE PARTNERSHIP TO DEVELOP TECHNOLOGY INFRASTRUCTURE: A CASE STUDY OF THE ECONOMIC RETURNS OF DNA DIAGNOSTICS

ALAN C. O'CONNOR and BRENT R. ROWE

114 Sansome Street, Suite 500, San Francisco, CA 94104, USA

1   INTRODUCTION

This paper is a case study of a public–private partnership undertaken as part of a US Advanced Technology Program (ATP) focused program designed to overcome gaps in the technology infrastructure supporting DNA diagnostics. The case study explores and illustrates the inter-connectedness of key technology infrastructure: technologies that increase the efficiency and efficacy of the products and services they enable, such as a piece of analytical equipment; protocols, standards, assays, and analytical methods developed to reap the greatest utility from analytical equipment and services and their output; and the processes and institutions that enable and support the underlying research and discovery of these methods and tools, such as research universities and government R&D programs.

Advanced DNA diagnostics technologies are a vital technology infrastructure with which researchers are finding new ways to diagnose and treat diseases and discover new medicines. These technologies – laboratory equipment, genomic data, assay techniques, and other tools – make practical use of our expanding knowledge of molecular biology and biochemistry.

They permit scientists to conduct robust analyses of disease susceptibility in humans, plants, and animals; forensics testing; disease identification; and drug efficacy studies. Most key medical discoveries and milestones achieved in the past decade were possible only because the DNA diagnostics technology infrastructure was in place to enable them. DNA diagnostics technologies are now critical to biotechnology and health-related research.

In the late 1980s and early 1990s, when ATP's Tools for DNA Diagnostics focused program was launched, the scientific community's understanding of molecular biology and genomics was increasing rapidly, as was the accumulation of genetic data. But tools had yet to be developed to efficiently acquire genetic information or to enable applications that held enormous potential for medical science (Abramowitz, 1996; Hodgson, 2000). ATP acted to fill the gap in the technology infrastructure by supporting early R&D of DNA diagnostic technologies that might not otherwise have been developed or whose introduction would have been significantly delayed because of underinvestment by private firms.[1] The aim of the focus program was to encourage the biotechnology sector to develop generic, inexpensive, and easy-to-use tools for rapid DNA analysis (Georgevich, 1997).

Biotechnology R&D is generally characterized by technologies requiring substantial investments in time, money, and effort to develop and sustain concepts through long incubation times. Before the focused program was created, the pharmaceutical industry and the investment community expected that large medical equipment suppliers would bring new analytical tools to market; however, the firms that met those expectations were predominantly small, start-up biotechnology companies founded by geneticists, molecular biologists, engineers, and their colleagues with significant technical savvy and application insight (Silverman, 1995). In the early years of biotechnology R&D, these firms generally had little access to capital and relied heavily on federal technology development and application awards, of which ATP was the largest, to continue their core research. ATP recognized significant technical and market barriers and responded by creating the focused program and awarding public-sector cost-sharing on a competitive basis for high-risk DNA diagnostics projects that promised significant public benefits (Abramowitz, 1996; Georgevich, 1997).

In this paper, we analyze ATP's largest and most ambitious Tools for DNA Diagnostics project, a joint project between Affymetrix and Molecular Dynamics that sought to overcome several key technical barriers to personalized medicine – the diagnosis, treatment, and management of patients' health based on their unique genetic make-up.[2] The research performed by two firms, who would not have otherwise collaborated or engaged in much of the research if it had not been for ATP's sponsorship, was critical to developing the technology infrastructure supporting medical and biotechnology research. Research outcomes yielded the development of advanced DNA microarray and DNA sequencing technologies, induced innovation at competitor firms, and supported the Human Genome Project.

This paper is organized as follows. Section 2 places this work within the larger body of innovation economics research. Section 3 reviews the two firms' project, the innovation process, and technology outcomes. Section 4 describes our approach to quantifying the impacts of this research. Sections 5 and 6 detail the economic impact calculations. Finally, Section 7 discusses qualitative benefits and implications.

---

[1] ATP was established as a program of the US National Institute of Standards and Technology (NIST) to create public–private partnerships to accelerate the development of high-risk, innovative technologies that promise significant benefits to the nation. ATP funds technology development projects using a cost-sharing method with industry partners who retain intellectual property rights to technology outcomes. For information about ATP's mission, please see *The Advanced Technology Program: Challenges and Opportunities*, Charles W. Wessner, Ed. (1999).

[2] The research findings in this paper are a subset of the findings of a broader examination of ATP's Tools for DNA Diagnostics focused program and project portfolio. The final report was released publicly in January 2007 and is available for download at http://www.atp.nist.gov/eao/gcr06-898.pdf.

2 LITERATURE REVIEW

The technology infrastructure is comprised of technologies that increase the efficiency and efficacy of the products and services as well as protocols, standards, assays, and analytical methods. Justman and Teubal (1995) describe the technological infrastructure as 'a set of collectively supplied, specific, industry-relevant capabilities, intended for several applications in two or more firms or user organizations' (p. 260). Tassey (1982, 1997, 2005) defines the technology infrastructure by using the term 'infratechnologies', which he defines as 'a diverse set of technical tools that are necessary to efficiently conduct all phases of R&D, to control production processes, and to execute marketplace transactions for complex technology-based goods' (2005, p. 92)

We offer an expansion of this definition to include the processes and programs that enable and support the underlying research and discovery into technological methods and tools, such as research universities and government R&D programs. For example, NIST and ATP therein, as well as other US government programs, such as the National Institutes of Health (NIH), Small Business Research Innovation (SBIR) grant program, can be considered part of the technology infrastructure because these programs' intent is to guide, sponsor, and encourage the development of technologies by private-sector organizations for applications that promise substantial positive social benefits.

The development process for the technology infrastructure has been studied extensively. The coordination of research partnerships between companies is credited with fostering much of this research (Hagedoorn et al., 2000; Baumol, 2001; Link and Scott, 2001; Link et al., 2002; Link et al., 2005). At the crux of the study of infrastructure technology is the idea that individual or shared research can have benefits that extend beyond one company or group of companies. The concept of such benefits was first discussed in Marshall (1920), and spillovers benefits have been the subject of many studies (e.g. Bresnahan, 1986; Jaffe, 1986, 1996; Bernstein, 1989). Another benefit is the idea of induced innovation; that is, when development at one company motivates another company (or companies) to develop a new technology more quickly to compete, and customers benefit based on more selection and faster time to market of products (Ruttan, 2001).

ATP itself has also been the focus of significant analysis since its origination. ATP funded a variety of case studies (e.g. Link and Scott, 2005; White and Gallaher, 2002; White and O'Connor, 2004; Pelsoci, 2007, 2005) and conceptual analyses (e.g. Jaffe, 1996; Mansfield, 1996; Fogarty et al., 2006). Among many published research articles, in 1998, the *Journal of Technology Transfer* sponsored a special edition entitled 'Symposium on Evaluating a Public Private Partnership: The Advanced Technology Program' (Ruegg, 1998). Other analyses of ATP include Link and Scott (2005) and Link (1999). This paper builds on past empirical research (e.g. Blind and Grupp, 1999; Link and Scott, 2005) on the impact of investments in the technology infrastructure and ATP's role in such by offering an analysis of the impact of one public–private partnership on the infrastructure supporting DNA diagnostics.

3 THE MIND DEVELOPMENT PROJECT

ATP awarded the MIND Development project to Affymetrix and Molecular Dynamics in 1994. The aim of the project was to develop a miniaturized, handheld integrated nucleic acid diagnostic device that could provide physicians with an inexpensive, easy-to-use, and fast tool for analyzing patients' blood samples and providing a clinical diagnosis. The companies' proposal set an overall goal of developing the full suite of instrumentation, assays, protocols, and data analysis and management systems necessary to make such a device a reality. Although ATP and the two firms considered the device's development to be a significant technological leap, ATP considered the two firms' capabilities a promising combination for overcoming key technical barriers related to genetic analysis, biological sample acquisition, and instrumentation. The project lasted 5 years, and ATP provided nearly one-half of the 5-year (1995 –2000) project's $57.2 million budget.[3]

Affymetrix was founded by academics who had invented DNA microarrays, which are glass wafers the size of a thumbnail tiled with probes made of genetic sequences. Researchers use DNA microarrays to investigate large numbers of genes simultaneously in blood or tissue samples. DNA microarrays are an important component of medical research because they document cells' responses to diseases and the effects of drug treatments (Gerhold *et al.*, 2002). Molecular Dynamics was a small molecular biology instrument manufacturer and had built Affymetrix's first microarray scanner.[4]

The two firms jointly set technical objectives but worked independently. Their strategy was to develop the constituent components of the device and bring them together when possible. Each firm would commercialize its own technology milestones. A DNA microarray would serve as the core of the handheld device, and Affymetrix set about adapting and miniaturizing its microarray technology for that purpose and developing needed sample preparation, measurement, and analysis systems. Molecular Dynamics set about developing advanced biochemistries and designing the device's instrumentation.

The ambitious aim of developing the handheld device was not accomplished, but several key technology infrastructure needs identified by ATP for DNA diagnostics were achieved. As research progressed, the market opportunity shifted from point-of-care technologies toward advanced research tools; thus, the two firms reoriented their technical goals and commercialization strategies. Each company commercialized technologies that substantially improved the efficiency and effectiveness of research in molecular biology.

In this paper, we quantify the laboratory efficiency gains from the contribution of these technologies to the molecular biology technology infrastructure supporting medical and scientific research. Affymetrix representatives indicated that their microarray technology was accelerated 1.5 years and that, although three-quarters of the commercialized work would likely have been developed in the absence of the project, ATP's support was critical to its commercial success. Each probe on a microarray was reduced in size from 50 to 25 microns, which increased microarrays' analytic capacity 4-fold. Affymetrix's ATP project work contributed significantly to microarrays' application environment, including measurement systems, assay protocols, and software for data management and analysis.

Molecular Dynamics' ATP-cofunded technologies greatly accelerated the acquisition of sequenced DNA. The need for improved DNA sequencing technologies was apparent during the earliest years of the Human Genome Project, the effort to acquire the full sequence of human DNA. For researchers to achieve their aim of understanding the link between human disease and certain genes, they first needed to decipher the sequence of the approximately 3 billion DNA base pairs contained in 23 pairs of human chromosomes.[5]

---

[3] The original project budget was $63.0 million, just under half of which would be provided by ATP. The project's official period of performance was February 1995 through January 2000, but this analysis simplified that period to whole calendar years. ATP projects are awarded on a cost-sharing basis, and Affymetrix and Molecular Dynamics matched $18.5 million and $10.1 million, respectively.

[4] In the decade following the project's award, Affymetrix became the dominant microarray producer and Molecular Dynamics ultimately became part of GE Healthcare, but at the time of the project award both were small, technology-based organizations.

[5] DNA in all living things is composed of four bases – adenine (A),thymine (T), guanine (G), and cytosine (C). Each strand of an organism's DNA will have these bases in a specific order, and the strands are complementary, where A on one strand bonds with T on the other, and C on one strand bonds with G on the other. Each rung in the double helix ladder of a DNA molecule is commonly referred to as a base pair (bp).

TABLE I   Productivity comparison of slab gel and high-throughput capillary DNA sequencers.

	Slab gel electrophoresis (ABI Prism 377)	Capillary array electrophoresis (MegaBACE 1000)
Instrument run time	6.5 h	2.5 h
Combined instrument run time and manual intervention time	6.83 h	2.75 h
Number of lanes	96 lanes	96 lanes
Average readlength	400 bps	650 bps
Pass rate	85%	98%
Consumables cost per sample (lane)	$0.50	$1.25

Through most of the 1990s, determining genetic sequences was costly and time consuming; even the most well-equipped laboratories were only able to acquire a small amount of one genetic sequence every few days (Regis, 1995; Meldrum, 2001). In collaboration with Richard Mathies at the University of California, Berkeley, Molecular Dynamics' ATP-cofunded project activities led to the development of the first high-throughput DNA sequencer, the MegaBACE 1000. A DNA sequencer is a laboratory instrument that determines the order of nucleotides that comprise pieces of DNA. The defender technology for sequencing DNA, slab gel electrophoresis, required careful handling, pouring, and placing of sensitive gels. Errors in gel placement, handling, or preparation often impeded data collection and required data verification steps. Molecular Dynamics developed a new sequencer that used capillary array electrophoresis (CAE). This technology was a liquid-based system that analyzed DNA fragments placed in capillary tubes, avoiding gel electrophoresis' manual processes and toxic materials while also providing higher data quality and greater throughput.

The efficiency of the new sequencers as compared to the old ones can be seen in measures of their output. The slab gel sequencers required an average of 6.5 h to complete one sequencing cycle in which 96 samples were analyzed. Each sample was read to a typical length of 400 base pairs (bps), for a total of 38,400 bps or 5900 bps/h. In contrast, Molecular Dynamics' MegaBACE required 2.5 h to complete one cycle and could read 96 samples to an average readlength of 650. Researchers could acquire more data (62,400 bps), more quickly (24,960 bps/h), and at a higher quality. The average percentage of that data that met quality standards was 98% for the MegaBACE vs. 85% for the slab gel instrument (see Tab. I).

The MegaBACE's introduction in 1997 induced innovation at Molecular Dynamics' principal competitor, Applied Biosystems, Inc. (ABI), the industry leader in sequencing technology that marketed slab gel sequencers. It was later learned that ABI had a similar capillary-based instrument in the early stages of development. ABI responded to the MegaBACE's introduction by accelerating development of its own capillary sequencer, the ABI Prism 3700 (Goozner, 2000; Shreeve, 2004; Karow, 2006). James Shreeve's (2004) The Genome War, a highly regarded description of the sequencing of the human genome, provides first-person accounts from insiders at ABI that the 3700 was accelerated by at least 1 year.

With the introduction of the MegaBACE and the accelerated introduction of the Prism 3700 sequencer, sequencing moved from a cumbersome process to a highly automated process that produced several times more data with near-perfect accuracy. High-throughput sequencers moved the genome project's target completion date for a finished draft forward from 2006 to 2003 (Hodgson 2000). The project was supposed to be completed in 2006, but a first draft of 90% of the genome was completed in June 2000. Significant downstream impacts on data analysis, outcomes, and research were enabled by the sequenced human genome.

4   ANALYTICAL APPROACH

Affymetrix's DNA microarrays and Molecular Dynamics' sequencer are infrastructure tools for acquiring information. Placing a value on the information acquired and the downstream scientific discovery enabled by these tools was not possible. In the absence of a system that could be easily modeled, we valued the technological improvements in terms of what it would have taken researchers to acquire the same data volumes with the defender technologies as with the new ones. The primary result of the improvements was considered to be a cost or price reduction to their end user. Thus, to quantify economic benefits, we follow the methodologies pioneered by Griliches (1958) and Mansfield *et al.* (1977).

Counterfactual scenarios – as employed by others (e.g. White and Gallaher, 2002; White and O'Connor, 2004; Link and Scott, 2005; Pelsoci, 2005, 2007) and described by Powell (2006) – were used to quantify net public benefits by estimating the hypothetical costs of generating the same volume of genetic data using the processes and technologies the ATP-cofunded innovations replaced.

Because returns to the innovator could not be estimated reliably, our analysis excluded private benefits and costs.[6] This study focused on quantifying net benefits accruing to end users (public benefits) and compared those benefits to ATP's portion of project expenses (public costs). Net public benefits from the ATP project were estimated by measuring resource savings from adopting technology outcomes, less adoption costs and the funds ATP invested in the project. We also quantified spillover benefits from induced innovation at ABI to the ATP-sponsored project; end user benefits from Prism 3700s installed in 1999 were included net of adoption costs.

Resource savings encompassed avoided equipment costs, fully burdened wages, and other expenses that end users would have otherwise incurred. For instance, if data volume were held constant, economic benefits would be the cost savings of using more efficient Affymetrix microarrays instead of the previous ones. Thus, our net public benefit estimates capture the value of having acquired the same information in the currency of the technology the project superseded.

Data to inform the technical and economic impact metrics were collected from primary and secondary data sources. Primary data sources included current and former representatives from the funded firms, end users, ATP, and individuals with significant domain expertise in and historical knowledge of the technologies and the events surrounding the technologies' development. Secondary sources included published articles in scientific and engineering journals, trade publications, and reports issued by government agencies.

5   CALCULATING ECONOMIC BENEFITS FROM AFFYMETRIX'S ATP ACTIVITIES

The economic analysis of Affymetrix's project outcomes quantified the public benefits of the 1.5-year acceleration of microarrays with a fourfold increase in probe density. The first Affymetrix microarray with a 25-micron probe size was introduced in early 1999. We valued the defender microarrays, consumables, and labor hours that would have been needed to acquire the same data volume as the improved microarrays did between 1999 and mid-2000.

---

[6] To quantify private impacts, we would need information on R&D expenditures and past/projected sales revenues. This information is typically confidential and difficult to identify because of technology interactions.

TABLE II   Avoided microarray expense benefits (2005$).

	1999	2000
Average unit price	$468	$452
Estimated unit sales	98,000	87,500
Avoided microarray assays	294,000	262,500
Maximum avoided microarray expenses	$137,592,000	$118,650,000
Maximum avoided consumables expenses	$58,800,000	$52,500,000
Maximum avoided labor expenses	$21,268,000	$18,989,000
Benefits attributable to ATP funding (25%)	$54,415,000	$47,535,000

We estimated the number of microarrays sold in 1999 through the first half of 2000 to be 98,000 and 87,500 units, respectively (see Tab. II).[7]

We calculated annual benefits by determining the benefits attributable to one improved microarray and multiplied those benefits by the unit sales estimates. Each improved microarray yielded the same amount of information as four defender microarrays. Implicit in claiming three times the actual number of units sold as a benefit is accepting the fourth unit as the public cost of adoption. Reagents, dyes, and other consumables estimated to cost $200 per microarray are needed to work with each microarray. Each microarray assay takes approximately 2 h of manual intervention, which we valued at $72.34 per hour.[8]

The total benefit cannot be attributed solely to the ATP project because Affymetrix likely would have developed some of the same commercialized technologies outside of the project. For example, Affymetrix needed the software, protocols, and supporting technologies for microarrays to gain market acceptance. Similarly, Affymetrix needed to shrink probe sizes because more densely tiled chips are more efficient for end users. The company believed that 75% of the commercialized work from the project would have been undertaken without the award. Therefore, we assumed that the remaining 25% approximates the public benefits from ATP sponsorship.

6   ESTIMATING BENEFITS FROM MOLECULAR DYNAMICS' ATP ACTIVITIES

Net public benefits from Molecular Dynamics' ATP-cofunded technologies were calculated as the benefits observed by users of MegaBACE 1000 instruments installed in 1997 through 2000 and those Prism 3700 instruments installed in 1999.[9] We calculated benefits for new installations through the counterfactual estimated introduction date of the Prism 3700 in 2000.

Benefits accruing to end users when few alternatives are available, such as during the tight market for sequencers in 1999–2000, were claimed. However, once a competitive product was available in sufficient quantity, public benefits attributable to ATP ended. Molecular Dynamics' production of the MegaBACE allowed end users to acquire capillary instruments for their

---

[7] Affymetrix's total full-year product sales are available from its filings with the Securities and Exchange Commission (SEC): $114.9 million (1999) and $196.1 million (2000). Probe array sales accounted for approximately 40% of total product sales during this period. The balance of product sales was for consumables and the instrumentation.

[8] Data collected by the US Bureau of Labor Statistics reveal that the average unburdened wage for a laboratory technician in 2004 was $17.56/h (BLS 2005). Adjusting for inflation and multiplying the result by 2.0 to account for benefits, payroll taxes, and employee administrative and overhead costs yield an average fully burdened hourly cost of $36.17. The labor expense benefit per avoided microarray experiment is $72.34.

[9] Data on the installed base of MegaBACE and ABI sequencers were obtained from company Forms 10-K and equivalent reports. Annual US MegaBACE installations for 1998–2000 were 90, 170, and 210 units, respectively. ABI installed 500 Prism 3700s in the United States in 1999.

TABLE III   Estimated installed base and associated sequencing volume, 1998–2005.

Year	Cumulative capillary sequencer installs	Midpoint of installed base	Acceptable output (million bps)	Number of runs-capillary instruments (thousands)	Raw data output-capillary instruments (million bps)	Raw data output-slab gel instruments (million bps)	Number of runs-slab gel instruments (thousands)
1998	0	45	4,003	65	4,084	4,709	123
1999	760	425	37,803	618	38,575	44,474	1,158
2000	970	865	76,940	1,258	78,511	90,518	2,357
2001	970	970	64,710	1,058	66,031	76,129	1,983
2002	970	970	64,710	1,058	66,031	76,129	1,983
2003	880	925	61,708	1,009	62,967	72,598	1,891
2004	210	545	36,358	595	37,100	42,774	1,114
2005	0	105	7,005	115	7,148	8,241	215

projects when they otherwise would have had to purchase the less efficient slab gel sequencers or forgo high-throughput sequencing altogether. We estimated that this continued through the end of 2000, before the sequencer market slowed following completion of the draft human genome (Coty, 2002). Beyond 2000, if the MegaBACE had not been available, end users would have chosen the 3700 instead and would have received the same benefits as from the MegaBACE sequencers. Net public benefits were the incremental counterfactual costs of using slab gel sequencers to achieve the same data volume as capillary sequencers, less adoption costs.

6.1   Estimating the installed base of capillary sequencers

The US installed base for which benefits were calculated totaled 470 MegaBACE sequencers and 500 ABI 3700 sequencers.[10] It was assumed to have grown linearly during any given year, allowing us to use the midpoint of the yearly installed base as a base from which to estimate the volume of data generated, and thereby the cost savings. Both the MegaBACE and the 3700 were estimated to have a useful life of 5 years, after which they would have no residual value (see Tab. III). The installed base grew through 2000 and began to decline in 2003 as instruments were retired. Thus, the last year for which benefits were calculated was 2005.

6.2   Estimating sequencing data production volumes

Estimated data production volume is a function of the number of instruments, how often the instruments were operated, the amount of data acquired from each run, and the amount of time required to complete one run, including instrument set up and other processes. Based on our interviews, we assumed that through 2000 (or until the first draft of the human genome was published) capillary sequencers were operated, on average, two shifts a day, 5 days a week. This equated to 4,000 h/year, per instrument. Following the completion of the human genome, and therefore beginning in 2001, many sequencing centers slowed their production rates. End users believe that most sequencers were operating, on average, one and a half shifts per day.[11]

---

[10] Approximate exports of 40–60% of sequencer production imply that similar benefits and costs accrued to non-US users, with the noted exception of the public technology development cost share. However, this research was sponsored by ATP; accordingly, the focus of our research and analysis was on the benefits to US end users.

[11] The majority of capillary sequencers purchased between 1999 and 2000 were installed at major genome centers and research laboratories that had adopted an industrial-scale production environment to sequence human, mouse, rat, wheat, and other genomes of significant scientific and commercial value. Private-sector laboratories were concurrently seeking out new genes for drug discovery. Many of these laboratories operated 24 h a day, 7 days a week, every week

TABLE IV   Benefits from introduction of capillary DNA sequencers (2005$).

Year	Labor benefits	Consumables benefits	Avoided equipment expenditures	Adoption costs-megaBACE 1000	Adoption costs-prism 3700	Public benefits-capillary DNA sequencers
1998	$5,307,000	−$1,968,000	$14,220,000	−$21,060,000		−$3,501,000
1999	50,126,000	−18,589,000	120,079,000	−39,780,000	−$165,500,000	−53,664,000
2000	102,021,000	−37,834,000	139,039,000	−49,140,000		154,085,000
2001	85,803,000	−31,820,000				53,983,000
2002	85,803,000	−31,820,000				53,983,000
2003	81,823,000	−30,344,000				51,479,000
2004	48,209,000	−17,878,000				30,331,000
2005	9,288,000	−3,444,000				5,844,000
Total	468,380,000	−173,699,000				292,540,000

Under these operating conditions, one MegaBACE would produce 90.8 million bps of raw data output per year.[12] In 2000, approximately 78.5 billion bps were sequenced, of which 98% were of acceptable quality. The corresponding data volume required from slab gel sequencers to achieve the same results would have been 90.5 billion, which would have required 2.36 million runs instead of the capillary instruments' 1.26 million. Table IV presents the estimated annual sequencing volume of acceptable data and presents a comparison of slab gel and capillary platforms for achieving the same.

6.3   Calculating public benefit-cost estimates

We calculated annual benefits as follows.

- *Avoided labor expenses*: The incremental 65 minutes required per run (Table 1) were monetized using a fully burdened $36.17 hourly wage to derive the annual labor benefit of using capillary sequencers: $102,020,000 in 2000.[13]
- *Avoided consumables expenses*: The consumables used by the capillary sequencers were more expensive than the slab gels' consumables. Laboratories measure the cost of consumables as the cost per lane, which is the cost of sequencing one DNA fragment in one capillary or gel lane one time.
- *Net equipment benefits*: The net equipment benefit is the difference between the savings on avoiding additional slab gel instrument purchases and the cost of adopting capillary instruments. Under the counterfactual scenario, it is assumed that labs initially would have had the same number of slab gel instruments as capillary instruments. For 1998, if around 123,000 runs were required, but only 45 slab gels were installed at those labs, they would only be able to complete approximately 39,000 runs if operated three shifts a day.[14] The deficit

---

of the year. However, units were also installed at smaller laboratories that operated less frequently. Assuming that all units were operating continuously would overstate benefits.

[12] Dividing the total number of shift hours per year (4,000 h in 1998) by the sum of the instrument's run and manual intervention times (2.75 h) yields the number of runs the instrument can yield in two shifts per year – about 1,455 runs. Each run sequences one plate of 96 samples, each of which would be read to 650 bps, on average.

[13] The calculation for capillary sequencers is 0.25 h/run × $36.17/h × 1.258 million runs ≈ $11,377,000. For slab gel sequencers, it is 1.33 h/run × $36.17/h × 2.357 million runs ≈ $113,398,000. It is important to note that the total number of shifts required per year under the counterfactual scenario would have exceeded three shifts per day. This means that many additional technicians would have been needed and additional slab gel sequencers would have been required. This analysis assumed that when a technician would not be setting up an instrument for a run that he or she would be free for activities in gel preparation, cleanup, and postrun lane retracking. Despite this assumption, additional 96-lane ABI 377 sequencers would have been required.

[14] The calculation for the number of runs possible for a unit operated in three shifts per year is (6,000 h/year)/(6.83 h/run) × 45 sequencers.

would need to have been met by installing approximately 95 more instruments to perform the remaining 84,000 runs. At a cost of nearly $150,000 each, the additional equipment expense would have been $14,220,000. Because of the 5-year equipment lifetime, installations from 1998 were available in later years. Labs would have had to install additional units in 1999 and 2000, but capacity would have been sufficient beyond 2000.

Adoption costs constituted the installed price per sequencer multiplied by the number of sequencers installed. The average price paid for the MegaBACE 1000 and ABI 3700 was $234,000 and $331,000, respectively, in constant 2005 dollars (Mardis, 1999).[15] Table 4 presents a time series of public benefits and costs. Total net benefits the public realized from Molecular Dynamics' project work were estimated to be $280.2 million, with most accruing during 2000, the year in which the initial draft of the human genome project was completed.

7 CONCLUSIONS AND IMPLICATIONS

The widespread impact of DNA diagnostics equipment and techniques and the use of such to support applications in many fields exemplify their characterization as part of the technology infrastructure. The purpose of DNA diagnostics research is to develop new tools and techniques that researchers and health care providers can leverage to solve complex biological questions (e.g. what genetic characteristics cause a certain disease) and enable better health care for the general public. The programs established to encourage innovation are themselves a part of the broader technology infrastructure because they support research through direct labor, coordination efforts, and, in the case of ATP, sponsorship of private-sector research.

ATP and the companies achieved many of their goals for the project. ATP accelerated the closure of a technology infrastructure gap and the two firms stated that they benefited financially through increased profits and licensing arrangements, although we were unable to access this information. ATP's support helped increase the prominence of a new industry. Representatives from Affymetrix and the former Molecular Dynamics believe that the success of the project and ATP's support encouraged other firms to develop and market technologies for what was becoming the pharmacogenomics and genomics marketplace. Affymetrix's ATP-supported software research may have spawned a new market that serves the computing needs of molecular biology applications.

Table V presents a time series of public benefits, ATP (public) costs, and net public benefits. Net public benefits that accrued over 1995–2005 were $359.8 million. Applying a 7% real discount rate[16] yields a net present value for the entire project of $215.6 million, which corresponds to an internal rate of return of 84% and a benefit-to-cost ratio of 8.7.[17] Further, spillover benefits such as induced innovation at ABI and downstream benefits from licensing agreements have increased the impact of this research dramatically.

Ultimately, the principal beneficiaries of these technologies are patients who receive more timely, better quality, and more effective health care because doctors, clinicians, and researchers have more powerful DNA diagnostic tools. The information generated – a sequenced genome, an expression profile of a diseased tissue sample, or an early warning of

---

[15] In nominal terms, the ABI Prism 3700 price was $100,000 more than the MegaBACE 1000 at $300,000. The incremental difference in price is partly explained by the fact that the 3700 had an automatic loading probe. ABI also had substantially more brand presence; an established reputation; and a more extensive sales, marketing, and service infrastructure than Molecular Dynamics had during the period covered in this analysis.

[16] We used a 7% real discount rate based on the US Office of Management and Budget's (OMB's) Circular Number A-94, which provides guidance for analyses of government investments.

[17] Note that our case study is based largely on interview data; thus, the results may be sensitive to interviewer bias.

TABLE V   Annual public benefits, public costs, and net public benefits-MIND development project (2005$).

Year	Public benefits—capillary DNA sequencers	Public benefits—advanced DNA microarrays	Combined public benefits	Total ATP cost share (public costs)	Net public benefits
1995				−$4,007,000	−$4,007,000
1996				−5,717,000	−5,717,000
1997				−8,678,000	−8,678,000
1998	−$3,501,000		−$3,501,000	−8,076,000	−11,577,000
1999	−53,664,000	$54,415,000	751,000	−8,192,000	−7,441,000
2000	154,085,000	47,535,000	201,620,000	−	201,620,000
2001	53,983,000		53,983,000	−	53,983,000
2002	53,983,000		53,983,000	−	53,983,000
2003	51,479,000		51,479,000	−	51,479,000
2004	30,331,000		30,331,000	−	30,331,000
2005	5,844,000		5,844,000	−	5,844,000
Total	292,540,000	101,950,000	394,490,000	−34,670,000	359,820,000

a gene that may make a patient more likely to contract an illness – have social impacts that are invaluable, as is the contribution to scientific knowledge accelerated technologies bring.

Although this analysis was confined to the funding of one specific research project, the methodology used is appropriate for any analysis of infrastructure technologies. Through the use of a counterfactual analysis, analysts can value technological improvement in terms of what it would have taken (e.g. labor hours) to achieve the same result (e.g. data analysis results) with the technology that was superseded.

This research is one of the first empirical studies to analyze different components of the technology infrastructure – analytical tools, protocols and assays, and technology development programs – and the resulting contributions to economic welfare. We also offer one of the first analyses that quantifies benefits from public – private partnerships to encourage the development of the biotechnology industry. Given biotechnology's potential to improve public health and economic development, economic analyses of investments in the underlying infrastructure that enables core scientific research present stakeholders with valuable tools for policy making. Further work in quantifying the impacts of publicly funded improvements to the biotechnology infrastructure will deepen our understanding of the role the public sector can play in this emerging sector and provide objective analyses for gauging performance and acquiring lessons learned.

Acknowledgements

The research supporting this paper was originally conducted under contract to ATP. The authors wish to extend their appreciation to current and former researchers at ATP and RTI who provided technical and editorial expertise over the course of the research, including Jeanne Powell, Michael Gallaher, Joel Sevinsky, Dallas Wood, Bill White, Stephanie Shipp, Michael Walsh, and Gradimir Georgevich.

References

Abramowitz, S. (1996) Towards Inexpensive DNA Diagnostics. *Trends in Biotechnology*, **14**(10), 397–401.
Baumol, W.J. (2001) When Inter-Firm Coordination Beneficial? The Case of Innovation. *International Journal of Industrial Organization*, **19**, 727–737.
Bernstein, J. (1989) The Structure of Canadian Interindustry R&D Spillovers, and the Rates of Return to R&D. *Journal of Industrial Economics*, **37**(3), 315–328.

Blind, K. and Grupp, H. (1999) Interdependencies Between the Science and Technology Infrastructure and Innovation Activities in German Regions: Empirical Findings and Policy Consequences. *Research Policy*, (28), 451–468.

Bresnahan, T. (1986) Measuring the Spillovers from Technical Advance: Mainframe Computers in Financial Services. *American Economic Review*, **76**(4), 742–755.

Bureau of Labor Statistics (BLS) (2005) Occupational Employment and Wages, 2004: 19–4021 Biological Technicians. Available online at: http://www.bls.gov/oes/current/oes194021.htm.

Coty, C. (2002) Mapping the Future of Sequencing. *Genomics and Proteomics*, **2**(7), 54–58.

Fogarty, M.S., Sinha, A.K. and Jaffe, A.B. (2006) ATP and the US Innovation System: A Methodology for Identifying Enabling R&D Spillover Networks. The Advanced Technology Program.

Georgevich, G. (1997) Tools for DNA Diagnostics: ATP Competition 98–08. Available online at: http://www.atp.nist.gov/atp/97wp-dna.htm; accessed 30 January 2007.

Gerhold, D.L., Jensen, R.V. and Gullans, S.R. (2002) Better Therapeutics Through Microarrays. *Nature Genetics Supplement*, **32**, 547–552.

Goozner, M. (2000) Patenting Life. *The American Prospect*, Online December 18, 2000.

Griliches, Z. (1958) Research Costs and Social Returns: Hybrid Corn and Related Innovations. *Journal of Political Economy*, **66**, 419–431.

Hagedoorn, J., Link, A.N. and Vonortas, N.S. (2000) Research Partnerships. *Research Policy*, **29**, 567–586.

Hodgson, J. (2000) Gene Sequencing's Industrial Revolution. *IEEE Spectrum*, **7**(11), 36–43.

Jaffe, A.B. (1986) Technological Opportunity and Spillovers of R&D. *American Economic Review*, **76**, 984–1001.

Jaffe, A.B. (1996) Economic Analysis of Research Spillovers: Implications for the Advanced Technology Program. The Advanced Technology Program.

Justman, M. and Teubal, M. (1995) Technological infrastructure policy (TIP): Creating Capabilities and Building Markets. *Research Policy*, **24**, 259–281.

Karow, J. (2006) For ABI, Developing Agencourt's Sequencing Technology is a High Priority. *GenomeWeb Daily News*, June 6.

Link, A.N. (1999) Case study of R&D Efficiency in an ATP Joint Venture. *Journal of Technology Transfer*, **23**(2), 43–51.

Link, A.N. and Scott, J.T. (2001) Public/private partnerships: Stimulating Competition in a Dynamic Market. *International Journal of Industrial Organization*, **19**, 763–794.

Link, A.N. and Scott, J.T. (2005) Evaluating Public Sector R&D Programs: The Advanced Technology Program's Investment in Wavelength References for Optical Fiber Communications. *Journal of Technology Transfer*, **30**(1/2), 241–251.

Link, A.L., Paton, D. and Siegel, D.S. (2002) An Analysis of Policy Initiatives for Promote Strategic Research Partnerships. *Research Policy*, **31**, 1459–1466.

Link, A.N., Paton, D. and Siegel, D.S. (2005) An Econometric Analysis of Trends in Research Joint Venture Activity. *Managerial and Decision Economics*, **26**, 149–158.

Mansfield, E. (1996) Estimating Social and Private Returns from Innovations Based on the Advanced Technology Program: Problems and Opportunities. The Advanced Technology Program.

Mansfield, E., Rapoport, J., Romeo, A., Wagner, S. and Beardsley, G. (1977) Social and Private Rates of Return from Industrial Innovations. *Quarterly Journal of Economics*, **91**, 221–240.

Mardis, E. (1999) Capillary electrophoresis Platforms for DNA Sequence Analysis. *Journal of Biomolecular Technology*, **10**, 137–143.

Marshall, A. (1920) *Principles of Economics*. London: Macmillan.

Meldrum, D.R. (2001) Sequencing Genomes and Beyond. *Science*, **292**, 515–517.

Pelsoci, T.M. (2005) Photonics technologies: Applications in Petroleum Refining, Building Controls, Emergency Medicine, and Industrial Materials Analysis. NIST GCR 05-879. Gaithersburg, MD: National Institute of Standards and Technology.

Pelsoci, T.M. (2007) ATP-Funded Green Process Technologies: Improving US Industrial Competitiveness with Applications in Packaging, Metals Recycling, Energy, and Water Treatment. NIST GCR 06-897. Gaithersburg, MD: National Institute of Standards and Technology.

Powell, J. (2006) Toward a Standard Benefit-cost Methodology for Publicly Funded Science and Technology Programs. NISTIR 7319. Gaithersburg, MD: National Institute of Standards and Technology.

Regis, E. (1995) Hacking the Mother Code. *Wired*, **3**(9), pp. 136–142. Available online at: http://www.wired.com/wired/archive/3.09/hood.html.

Ruegg, R.T. (ed) (1998) *The Journal of Technology Transfer. Symposium on Evaluating a Public Private Partnership: The Advanced Technology Program*, **23**(2).

Ruttan, V.W. (2001) *Technology, Growth and Development: An Induced Innovation Perspective*. New York and Oxford: Oxford University Press, pp. xvi, 656.

Shreeve, J. (2004) *The Genome War: How Craig Venter Tried to Capture the Code of Life and Save the World*. New York: Alfred A. Knopf.

Silverman, P. (1995) Commerce and Genetic Diagnostics. *Hastings Center Report*, **25**(3), 15–18.

Tassey, G. (1982) Infratechnologies and the Role of Government. *Technological Forecasting and Social Change*, **21**, 163–180.

Tassey, G. (1997) *The Economics of R&D Policy*. Westport, CT: Greenwood Publishing Group (Quorum Books).

Tassey, G. (2005) Underinvestment in Public Good Technologies. *Journal of Technology Transfer*, **30**(1/2), 89–113.

Wessner, C.W. (1999) *The Advanced Technology Program: Challenges and Opportunities.* Washington, DC: National Academy Press.

White, W.J. and Gallaher, M.P. (2002) Benefits and Costs of ATP Investments in Component-Based Software. NIST GCR 02-834. Gaithersburg, MD: National Institute of Standards and Technology.

White, W.J. and O'Connor, A.C. (2004) Economic Impact of the Advanced Technology Program's HDTV Joint Venture. NIST GCR 03-859. Gaithersburg, MD: National Institute of Standards and Technology.

RESEARCH NETWORKS AS INFRASTRUCTURE FOR KNOWLEDGE DIFFUSION IN EUROPEAN REGIONS[†]

LORENZO CASSI[a,b], NICOLETTA CORROCHER[a,c], FRANCO MALERBA[a]
and NICHOLAS VONORTAS[d]

[a]*CESPRI, Bocconi University, Milan, Italy;* [b]*ADIS, Université Paris Sud, Orsay Cedex, France;*
[c]*Department of Economics, NFH, University of Tromso, Tromso, Norway;* [d]*CISTP and Department
of Economics, George Washington University, Washington DC, USA*

1 INTRODUCTION

The role of networks in disseminating information and ideas, providing access to resources, capabilities and markets, and allowing the combination of different pieces of knowledge has become of critical importance for innovation and, by extension, for economic competitiveness. During the past couple of decades, the governments of advanced countries have made a strong effort to promote cooperative research, particularly within the European Union (EU) (Caloghirou *et al.*, 2002). In the pursuit of a more competitive European economy, the European Commission has built international research networks through the Framework Programmes (FP) on research and technological development. The FPs have provided a systematic process

---

[†]This paper draws on the report 'Networks of Innovation in Information Society: Development and Deployment in Europe', European Commission, DG Information Society and Media, 2006. The contents of the paper do not necessarily reflect the views and policies of the European Commission. The paper presents the analysis and opinion of the authors who are exclusively responsible for any mistakes and misconceptions.

for reaching a number of goals including, among others, the integration of European research and technological development across member states.

This paper focuses on the complementarity between research and deployment network infrastructures in fostering the diffusion of innovation-related knowledge. It examines the structure of collaborative networks and knowledge transfer between research and diffusion activities in the field of information and communication technology (ICT) in the EU as a whole, and in some specific European regions in more detail. In particular, it analyses the linkages between the research networks built through the FP6 in the thematic area 'Applied Information Society Technologies (IST) Research Addressing Major Societal and Economic Challenges' on the one hand, and the diffusion networks built through EU programmes (eTen and eContent) and regional programmes on the other.

The paper is organised as follows. Section 2 presents a brief literature review on the role of networks in bridging research and knowledge dissemination, especially at the regional level. Section 3 illustrates the methodology and describes the available data. Section 4 reports the results: it characterises the research and diffusion networks, stresses the role of the key network actors, and investigates the complementarities between research and knowledge diffusion networks. Section 5 concludes and discusses policy implications.

2   CONCEPTUAL FRAMEWORK

Science, technology and innovation networks are regarded as the emerging organisational mode in environments of complex technologies and rapid technological advance. Success in knowledge-intensive industries depends on organisational learning and commercialization of technologies across different networks. Networks serve as a locus for innovation, because they provide more timely access to external knowledge and resources, represent a test for internal expertise and learning abilities, and give better monitoring and control over fast-moving developments (Powell *et al.*, 1996; Gulati, 1999; Cowan and Jonard, 2004).

Science, technology and innovation networks have also gained momentum in the policy agenda of the member states of the EU. They have been perceived as an integral part of the efforts of the EU to develop the European Research Area (ERA) by integrating the systems of member states into a coherent whole (European Commission, 2000). The creation of the ERA is viewed as a critical step towards the development of a broad infrastructure for scientific and technological development, i.e. a set of interconnected elements that support research and diffusion in Europe, and facilitate the circulation of information and knowledge, the development of transnational organisational forms, the definition of common standards and the promotion of shared values.

To this end, the main policy tool has been the FP (Peterson and Sharp, 1998). Several studies have started to investigate the effectiveness of the FP in building such an infrastructure (e.g. Caloghirou *et al.*, 2004 and 2005; Breschi and Cusmano, 2004; Roediger-Schluga and Barber, 2006). Breschi and Cusmano (2004) and Roediger-Schluga and Barber (2006) focus on R&D networks promoted under the first five FPs and show that the FP funding schemes support the construction of complex networks with structural properties that facilitate dissemination. Moreover, it is shown that there is a significant overlap of participants for consecutive FP and recurring patterns of collaboration amongst the same organisations: 'This core may constitute the backbone of the present European research area' (Roediger-Schluga and Barber, 2006, p. 36). In an assessment of IST in FP6, Breschi *et al.* (2007) find that the examined IST research programmes played an important role in generating and diffusing knowledge, as they managed to attract key industry players and boosted network connectivity.

Existing studies concentrate on the effectiveness of research networks at the European level. A key issue that has been much less analysed refers to how these research networks impact on regional systems and how they interact with research and diffusion activities carried out at the regional level.[1] As Storper (1997) has emphasised, however, one of the most relevant issues in a knowledge-based economy is the tension between globalisation and 'territorialisation', the latter referring to the development of knowledge-intensive regional clusters. Similarly, Bathelt *et al.* (2004) have indicated the need for complementarities between close and distant interaction in order to foster an effective process of knowledge creation and dissemination and, consequently, for policies able to balance efforts in developing of 'global pipeline' (e.g. international collaboration) with efforts in generating and promoting local social capital (Coleman, 1988). The main aim of this paper is to investigate the major complementarities between the ICT research network built through the FPs and the diffusion networks built through both dedicated EU funded programmes and other national and regional programmes in ICTs that focus more on technology exploitation and development.

3   METHODOLOGY AND DATA

3.1   European Level Networks

We focus on the innovation and diffusion projects within the technological domains of the thematic area 'Applied IST Research Addressing Major Societal and Economic Challenges' of FP6.[2] This thematic area combines cooperative research projects through the FP and technology diffusion projects through the EU programmes eTen and eContent on the one hand, with national/regional programmes of technology development, transfer and commercialization on the other. eTen was designed to help the dissemination of telecommunication networks-based services (eServices) with a trans-European dimension. It focused strongly on public services, particularly in areas where Europe has a competitive advantage. eContent was a market-oriented programme, which aimed at supporting the production, use and distribution of European digital content and to promote linguistic and cultural diversity in the global networks. We identify organisations participating in FP6, eTen and eContent projects and use them as the initial sample for network analysis (Tab. I).

The characteristics of the covered projects and organisations are displayed in Table II.

We build two partnership networks on the basis of this information: a research network and a diffusion network. We assume that if two organisations participate in the same project, they are directly linked. Our analysis assumes that each of these links represents a channel of collaboration, knowledge exchange and information spillovers.[3] We use network analysis software tools (Wasserman and Faust, 1994) to examine networks' structural properties, interactions and overlaps, as well as the specific role played by organisations acting as hubs and/or gatekeepers.

---

[1] Regional and research policies in the EU are seen as closely interlinked and, to a certain extent, interdependent. Increased regional cohesion and competitiveness are considered to be partly dependent on the existence of a suitable research infrastructure. See for example http://cordis.europa.eu/fp7/regional_en.html.

[2] IST has been a core investment area in research and technological development since the initiation of the FPs in the early 1980s. This investment had been encapsulated in a host of well-known RTD programmes such as ESPRIT I-IV, RACE I-II, ACTS, DELTA, DRIVE, TAP I-II, and AIM. Such programmes and their derivatives were placed under the overall IST thematic priority in FP5 that has continued in the current FP6. The IST thematic priority is also featured prominently in the new FP7.

[3] We consider all the participants in a project having similar roles, i.e. we do not assign any specific role to the prime contactor of the project.

TABLE I   Network data.

	IST research projects	*IST diffusion projects*
Description	European network formed by organisations participating in FP6 IST – TA1 projects	European network formed by organisations participating in eTen and eContent projects
Data source	Internal EC database (not publicly available)	Internal EC database (not publicly available)
Period	First four Calls of FP6, 2002–2005	eTen: 2000–2005; eContent: 2002–2005

TABLE II   Research and diffusion projects and organisations.

	IST research projects	*IST deployment projects*
Participants	4198	2008
Projects	249	287
Participants per project	17	7
Organisations	2417	1634
Projects per organisation	1.7	1.2

3.2 Regions

In order to obtain more detailed information, we have investigated research and diffusion activities within specific regions, by complementing the aggregate network analysis mentioned above with a series of in-depth interviews across several regions (NUTS 2 level). We have selected nine regions that represent the gamut of science, technology and economic capabilities in Europe. These regions represent different geographical areas: Central Europe (Rhône-Alpes, Bremen, East Wales); Northern Europe (North Jutland[4], Lansi Suomi); Southern Europe (Attiki, Emilia Romagna, Norte); and a new member state (Malopolskie).

In these regions, we have considered networks supported by instruments that are more focused on regional development such as the European Structural Funds and other national/regional funds. Our analytical goal has been to identify different patterns of network collaboration and knowledge transfers between research and diffusion activities within these regions. In-depth field interviews regarding projects carried out in the different regions have been conducted with a set of carefully selected organisations, in order to support the quantitative network analysis and to better understand the linkages between innovation and diffusion processes at the regional level. The interviews add critical information on the value of links and connections within the ERA provided by the EC-funded activities.

We selected two subsets of interviewees per region, one from our aggregate network analysis that allows us to identify a group of large and small effective producers participating to FP6 and/or eTen and eContent projects, and one from national/regional projects, which allows us to identify organisations that have a strong diffusion record. We interviewed 62 regional actors including representatives of companies (22), of public research centres (18), of universities (13) and of government and quasi-government organisations (9) that facilitate IST diffusion in the selected thematic area and in the selected member state(s) and region(s).

---

[4] This region is NUTS 3 level.

4 EMPIRICAL ANALYSIS

This section presents the results of our investigation, which combined network analysis on data from EU research and diffusion programmes with information from the interviews carried out within the selected regions. We first illustrate the structural properties of research and diffusion networks at the EU level. We then examine the characteristics of network hubs that represent critical actors in strengthening connectivity within the networks. We subsequently turn to investigate the complementarities between research and diffusion networks and in doing so, we place a particular emphasis on the role of gatekeeper organisations. Finally, we look at research and diffusion networks and analyse their overlap at the regional level.

4.1 Research and Diffusion Networks' Characteristics at the European Level

The differences between the structural properties of the two networks depend mainly on the size (number of participants) of each network. Research projects tend to have significantly more participants than diffusion projects (Tab. III).

Both networks are highly connected. Most participants are in the largest components, implying that they are connected in some way to each other.[5] The research network appears, however, to support significantly higher exchange of information compared to the diffusion network given that about 98% of organisations are in the largest component of the former compared to about 71% of organisations in the latter.

More striking differences between the research and the diffusion networks emerge, if the giant bi-component is considered. In order for a set of nodes to be classified as a bi-component, all nodes must be reachable from any other at least via two (and not only one) different paths. This feature implies that organisations belonging to a bi-component have a higher probability to receive the information spreading around the network than an organisation belonging to a component. The bi-component of the research network has almost the same size as the largest component (2340 instead of 2373), while the bi-component of the diffusion network is much smaller: 733 organisations instead of 1154. This means that only 63% of the organisations belonging to the giant component have also *another* path connecting to the others. Therefore, in the diffusion network, the number of organisations connected to each other is proportionally smaller than in the research network and, even for those who are connected, the connection

TABLE III   Network characteristics.

	IST research network	IST diffusion network
Number of nodes (organisations)	2417	1634
Number of edges (links)	61686	7422
Network density	0.02	0.006
Giant component	2373	1153
Giant bi-component	2340	733
Average degree	51.04	9.08
Average distance*	2.5	5.08
Max distance*	5	11
Clustering coefficient*	0.0377	0.1292

*These indexes refers to the giant component.

---

[5] More formally, a component is a subpart of a network where there exists at least one *path* (i.e. an alternating sequence of node and edges) linking all its nodes. In other terms, all the nodes belonging to a component have to be reachable at least in one way.

is weaker. These differences in the connectivity of the two networks reflect both the institutional features and the objectives of the two types of programmes, and probably the fact that the diffusion network deals with more focussed activities regarding marketable products.

Information flows more easily in research networks than in diffusion networks. The average distance[6] in the research network is lower than in the diffusion network: any node can reach any other node in the research network in 2.5 steps, on average, compared to five steps in the diffusion network. However, diffusion activities are locally more cohesive and dense as suggested by the value of the clustering coefficient that is greater for the diffusion network than the research network.[7]

Despite such differences, however, both networks are well structured to be effective and useful as knowledge systems. Their structural properties, i.e. low-average distance and high-clustering coefficient,[8] point out that both networks have *small world* properties (Watts and Strogats, 1998).

If the research and diffusion networks are considered together (i.e. all the organisations participating in FP6 and the organisations participating in eTen and eContent as members of the same network) the giant component[9] (which includes 3499 organisations (92.7%)) is characterized by an average distance of 3 (Tab. IV). This means that the overall network is well connected, as each organisation is on average three steps away from any other. In other words, each organisation has relatively easy access to information.

Interestingly, however, the research network and the diffusion network overlap very little. Only 277 organisations[10] participate in both networks. The two networks overlap even less in terms of links: the research and the diffusion networks have only 131 links in common. There are 3011 links among the 277 organisations participating in both networks and these links can depend on a partnership either in a research project or in a diffusion project. About 2526 out of 3011 (83.89%) links are related exclusively to research project participations, 354 (11.76%)

TABLE IV   Global IST research and diffusion network: structural properties.

	IST network
Number of nodes (organisations)	3774
Number of edges (links)	68,977
Network density	0.0097
Giant component	3499
Giant bi-component	3150
Average degree	36.55
Average distance*	3
Max distance*	9
Clustering coefficient*	0.0138

*These indexes refers to the giant component.

---

[6] The *distance* between two nodes is given by the shortest path connecting them and it is equal to the number of edges separating the two nodes. If there is no path connecting two nodes, the distance is assumed to be infinite.

[7] The clustering coefficient for a node is the proportion of links between the nodes within its neighbourhood divided by the number of links that could possibly exist between them. The clustering coefficient for the whole network is the average of the clustering coefficient for each node and grasps the level of social capital, since it measures how many *direct* partners of a specific organisation collaborate with each other.

[8] Here *low-average distance* means that the network has the same value of a random network with the same size and density, *high-clustering coefficient* means that the network has a value that is much greater than the value of the random network.

[9] The giant bi-component is slightly smaller: 3150, i.e. the 90% of the size of the giant component.

[10] This includes 11.5% of the organisations participating in the research network, 16.9% of the organisations participating in the diffusion network, or 7.3% of the total number of organisations (3774).

only to diffusion project participations and only 131 (4.35%) depend on participations in both programmes.

4.1.1 The Role of Network Hubs

Network hubs are key actors within the networks. A hub may be defined as a node with either a large number of connections or a node that is highly influential as a network connector, i.e. one that connects nodes that would otherwise remain unconnected. Hubs have an extremely important role in networks as they facilitate, more than other network participants, the rapid and effective dissemination of knowledge even to the most peripheral sections of the network. More formally, this definition of a network hub can be captured by two indicators: (i) degree centrality,[11] (ii) betweenness centrality.[12] Degree centrality and betweenness centrality have been calculated for all organisations: we have built a synthetic index that ranks organisations according to their performance in terms of both these indicators. Hubs have, then, been defined as the top 2% of the organisations on the basis of this ranking. This share was chosen on the basis of the observation that the top 2% percent of organisations manage 30% of all links.[13] This procedure has been applied to each network, resulting in the definition of two types of hubs: research hubs (48 organisations from FP6) and diffusion hubs (32 organisations from eTen and eContent).

As anticipated, the *research network* is dominated by higher education and research institutions, while the *diffusion network* is dominated by private companies and other organisations.[14] It is interesting to notice, however, that higher education institutions are also active in the diffusion network. Five 'other organisations' that appear as hubs in the diffusion network include three city councils, a regional government and a municipal company.

We also observe key differences in the role of hubs at the local *vs.* national level, when we compare research and diffusion hubs. Distinguishing between hub linkages with organisations located in the same country and links with organisations located in the same region (NUTS 2), excluding the largest multinational corporations and National Research Centres, and considering only the EU15 countries, we can identify 28 research hubs and 26 diffusion hubs. Looking at the behaviour of these hubs, we can advance the following points:

- Diffusion hubs act more locally than research hubs.
- National links in research are more than twice as many as national links in diffusion, and regional links in research are more than three times as many as regional links in diffusion.
- Differences between the linkage patterns of different types of hubs emerge. In the research network, private companies are less geographically limited, while the opposite is true for the diffusion network. In the diffusion network, the 'other organisations' are those with the most localized links. Their regional links are more than twice the average number. These actors indeed play a key role in diffusion at the regional level. Academic hubs, on the contrary,

---

[11] Degree centrality is defined as the number of lines incident with a node. In the context of this study, degree centrality is defined as the number of other organisations with which the focal organisation has a relational tie.

[12] Betweenness centrality is defined as the fraction of shortest paths (i.e. the minimum number of lines connecting two nodes) between node pairs that pass through the node of interest. It is a measure of the influence a node has over the spread of information and knowledge through the network. The basic idea is that a node that lies on the information path linking two other nodes is able to exercise a control over the flow of knowledge within the network.

[13] The 2% cut-off is obviously arbitrary. However, this arbitrariness in the cut-off value is hard to avoid in similar exercises. We considered different values (both higher and lower than 2%) in order to check for robustness. The main results are not affected. Alternatively, hubs could have been defined on the basis of threshold values for centrality. This becomes impractical, however, because of the need to compare across different types of networks of different sizes.

[14] Percentages of total organisations are not reported here. They are available upon request.

do not show any differences in the two networks as far as the localisation of their links is concerned. [15]

4.1.2   The Role of Gatekeepers in Bridging Research and Diffusion Networks

In our framework, *gatekeepers* are organisations that link the research with the diffusion network. By doing so, they allow others to access information and capabilities developed in other networks and contexts.

As seen in Figure 1, gatekeepers are positioned in both networks. In our analysis, 277 organisations are identified as having this bridging position. Some of these organisations are also hubs, and this has implications in terms of their connectivity within the network. 27 out of 48 (56.2%) hubs in the research network and 22 out of 32 (68.7%) hubs in the diffusion network are also gatekeepers. It is worth noticing that 11 organisations are hubs in both networks: they could be classified as the strongest gatekeepers in our sample. We hypothesize that gatekeepers are in a unique position to speed up the process of innovation and technology diffusion, since they work as bridge between the two different networks.

Higher education institutions and research organisations are more numerous than others as gatekeepers, accounting for about one-third of the total each. However, industrial organisations are also active as gatekeepers (about a quarter of the total) and, within this group, small and medium-sized enterprises (SMEs) play an active role, representing 17% of these bridging organisations.

The variety of different organisational types acting as gatekeepers means that different kinds of knowledge are exchanged and shared across the networks. Our field interviews strongly confirmed this hypothesis. Higher education and research institutes develop and diffuse advanced and frontier knowledge to the network. On the contrary, companies provide links to the market and market information feedbacks so that research can be more focussed on market relevance. A highly functional network would need gatekeepers from the different sectors in order to exchange and integrate different types of information and knowledge. The linkage pattern between the research and the diffusion networks was discussed earlier (Tab. IV). The important role of gatekeepers in linking research and diffusion networks is highlighted by the fact that one-third of all links in both the research network and the diffusion network connect gatekeepers to other organisations in these networks. Simply put, about one-third of all links in either network involve the relatively few organisations (277) that bridge the two networks together.

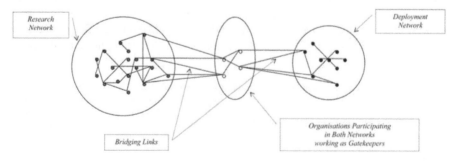

FIGURE 1   Gatekeepers.

---

[15] Again, figures with data and numbers are not reported here. They are available upon request.

Our field analysis has pointed out that many organisations that are active players in the research networks are often not aware of diffusion opportunities. The opposite also happens frequently: poor links between research and diffusion arise in the case of organisations, which are actively involved in diffusion activities but are not tied into the research network. On the contrary, and as already shown by the network analysis above, gatekeepers are generally well aware of the diffusion opportunities at the international, national as well as regional level. They help integrate firm-specific competencies with other organisations, which can provide insights and experience and allow the application of the know-how developed within the research network to specific regional projects. The intermediary function of gatekeepers, deeply integrated in both the research and the diffusion networks, is therefore quite important.

Pushing the issue of complementarities between the research and diffusion networks and the role of gatekeepers in them, we have juxtaposed the research network (FP6) with a network including both the research links and the diffusion links of the same organisations (Tab. V). An example is shown in Figure 2.

Similarly, we have juxtaposed the diffusion network (eTen, eContent) with a network including both the diffusion links and the research links of the same organisations (Tab. VI).

A striking result is how little the research network is affected by the inclusion of the technology diffusion linkages of its participants. All the structural properties barely change (Tab. V). In contrast, the structural properties of the diffusion network change significantly when the research links of its participating organisations are introduced (Tab. VI). The inclusion of the research links raises the degree of connectivity of the diffusion network. For example,

TABLE V   Research network and diffusion links: structural properties.

	IST research network	IST research plus diffusion links
Number of nodes (organisations)	2417	
Number of edges (links)	61,686	62,040
Network density	0.02	0.02
Giant component	2373	2375
Giant bi-component	2340	2353
Average degree	51.04	51.34
Average distance*	2.5	2.5
Max distance*	5	6
Clustering coefficient*	0.0377	0.0375

*These indexes refer to the giant component.

A simplified version of the
IST RESEARCH Network

A simplified version of the
IST RESEARCH plus DIFFUSION links

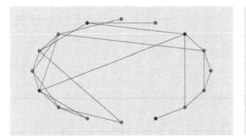
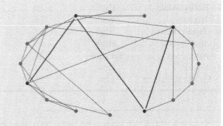

FIGURE 2   An example of how the IST research networks plus diffusion links are built up.

TABLE VI   Diffusion network and research links: structural properties.

	IST diffusion network	IST diffusion plus research links
Number of nodes (organisations)	1634	
Number of edges (links)	7422	9948
Network density	0.006	0.007
Giant component	1153	1401
Giant bi-component	733	1072
Average degree	9.08	12.17
Average distance*	5.08	3.65
Max distance*	11	9
Clustering coefficient*	0.1292	0.0434

*These indexes refer to the giant component.

both the size of the giant component and the size of the giant bi-component increase significantly. Furthermore, the inclusion of research links reduces the average distance between the participants.

Therefore, an important effect of the IST research network is the enlargement and widening of the number of organisations involved in sharing and exchanging knowledge and information at the regional level and the speeding up of knowledge circulation among the diffusion network organisations.

4.2   Research and Diffusion Networks in Selected Regions

In order to examine more in depth the links between the research networks and the diffusion networks, a similar analysis has also been carried out for the nine specific regions mentioned earlier (Tab. VII).

In general, each regional network in the nine regions has a higher density than the density of the overall network, suggesting that being co-localized makes it more likely to be connected. Attiki and Emilia Romagna – regions with low capability in science, technology and economy measured in terms of a set of indicators of R&D development, human capital, and industrial structure[16] – have the highest number of organisations participating in IST research and diffusion networks. The latter signals the important role of the European programmes in

TABLE VII   Regional networks: structural properties.

Region	STE strength	IST network organisations	Research network Organisations	Research network Density	Diffusion network Organisations	Diffusion network Density
UK – East Wales	High	2	1	–	1	–
FR – Rhône-Alpes	High	20	12	0.15	9	0.11
DE – Bremen	High	16	10	0.53	9	0.27
DK – North Jutland	High	3	3	0.66	0	–
FI – Lansi Suomi	High	11	10	0.53	1	–
PT – Norte	Very low	22	13	0.35	9	0.11
GR – Attiki	Low	116	56	0.14	84	0.039
IT – Emilia Romagna	Low	54	25	0.14	38	0.11

[16] Source: EUROSTAT, average on 1999–2004. We used the following indicators: GERD per capita; R&D personnel per inhabitant; human resources in science and technology; percentage of total employment in high-technology manufacturing; percentage of total employment in knowledge-intensive services.

TABLE VIII   Regional networks: hubs and external connections.

Region	Research network			Diffusion network		
	Organisations	Hubs	Connection to external hubs	Organisations	Hubs	Connection to external hubs
UK – East Wales	1	0	0	1	0	0
FR – Rhône-Alpes	12	2	0.11	9	0	0
DE – Bremen	10	0	0.06	9	0	0.021
DK – North Jutland	3	0	0.09	0	–	–
FI – Lansi Suomi	10	0	0.075	1	0	0
PT – Norte	13	0	0.089	9	0	0.003
GR – Attiki	56	2	0.11	84	2	0.017
IT – Emilia Romagna	25	0	0.06	38	4	0.026

terms of inclusion and cohesion, and are illustrative examples of the effectiveness of the FP6 in strengthening the connection between research and diffusion.

Fielding large number of organisations, however, does not necessarily imply that the region has a stronger *connection to external hubs*, as Table VIII shows.[17] In fact, it is the presence of hubs in a region (this is the case of Attiki and Rhône-Alpes for research and of Emilia Romagna for diffusion) that increases the connectivity of the region to other external hubs.

It was reported that the deployment of product- and process-specific knowledge developed by the research network is not always possible due to the lack of sufficient infrastructure to support market introduction. One of the most important issues emerging in the field analysis is the relatively weak linkage between organisations with ideas and regional deployment networks. Notable exceptions exist, of course. An example is the University of Cardiff that actively coordinates a number of local and national activities in addition to EU projects and brings together a lot of local resources.

The complementarity between the two networks is confirmed by the limited overlap between the research and diffusion networks (Tab. IX).

The overlap between IST projects and structural funds is even smaller: there are no explicit links between the participation in IST networks and the use of structural funds. Structural policy instruments focus mainly on funding projects that improve the level of employment in a region, while programmes such as the FP6 prioritise different thematic topics. Given that the priority for regional funds is to help the transition to knowledge society and sustainable

TABLE IX   Overlap between research and diffusion networks by region.

Region	Overlap between research and diffusion network		Overlap between IST networks and structural funds	
	Organisations	Links	Research	Deployment
UK – East Wales	0	–	–	–
FR – Rhône-Alpes	1	0	1	2
DE – Bremen	3	0	1	2
DK – North Jutland	0	–	0	–
FI – Lansi Suomi	0	–	3	0
PT – Norte	0	–	6	3
GR – Attiki	24	8	17	16
IT – Emilia Romagna	7	0	5	8

---

[17] The *connections to external hubs* are calculated as the ratio between existing links among regional organisations and hubs located out of region and the potential ones.

development,[18] however, one could argue for stronger linkages across networks to increase knowledge flows.

In general, ICT diffusion activities are not always closely tied to the strategies of the regional governments. There seem to be some differences between the examined Northern European regions, where there is a little coordination with regional strategies, and the examined Southern European regions, where coordination activities take place more frequently. One relevant finding from the interviews is that large organisations are informed of and exploit regional links, while SMEs are often not aware of the existence of regional strategies for ICT diffusion and do not have resources and capabilities to efficiently use them.

Finally, often organisations are reportedly unaware of any regional strategy that affects them. In many cases, they do not have precise information about where they could get assistance with regional diffusion and are not aware of direct links between national and regional networks in deploying ICT products developed within IST research projects. This is probably due to the fact that organisations are aware just of first tier (direct) linkages, but are less conscious of second and third tier linkages. That is to say that, while the overall network (research and diffusion) appears to be well connected when looking at the quantitative data, information about diffusion projects and about potential indirect linkages with hubs and gatekeepers still remains scarce in the regions, especially for small companies.

5 CONCLUSIONS AND POLICY IMPLICATIONS

The stronger emphasis on innovation and the quest for balancing supply and demand side effects of technological advancement in Europe implies that both research and diffusion linkages have become a core policy concern and that their analysis deserves intense and deep scrutiny. Both the economic literature and the agenda of European policy makers have recognized for some time now that networks are key means for the development of new knowledge and the diffusion of knowledge into products and processes.

From a policy perspective, the creation of an international infrastructure and interconnected networks for science and technology has represented a main concern in the design of the recent FP of the European Commission. Some recent empirical contributions have investigated the effectiveness of these programmes and have found positive results. However, much less has been done so far with reference to the relation between European research networks and regional diffusion programmes. The present work aimed at examining the links and complementarities between research and diffusion networks developed through EU and national/regional funding, using tools from social network analysis and interviews in a selected number of regions.

Diffusion networks were found to be considerably strengthened by the research networks. Research networks complement regional knowledge dissemination by providing net link additions, presumably allowing many more organisations to be interconnected than would have been otherwise the case, thus supplementing knowledge exchange and broadening the diffusion of information within the network. In particular, the research network increases the number of the organisations that are involved in sharing and exchanging knowledge through

---

[18] As Table IX shows, only in Attiki there is a substantial overlap of organisations and links between research and diffusion networks, and between these networks and structural funds. However, one may recall that Attiki is a capital city region with a major concentration of national industry, quite different from the rest of the regions examined. Furthermore, Greeks are, in relative terms, the most frequent postgraduate students abroad and this helps establish social networks that allows them to make connections within Europe. Finally, structural funds within Greece are strongly supported by government intervention.

the diffusion network. It also speeds up information transmission among its organisations by lowering the average distance among them.

Two (related) types of actors maintain the connections within each network and across the research and the diffusion networks: hubs and gatekeepers.[19] Hubs play a critical role in maintaining the ties of the smaller and more isolated members within the networks. They diffuse technological and market information, help define standards for emerging products and provide demand (applications) for research results. It is the actual presence of hubs in a region that increases the connectivity of the region to others. Gatekeepers bridge the research and diffusion networks, thus helping both to disseminate knowledge of all kinds through various knowledge channels and to provide access to resources and opportunities. The intensity of the activity of individual gatekeepers is remarkable. Even though a relatively small number of organisations falls into this category, they are responsible for one-third of the links in each network (research and diffusion). The vast majority of these links connect gatekeepers and other organisations.

Multinational corporations participate in research networks and in large scale projects that link research and diffusion. In doing so, they allow smaller organisation to access resources such as technical and market knowledge to a larger extent than would have been possible otherwise. SMEs appear to be important players in diffusion activities. They are deeply rooted in their respective territories and represent very efficient agents when it comes to deploying specific applications and to building relationships with regional authorities.

Our findings have useful policy implications. They support the idea of creating virtual regional innovation systems in order to overcome the tension between global research activities and local diffusion activities. While research across the ERA is highly networked, regional diffusion networks are less interconnected. Moreover, IST research and knowledge diffusion networks are not always strongly connected. It is for these reasons that gatekeeper organisations play a critical role in the networks by providing interconnections across them. Regions could involve more of these types of organisations in order to bridge the gap between research and knowledge diffusion more effectively and to harness the outcomes from FP projects. Both research and diffusion networks appear to be effective in information dissemination, the latter more so at the regional level.

However, having a large number of organisations in the network does not guarantee extensive linkages to the outside world; the inclusion of hubs among them does. Since the presence of hubs in a region raises disproportionately the connectivity of the region with others, the attraction of such organisations to a region certainly makes sense. Large research and business organisations are critical for bridging research and diffusion as they possess financial, technical, human and locational resources to manage the ensuing complexity. The message here is that regions may find it advantageous to support the presence of such large organisations in their territories. In addition to diffusing technological and market information, helping define standards for emerging products, and providing demand (applications) for research results, the role of such organisations in networks is to promote SMEs beyond their limited geographical areas.

At present, however, regional strategies for economic development and ICT diffusion seem relatively unknown to the network participants that we examined. In many cases, organisations focused on the global marketplace in their development process disregarding the regional level. This may be appropriate for frontier research but it is not the most effective way for innovation diffusion. Increased awareness of opportunities should be the first step. In order to promote knowledge diffusion, national governments must play a catalytic role by initiating and supporting mechanisms for inter-regional cooperation and collaboration.

---

[19] The two sets are not independent: several, but not all, gatekeepers are also hubs.

Acknowledgements

The authors acknowledge generous funding by the DG and its evaluation unit C3, for carrying out the background evaluative study. In particular, Peter Johnston and Frank Cunningham from that unit were instrumental in the success of the study. The authors also wish to thank various participants to workshops in Brussels and two referees for their useful comments. The authors would also like to acknowledge the financial support of the Italian Ministry of Education, Universities and Research (FIRB, project RISC – RBNE039XKA).

References

Bathelt, H., Malberg, A. and Maskell, P. (2004) Clusters and Knowledge: Local Buzz, Global Pipelines and the Process of Knowledge Creation. *Progress in Human Geography*, **28**, 31–56.

Breschi, S., Cassi, L. and Malerba, F. (2004) A Five-Industry Analysis of Co-citation Networks. Working Paper for the STI-NET Project. European Commission, April.

Breschi, S., Cassi, L., Malerba, F. and Vonortas, N. (2007), Networked Research: European Policy Intervention for Information & Communication Technologies. Mimeo, Bocconi University.

Breschi, S. and Cusmano, L. (2004) Unveiling the Texture of a European Research Area: Emergence of Oligarchic Networks Under EU Framework Programmes. *International Journal of Technology Management*. Special Issue on Technology Alliances, **27**(8), 747–772.

Caloghirou, Y., Constantellou, N. and Vonortas, N.S. (eds.) (2005) *Knowledge Flows in European Industry: Mechanisms and Policy Implications*. Routledge.

Caloghirou, Y., Vonortas, N.S. and Ioannides, S. (2002) Science and Technology Policies Towards Research Joint Ventures. *Science and Public Policy*, **29**(2), 82–94.

Caloghirou, Y., Vonortas, N.S. and Ioannides, S. (eds.) (2004) *European Collaboration in Research and Development: Business Strategy and Public Policy*. Northampton, MA: Edward Elgar.

Coleman, J.C. (1988) Social Capital in the Creation of Human Capital. *American Journal of Sociology*, **94**, 95–120.

Cowan, R. and Jonard, N. (2004) Network Structure and the Diffusion of Knowledge. *Journal of Economic Dynamics and Control*, **28**(8), 1557–1575.

European Commission (2000), Toward a European Research Area. COM 2000/6.

Gulati, R. (1999) Network Location and Learning: The Influence of Network Resources and Firm Capabilities on Alliance Formation. *Strategic Management Journal*, **20**(5), 397–420.

Peterson, J. and Sharp, M. (1998) *Technology Policy in the European Union*. London: Macmillan Press.

Powell, W.W., Koput, K.W and Smith-Doerr, L. (1996) Inter Organizational Collaboration and the Locus of Innovation: Networks of Learning in Biotechnology. *Administrative Science Quarterly*, **41**, 116–145.

Roediger-Schluga, T. and Barber, M.J. (2006) The Structure of R&D Collaboration Networks in the European Framework Programmes. UNU-MERIT Working Papers, p. 36.

Storper, M. (1997) *The Regional World: Territorial Development in a Global Economy*. London : Guilford Press.

Wasserman, S. and Faust, K. (1994) *Social Network Analysis*. Cambridge: Cambridge University Press.

Watts, D. and Strogatz, S.H. (1998) Collective Dynamics of 'Small World' Networks. *Nature*, **393**, 440–442.

INTELLIGENT MACHINE TECHNOLOGY AND PRODUCTIVITY GROWTH

DAVID P. LEECH[a,b] and JOHN T. SCOTT[c]

[a] Business Division, Villa Julie College, Stevenson, MD, USA; [b] TASC, Inc., 1101 Wilson Blvd, Suite 1600, Arlington, VA 22209, USA; [c] Department of Economics, Dartmouth College, Hanover, NH 03755, USA

1 INTRODUCTION

Intelligent machine technology (IMT) is the application of computer-based knowledge to enable machines capable of using human-like behavior to perform tasks – that without the technology would be performed by humans – in complex and dynamic industrial environments.[1] IMT is in part enabling technology in that it will allow new machine-intensive and labor-saving production techniques across a wide range of industries.[2] It is in part infrastructure technology in that it will ideally conform to standards ensuring it will provide access across industries to human-performance-like, machine-based, generic technology that is necessary for the development of innovative labor-saving processes.[3] IMT is evolving from current

---

[1] We use the non-technical, descriptive term 'human-like' behavior; for both technical and philosophical reasons, 'human-level' behavior might be more apt. IMT is computational technology that senses its environment and adjusts its behavior based on modeling of interaction with that environment and evaluation to achieve goals. It can be encapsulated in a computer program, an intelligent sensor, or a robot. Examples of IMT include machine systems such as computer-aided design technologies, computer numerically controlled machine tools, computer controlled inspection systems, enterprise integration information systems, just-in-time production scheduling and inventory control technologies, internet technologies that enable out-sourcing to the most efficient suppliers, and multi-spectral measurement systems for construction site metrology and other applications.

[2] See Link and Siegel (2007, p. 97) for definition and discussion of enabling technologies.

[3] Link and Siegel (2003, p. 63, p. 78) define infrastructure technology and explain its role in innovation.

successes in computer-aided industrial operations; in that sense, *new* IMT is incremental innovation. However, the advances anticipated in intelligent machines, as they become capable of assuming industrial tasks currently performed by humans, support the view that the next two decades will see IMT emerging as radical innovation.[4] International competitiveness will require firms to use new IMT.[5] Hence, IMT-induced productivity growth is important to a nation's firms and merits the attention of their government's technology policy.[6]

This paper provides preliminary estimates of the productivity impact of IMT and the rate of return to IMT research and development (R&D) over the next two decades. To develop the estimates, we focus on a sample of firms operating in IMT development and applications in the automotive, aerospace, and capital construction industries. The paper adapts economists' traditional productivity growth model to enable the use of industrial experts' forecasts of a few key parameters of the model to form the estimates of productivity growth and rate of return. IMT-induced productivity growth has been widely anticipated because of the established industrial successes of computer-aided design, analysis, scheduling, inventory control, and numerical control, along with rapid developments in the understanding of how to build intelligent machines. The experts at the National Institute of Standards and Technology (NIST) and in industry with whom we have spoken anticipate that over the next two decades, intelligent machines will be closing the gap between their levels of performance and human levels of performance for specific industrial tasks. Closing the gap is an important policy issue and necessary to ensure continued productivity gains for the twenty-first century industries.[7] It is also exciting from a philosophical as well as technological standpoint as machines progress from winning chess matches to human-like performance of complex tasks in industry.[8] With the exciting prospects in mind, we estimate the range of likely productivity effects by combining the knowledge of the experts with economists' models of productivity.

The approach developed here for the study of IMT-induced productivity growth rates and IMT R&D rates of return is an application based on a very large and well-established literature about productivity growth and rates of return to R&D. For review of that large literature, see Link and Siegel (2003). For a focus on the disaggregated components of productivity, see Tassey (2005). In the present paper, we focus entirely on identifying the effect of one disaggregated component – namely, IMT.

Section 2 explains the measure of IMT-induced productivity growth. Section 3 then describes the sample and provides the productivity growth estimates. Section 4 explains the measure of the rate of return to IMT R&D. Section 5 then provides the rate of return estimates.

---

[4] Link and Siegel (2007, p. 126) provide a window to the literature about radical technologies; IMT is arguably a special case of such dramatic departures in process technology – special because of its pervasiveness, yet radical in the potential for transforming competition in individual industries.

[5] For example, see the description of IMT increasing the productivity of German automobile manufacturer BMW AG in Gumbel (2007).

[6] IMT development entails multidisciplinary research requiring sound technology policy. IMT is an emerging *system* technology, both technically – requiring the integration of technologies governing, as explained by Albus and Meystel (2001, pp. 17–18), sensory processing, world modeling, value judgment, and behavior generation – and institutionally – requiring the collaboration and integration of public, quasi-public, and private sector institutions specializing in basic scientific research, generic technology development, and infratechnology development. See Albus and Meystel (2001, pp. 145–152) regarding complexity of IMT and Tassey (1997) regarding complexity of technology and demands of multidisciplinary research. See Tassey (2005) regarding interaction of institutions in a successful national innovation system.

[7] See US Domestic Policy Council (2006). The goals for the American competitiveness initiative discussed there include capability and capacity in nano-manufacturing, intelligent manufacturing capabilities, and related sensor and detection capabilities.

[8] Computer programs not only play chess, they handle airline reservations, manage financial transactions, control inventories, verify customer identifications, dispense bank drafts, and track package shipments. Respected technologists believe the realization of 'digital people' and 'engineered minds' (autonomous machines) is palpably close (Albus and Meystel, 2001, p. 146).

Section 6 concludes with discussion of the importance of government support for IMT R&D investments.

2 THE MEASURE OF IMT PRODUCTIVITY GROWTH

Our estimation method focuses exclusively on new, IMT-induced growth in output, because we construct the measure of IMT-induced productivity growth as an effect above and beyond the effects for all sources of output growth other than the advance in IMT knowledge. Thus, the growth in output that we identify is that growth that is not explained by the growth in inputs other than IMT knowledge. Stated differently using the conventional categorization of inputs, we focus on only the growth in output that is not explained by growth in labor, in capital goods, in materials, in knowledge capital other than IMT knowledge stock, and in exogenous trends in output growth.[9]

To ensure a consistent focus for our respondents in industry (discussed in Sec. 3), we began with industry-specific credible future scenarios for the likely advances over the next two decades for IMT applications in the automotive, aerospace, and capital construction industries. The future scenarios were developed in consultations with a group of well-respected technology specialists from NIST, industry associations, and academe. The group of specialists also helped us to gain access to knowledgeable individuals within the selected private sector firms surveyed.[10]

To isolate the anticipated IMT-induced growth in output, respondents were asked their expectations about several parameters, which are defined in Table I. Gamma (γ) is defined to be the computational capability multiple – the increase in computational capability per unit of cost – anticipated for the computational tasks used in their industry over each of the next two decades. For example, if computational power per unit of cost for the industry were anticipated to grow by an order of magnitude over the next decade, then $\gamma = 10$.

TABLE I The IMT productivity parameters.

Parameter	Definition	Empirically based theoretical range (mean)[a]
Gamma (γ)	Computational capability multiple showing the increase in computational capability per unit of cost for the industry's computational tasks	1–35 (7.95)
Alpha (α)	Proportion of an industry's tasks as measured by their costs that can benefit from the application of new IMT	0.0–0.67 (0.325)
Beta (β)	Output quality multiple showing the increase in value of the industry's output attributable to new IMT	1–10 (4.55)

[a]The lower limit is simply the case of no effect – that is, there are no gains in computational capability or in output quality, and hence the multiples γ and β are 1, and none of the industry's tasks can benefit and hence the proportion α is 0. For the upper limit, we can of course only speculate regarding γ and β, and α's admissible upper limit of 1 is not particularly informative. We have responses from industry for each of the next two decades, and also given R&D with typical conditions for appropriating returns versus complete appropriation. To provide a sense of the realistic range for these parameters, reported here, for the upper limits, is the largest value reported by any of the respondents for either of the next two decades given R&D with typical conditions for appropriating return. In parentheses are the average responses for those two decades given the typical conditions. The figures here are based on 18 observations – one in each of the two decades from each of the nine respondents providing the information.

---

[9] Solow's (1957) seminal paper focused on a much more inclusive residual – namely, the residual productivity growth rate after the growth rates in capital and labor were controlled. See Link and Siegel (2003, pp. 27–28) for a discussion of Solow's residual.

[10] A complete list of the technology specialists with whom we consulted and their affiliations as well as the detailed future scenarios are provided in Leech et al. (2006).

Alpha (α) is defined to be the proportion of the industry's tasks as measured by their costs that can benefit from the application of new advanced machine intelligence. For example, if one-half of a manufacturing industry's costs are taken by tasks that can benefit from applications of advances in intelligent machines or systems, then $\alpha = 1/2$.

Finally, beta (β) is defined to be the output quality multiple. For example, if the applications of advanced machine intelligence are expected to increase the value of the industry's output by 25%, then $\beta = 1.25$.

Output at time t is Q_t. The cost of the factors of production, the inputs, at time t is F_t. An industry's total factor productivity is the ratio of the value of its output to the cost of its inputs, or $\text{TFP} = Q_t/F_t$. At time $t + \delta t$, the cost of the factors of production will be $\alpha(F_t/\gamma) + (1 - \alpha)F_t$. At time $t + \delta t$, the industry's total factor productivity given the effects of new IMT is $\text{TFP}_t = \beta Q_t/F(1 - \alpha + (\alpha/\gamma))$. Then, with a dot over a variable to denote its change per unit of time, the growth rate in total factor productivity induced by the new IMT is:

$$\left.\frac{\overset{\bullet}{\text{TFP}}}{\text{TFP}}\right|_{\text{new IMT}} = \frac{(Q_t/F_t)\,(\beta/(1 - \alpha + (\alpha/\gamma))) - Q_t/F_t}{Q_t/F_t} \tag{1}$$

where $\overset{\bullet}{\text{TFP}}/\text{TFP}|_{\text{new IMT}}$ is the notation to indicate the contribution of new IMT to the growth rate in total factor productivity, Q_t/F_t.[11]

To understand the relations captured by Eq. (1), denote $(\beta/(1 - \alpha + (\alpha/\gamma))) = (1 + r)$. Then,

$$\left.\frac{\overset{\bullet}{\text{TFP}}}{\text{TFP}}\right|_{\text{new IMT}} = \frac{(Q_t/F_t)(1 + r) - (Q_t/F_t)}{Q_t/F_t} = r \tag{2}$$

is the growth rate in productivity attributable to new IMT. Observe that the productivity growth multiple $(1 + r)$ increases as the quality multiple β increases. Also note that the productivity multiple increases as the fraction $1 - \alpha + (\alpha/\gamma)$, the multiplier for the factor cost F, gets smaller. The $(1 - \alpha)$ part of that denominator is the portion of cost that is not affected by IMT, so it gets smaller as α gets bigger. And the (α/γ) part of the denominator gives the portion of cost affected by IMT divided by the IMT capability multiple. The bigger that multiple, the smaller are costs, and the bigger is α, the more important that cost reduction is. So F, the start of period cost, is averaged in with a weight of $(1 - \alpha)$ with the new end-of-period cost, and F/γ, the end-of-period lower cost because of the improved IMT, gets averaged in with a weight of α.

We conclude this section with an intuitive summary statement as follows. Total factor productivity Q/F is the ratio of output's value to inputs' cost, and $\beta/(1 - \alpha + (\alpha/\gamma))$ is the productivity multiple induced by new IMT. Its numerator is the multiplier for the value of output because of the increase in its quality due to IMT improvements. Its denominator is the multiplier for costs (it will be a fraction between 0 and 1) because of the improvement in IMT. If α were 0, then the multiplier would be 1 since costs would not be reduced. If α were 1, then the multiplier would be $1/\gamma$, the reciprocal of the cost improvement multiple (two times

---

[11] We have then a very specialized portion of the residual in the original Solow (1957) formulation. Solow's residual reflected the growth rate in output not explained by the growth rates in labor and capital. That residual was classically attributed to an exogenous rate of output growth and the rate of growth in the stock of knowledge. Here we have focused on the residual attributable solely to new IMT.

the capability implies one-half the cost). Of course, α will in general be a fraction, so the denominator multiple is saying that part $(1 - \alpha)$ of the start of period cost F is unchanged, while the other part (α) gets reduced by the fraction $1/\gamma$.

3 THE ESTIMATES OF IMT PRODUCTIVITY GROWTH

To estimate IMT-induced productivity growth over the next two decades, we surveyed 14 firms.[12] The complete survey instrument is provided in Leech et al. (2006). Equation (1) is estimated using the survey responses of the nine companies that provide all of the necessary information. Thus, we rely on expert opinion gleaned from a survey of knowledgeable individuals in industry; that approach results in a small sample, and the limitations of such a sample must be acknowledged at the outset.[13]

We calculate 95% confidence intervals for the means that we present to allow us to capture the uncertainty about the true means for the variables of interest to us. Nonetheless, we emphasize that we would certainly prefer to have a larger sample, and the measures of productivity growth and R&D rate of return that we develop and integrate with survey data can be applied to larger samples if they become available.

Using the conventional categorization of inputs, we focus on only the growth in output that is *not* explained by growth in labor, in capital goods, in materials, in knowledge capital other than IMT knowledge stock, and in exogenous trends in output growth.[14] Table II shows the estimates of the IMT-induced productivity growth rate g per decade, and those rates are converted into compound annual rates of growth shown in Table III.

TABLE II   Anticipated IMT-induced productivity growth rate, g, per decade[a].

Decade	Number of observations	Mean	Standard Error[b]	95% Confidence interval[c]
2006–2015	9	3.69 (369%)	1.13*	1.08–6.31
2015–2025	9	7.38 (738%)	1.95**	2.89–11.87

[a]The period of analysis for this table is 9 years in length for the 2006–2015 scenario, and 10 years in length for the 2015–2025 scenario.
[b]The estimated mean's level of significance for a two-tailed test (based on the t-statistic = the ratio of the coefficient to the standard error) against the null hypothesis of a zero growth rate: * = 0.02, ** = 0.01.
[c]Based on the information provided by the respondents and the model, the anticipated IMT-induced productivity growth rate is within the reported range with probability 0.95. For example, for the first decade the anticipated IMT-induced productivity growth rate is in the range from 108 to 631% with probability 0.95. The reported means provide the point estimates – the expected outcome for the anticipated growth rate.

---

[12] The 14 companies with which we discussed IMT and to which we are grateful for the insights provided by their representatives are Boeing Company, Bechtel Corporation, CH2M Hill, CNH Global, Daimler-Chrysler Company, FANUC Robotics of America, Ford Motor Company, Foster-Miller, Inc., iRobot Corporation, John Deere, Mag IAS, Okuma, Northrop Grumman Corporation, and Toyota Corporation.

[13] We chose experts and firms in industry by using patent data to identify individuals and companies with a considerable stock of applied knowledge about IMT and also by consulting with a group of distinguished technology specialists from NIST, industry associations, and academe.

[14] Even infrastructure technology support from government and cooperative R&D in the industry are held constant at their accustomed levels in recent years. When respondents provided their estimates that have been used with the model to make predictions about IMT-induced productivity gains and about IMT R&D rates of return, the respondents were asked to assume that industry and government activities such as cooperative R&D and government support with infrastructure technology continue in the accustomed way. Estimates about quality multiples and computational capability and so forth are provided for the upcoming two decades and productivity growth rates and rates of return on investment are then derived.

TABLE III   Annual compound rate of anticipated IMT-induced productivity growth[a].

Decade	Annual rate of productivity growth
2006–2015	0.187 (18.7%)
2015–2025	0.237 (23.7%)

The rates in Table II using the decades as the period of analysis are converted into compound annual rates of growth r. Thus, given that g for the first decade is 3.69 (or 369%), the corresponding value of r is r such that we have $(1+r)^9 = 1 + g$. With $g = 3.69$, r solves as 0.187 or 18.7%. There are 10 years covered for the decade 2015–2025. Thus, with the decade growth rate for the second-decade scenario being 7.38 (738%), we have $(1+r)^{10} = 1 + g$, and the compound annual rate of growth r solves as 0.237 or 23.7%.

[a] For the 9-year span 2006–2015 and the 10-year span 2015–2025.

4   THE MEASURE OF IMT R&D RATE OF RETURN

Equation (1) when combined with IMT R&D intensity allows us to estimate the rates of return to IMT R&D. We have isolated the IMT-induced rate of growth in production. That growth rate is the rate of growth in output that is *not* explained by exogenous growth or by the rate of growth in other inputs – such as labor, physical capital goods, materials, and other types of R&D including government-provided infrastructure R&D. Thus, the IMT-induced rate of growth in production is:

$$\left. \frac{\dot{TFP}}{TFP} \right|_{new\ IMT} = \frac{\dot{Q}}{Q} - \lambda - \sum_j \eta_j \frac{\dot{X}_j}{X_j} \qquad (3)$$

where Q denotes output, X_j denotes the jth input other than IMT-knowledge stock, η_j denotes the elasticity of output with respect to the jth input, and λ denotes the exogenous rate of growth in output.

The IMT-induced rate of growth in productivity equals the product of the elasticity of output Q with respect to the IMT-knowledge stock R and the rate of growth $\dot{R}/R$ in that IMT-knowledge stock, where $\dot{R} \equiv dR/dt$ and t denotes time. Therefore, the IMT-induced rate of growth in production – the part of the growth rate for output due entirely to IMT-induced growth in output – can be written as the product of the rate of return, dQ/dR, to IMT R&D and the IMT R&D intensity, $\dot{R}/Q$ (the ratio to output of IMT R&D spending during the period) because:

$$\frac{\dot{Q}}{Q} - \lambda - \sum_j \eta_j \frac{\dot{X}_j}{X_j} = \eta_R \frac{\dot{R}}{R} = \frac{dQ}{dR} \frac{R}{Q} \frac{\dot{R}}{R} = \frac{dQ}{dR} \frac{\dot{R}}{Q} \qquad (4)$$

As Link and Siegel (2003, p. 72) observe, the formulation of the rate of return to R&D capital stock given in Eq. (4) ignores depreciation in the R&D capital stock and for that reason using the formulation to estimate the rate of return is expected to give a downward biased result here.[15] Link and Siegel (2003, p. 72) also discuss another source of downward bias when the formulation in Eq. (4) is used with total factor productivity growth rates in the typical econometric study. Namely, as Schankerman (1981) explained, to some extent R&D expenditures are already reflected in the measures of capital and labor for which growth rates, $\sum_j \eta_j (\dot{X}_j/X_j)$, are subtracted from the rate of growth in output to get the residual to be attributed to exogenous growth rate, λ, and the growth rate in R&D capital stock. Thus, the

---

[15] For technical details about why we anticipate a downward bias in the estimated rate of return when, as in the present case, we are estimating a social rate of return, see Scherer (1984, p. 283, endnote 7).

effect attributed to R&D is typically an 'excess rate of return' – a return above and beyond that already captured by the growth in other inputs that to some extent will reflect R&D investments. The 'double-counting' source of downward bias in the estimate of dQ/dR is less likely in our application of the formulation in Eq. (4), because in effect, by asking for estimates of α, β, and γ as described in Sec. 2, we have asked the expert industrial respondents to estimate directly the left-hand side of Eq. (4) – that is, we ask them to estimate directly the productivity effect that is attributable to new IMT.

5 THE ESTIMATES OF IMT R&D RATE OF RETURN

From the method explained in Sec. 2, we have derived each respondent's estimate of $(\dot{Q}/Q) - \lambda - \sum_j \eta_j(\dot{X}_j/X_j)$, the IMT-induced rate of growth in productivity for the industry of an IMT-user respondent and for the industries to which an IMT-developer sells IMT. From the survey responses, we estimate for each respondent the appropriate industry IMT R&D intensity, $\dot{R}/Q$. The respondents have provided multiples to convert company-level data about $\dot{R}$ and Q to industry-level data.

We include in $\dot{R}$ not only the downstream IMT R&D of the using industries, but as well we include the upstream IMT R&D done by IMT developers who sell IMT to the using industries. The sample of IMT developers covers a wide range of IMT, and the respondents provide multiples to convert company-level IMT R&D for the developers into industry totals including all of their competitors. The total industry-wide upstream IMT R&D of the IMT developers is then allocated to the downstream IMT-using industries in the proportions of all IMT patents taken by patents assigned to those downstream industries.[16]

For each respondent, we then have for each decade an estimate of the IMT-induced rate of growth in productivity and an estimate of IMT R&D intensity. Following Eq. (4), dividing the productivity growth rate by the R&D intensity for each of the nine observations provides an observation of the rate of return dQ/dR on IMT R&D. Table IV shows the rates of return with each entire decade as the period of analysis, and Table V shows the compound annual rates of return.

Those annual rates of return are somewhat more than 70%, somewhat higher than most of the estimates, using a variety of models and methods, for the rates of return to firms' overall R&D investments, reviewed by Link and Siegel (2007, Table 4.4, pp. 48–49). In the large literature they review, a majority of the estimated rates of return to firm R&D were in

TABLE IV Anticipated rate of return, i, to IMT R&D per decade[a].

Decade	Number of observations	Mean	Standard error[b]	95% Confidence interval[c]
2006–2015	9	154.85 (15,485%)	53.95*	30.45–279.25
2015–2025	9	229.25 (22,925%)	54.07**	104.56–353.94

[a]The period of analysis for this table is 9 years in length for the 2006–2015 scenario and 10 years in length for the 2015–2025 scenario.
[b]The estimated mean's level of significance for a two-tailed test (based on the t-statistic = the ratio of the coefficient to the standard error) against the null hypothesis of a zero rate of return to IMT R&D: * = 0.03, ** = 0.01.
[c]Based on the information provided by the respondents and the model, the anticipated rate of return to IMT R&D is within the reported range with probability 0.95. For example, for the first decade the anticipated IMT R&D rate of return is in the range from 3045 to 27,925% with probability 0.95. The reported means provide the point estimates – the expected outcome for the anticipated IMT R&D rate of return.

---

[16] The patent proportions were provided by 1790 Analytics Inc.

TABLE V Annual compound anticipated rate of return to IMT R&D[a].

Decade	Annual rate of return to IMT R&D
2006–2015	0.752 (75.2%)
2015–2025	0.723 (72.3%)

Table 4's IMT R&D rates of return using the decades as the periods of analysis are converted into compound annual rates of return, s. Thus, given that i for the first decade is 154.85 (or 15,485%), the corresponding value of s is s such that we have $(1 + s)^9 = 1 + i$. With $i = 154.85$, s solves as 0.752 or 75.2%. There are 10 years covered for the decade 2015–2025. Thus, with the decade IMT R&D rate of return for the second-decade scenario being 229.25 (22,925%), we have $(1 + s)^{10} = 1 + i$, and the compound annual rate of growth s solves as 0.723 or 72.3%.
[a] For the 9-year span 2006–2015 and the 10-year span 2015–2025.

the range of roughly 30% to 40%. None of the rates of return they report for total R&D or company-financed R&D are as large as the ones we estimate in Table V. However, we are not only estimating anticipated rates of return, rather than actual rates of return, but also we are examining just IMT R&D; and moreover, we have estimated a social, rather than a private, rate of return to the firm.

The rates of return to IMT R&D are social rates of return because they reflect the benefits and costs to society as a whole rather than solely to the developers and users of IMT that make the IMT R&D investments. On the benefits side, we have social rather than private rates of return because we estimate the gains from increased amounts of output from given resources and from reduction in resources used for given outputs, whether or not the private investors appropriate all of those benefits. We obtain estimates of the rate of growth in output made possible by the new IMT. The sales (the additional output times the price realized from the output) from those output gains will not typically equal the social value of the increased output because of the spillovers to consumer surplus (value to consumers above and beyond what they pay) and those spillovers increase with the competition faced by the firms making the R&D investments. On the costs side, in estimating the rate of return to IMT R&D investment, we have a social, rather than private, rate of return because we have included the costs of R&D investments made upstream (in the IMT-developers' industries) that are embodied in the IMT used in the downstream industries. The method weighs social benefits against social costs, resulting in a social rate of return to IMT R&D investments.

The estimates in Tables IV and V are conservative for a couple of reasons. The fact that we include in R&D intensity the upstream R&D that is useful for the downstream IMT-using industries – as is appropriate in order to have all of the social costs from which social benefits are derived – will make our estimates of the rate of return to IMT R&D smaller than would be the case if – as typically happens – the analysis did not account for R&D embodied in purchased technology.[17]

To be even more conservative in our estimation of the IMT R&D rates of return, we have included in the 'R&D' spending what Scherer (1984, chapter 8) refers to as 'launching costs'. The survey asked the respondents to estimate the amounts that they would spend to advertise the new IMT-based features, teaching customers about the new quality of the newly developed IMT-based products and services, and successfully launching them. Such expenditures to successfully launch new or newly improved goods are an important part of successful R&D because without them the benefits from the R&D would not be realized. Those costs are part of

---

[17] Some studies have accounted for R&D embodied in purchased inputs. A prominent example is Scherer (1984, chapter 3 and chapter 15). For a review and further development of the idea that benefits of R&D done outside the using industry affect R&D rates of return, see Scott (1993, chapter 9).

the social costs of introducing the new and newly improved IMT-based products and services and as such they have been included with the R&D spending to determine the R&D intensity used in calculating the rate of return. The approach of course lowers our estimates of the rate of return on the IMT R&D.

6 CONCLUDING OBSERVATIONS

Our study of IMT has implications for technology policy. IMT-induced productivity growth is expected to be substantial and expected social returns to IMT R&D are high. Moreover, the surveyed firms report that they would invest much more in IMT R&D if they could appropriate all of those social returns. The anticipated R&D investments reported for the scenarios described in Tables II–V assumed that the companies investing in IMT R&D would appropriate returns to the extent that they typically do, with much of the benefit spilling over to other producers and consumers. We asked them how much they would invest if, instead, they could appropriate all of the returns generated by their IMT R&D investments. If IMT developers and users could appropriate all of the returns from their IMT R&D investments, they would invest much more in IMT, with their IMT R&D intensities roughly doubling. Table VI compares the R&D intensities for the two decades under the alternative assumptions of typical conditions for appropriating returns versus complete appropriation of returns. Given the typical finding that incomplete appropriation of returns reduces R&D investment below the socially desirable level, the findings in Table VI support the need for government support of IMT R&D investments to overcome the market failure of underinvestment in socially valuable IMT R&D.

The respondents' opinions reinforce the idea that government-supported IMT R&D investments are an important source of the growth in the IMT-knowledge stock that will underlie the IMT-induced productivity gains. Each respondent was asked about the significance of government-funded R&D for the future developments anticipated by 2025. Significance was assessed on a scale from 1 to 10 with 1 indicating no perceptible influence of government-funded R&D, 5 implying that the government-funded R&D was or was expected to be an *important source* of information, and then the higher numbers indicate increasingly that government-funded R&D significantly affects or is expected to affect the direction and effectiveness of the establishment's R&D. The 14 respondents provided assessments of the importance of government-funded R&D for IMT advances over the upcoming years. The average response was 5.79 with a 95% confidence interval from 4.33 to 7.24. Clearly the

TABLE VI   Anticipated IMT R&D intensity per decade for typical versus complete appropriation of returns[a].

Decade/appropriation	Number of observations	Mean	Standard error[b]	95% Confidence interval[c]
2006–2015/typical	9	0.0300	0.00484*	0.0188–0.0412
2006–2015/complete	9	0.0593	0.0116*	0.0324–0.0861
2015–2025/typical	9	0.0332	0.00706**	0.0169–0.0495
2015–2025/complete	9	0.0766	0.0244***	0.0202–0.133

[a]The respondents were asked about their R&D investments given customary or typical conditions for appropriating returns and then alternatively given the counterfactual situation of complete appropriation of returns. As discussed in the text, the R&D here includes 'launching costs' and the upstream R&D embodied in the using industry's IMT.
[b]The estimated mean's level of significance for a two-tailed test (based on the t-statistic = the ratio of the coefficient to the standard error) against the null hypothesis of a zero IMT R&D intensity: * = 0.001, ** = 0.002, *** = 0.02.
[c]Based on the information provided by the respondents and the model, the anticipated IMT R&D intensity is within the reported range with probability 0.95. The reported means provide the point estimates – the expected outcome for the anticipated IMT R&D intensity.

respondents believe that government funding of IMT R&D will be important if the anticipated developments in IMT are to be achieved.

The respondents also report that compliance with industry technical standards is essential to their marketing and sales efforts for new IMT-based products and services. The need for effective standards is undoubtedly an important reason the respondents say government support of IMT investment is needed. Using a scale of 1–10, with 1 denoting that compliance with standards is insignificant and with 10 indicating that compliance with standards is *essential* to the sales and marketing strategy, there were nine respondents. Their mean response was 7.56 with a 95% confidence interval from 6.11 to 9.00. Clearly the respondents believe compliance with industry technical standards is important for the success of the next generations of IMT-based products. Such standards have been important to date. There were 13 respondents providing an evaluation of the importance of standards for IMT-based goods and services to date. Their average assessment was 7.54 with a 95% confidence interval from 6.90 to 8.17.

Although there is considerable uncertainty about the future advances in IMT, we conclude with a cautious summary and suggestions for future research.[18] In sum, our respondents anticipate IMT will generate substantial productivity growth over the next two decades. They report that their IMT R&D intensity would roughly double if they could appropriate all of the returns from the R&D, implying that the value created by their IMT R&D spills over to other firms to a substantial extent. They also report that government-funded IMT R&D has been and will continue to be important for the achievement of IMT advances. The generality of our findings is limited by our small sample size, and an important task for future research will be to increase the sample size. Developing surveys of academics and researchers in industrial laboratories, as well as surveying more firms with operations based in a variety of countries, will make possible a breakdown of the results by industry and allow estimates with smaller confidence intervals.[19]

Acknowledgements

We thank Albert N. Link and two anonymous referees for numerous helpful comments that have been incorporated into the final version of the paper.

References

Albus, J. and Meystel, A. (2001) *Engineering of Mind: An Introduction to the Science of Intelligent Systems*. New York: John Wiley & Sons.

Gumbel, P. (2007) BMW Drives Germany. *Time*, **170**(3), ProQuest document ID 1300201821. Available online at: http://proquest.umi.com/pqdweb?did=1300201821&sid=1&Fmt=3&clientId=4347&RQT=309&VName=PQD.

Leech, D., Burke, J., Russell, M., Waychoff, C. and Scott J.T. (consultant) (2006) *Future Economic Impacts of Investments in Intelligent Machine Technology, 2006–2025, Final Report to the National Institute of Standards and Technology*. Arlington, VA: Northrop Grumman.

Link, A.N. and Siegel, D.S. (2003) *Technological Change and Economic Performance*. London and New York: Routledge – Taylor & Francis Group.

Link, A.N. and Siegel, D.S. (2007) *Innovation, Entrepreneurship, and Technological Change*. Oxford: Oxford University Press.

Schankerman, M.A. (1981) The Effects of Double-counting and Expensing on the Measured Returns to R&D. *Review of Economics and Statistics*, **63**(3), 454–458.

Scherer, F.M. (1984) *Innovation and Growth: Schumpeterian Perspectives*. Cambridge, Massachusetts and London: MIT Press.

---

[18] We gain insight about the uncertainty of future advances in IMT from the range of the respondents' responses about γ, α, and β and hence the range for predicted IMT-induced productivity growth.

[19] Although a number of the corporations surveyed are multinational, the survey is focused on the US; future surveys should broaden the sample.

Scott, J.T. (1993) *Purposive Diversification and Economic Performance*. Cambridge and New York: Cambridge University Press.

Solow, R.M. (1957) Technical Change and the Aggregate Production Function. *Review of Economics and Statistics*, **39**(3), 312–320.

Tassey, G. (1997) *The Economics of R&D Policy*. Westport, Connecticut: Quorum Books.

Tassey, G. (2005) The Disaggregated Technology Production Function: A New Model of University and Corporate Research. *Research Policy*, **34**(3), 287–303.

US Domestic Policy Council (2006) *American Competitiveness Initiative: Leading the World in Innovation*. Washington, DC: Office of Science and Technology Policy.

TO ADMIT OR NOT TO ADMIT: THE QUESTION
OF RESEARCH PARK SIZE

STEPHEN K. LAYSON, DENNIS P. LEYDEN and JOHN NEUFELD

Department of Economics, University of North Carolina at Greensboro, Greensboro NC 27402, USA

1   INTRODUCTION

Research parks can have a significant impact on commercial research and development activities and are an important component of a nation's innovation system.[1] By providing a venue for research firms and organizations to operate in close proximity, they enable easier communication among professionals in different organizations, enhancing the research productivity of all of them. They enable communities to leverage technology-based growth into economic development, and they facilitate advancement through the stages of technology-based economic activity by reducing relevant market transactions especially with respect to technical labor.[2] These benefits have made the development of research parks a goal of public policy in the United States and in other countries. On July 22, 2004, Senator Bingaman introduced a Bill, S. 2737, 'The Science Park Administration Act of 2004,' to facilitate the development of science parks. The premise on which the Bill was based is: 'It is in the best interests of the Nation to encourage the formation of science parks to promote the clustering of innovation through high technology activities.' Building on the premise of S. 2737,

---

[1] According to Link and Scott (2006), the term science park is more common in Europe and Asia and the term research park is more common in the United States. See Link and Scott (2003, 2006) for alternative definitions of a university research park.

[2] For support of these assertions about the economic role of a research park, see Link and Scott (2007).

Senator Pryor introduced on May 11, 2007 a Bill, S. 1373, the 'Building a Stronger America Act.' S. 1373 provides grants and loan guarantees for the development and construction of science parks to promote the clustering of innovation through high technology activities. As of 2002, the United States had 81 parks operating with approximately 30 additional planned. University involvement in creating and managing research parks is widespread but not universal.[3]

Their importance highlights the needs for more knowledge about how science parks 'work,' who locates within a park and why, and the scope of leverage that parks provide tenants and the region where they are located. In the United States, at least, park formation is growing and gaining increased public policy attention. Leyden, Link and Siegel (2008) have provided an initial theoretical examination of why a firm locates in a university research park. This paper examines the issue of what determines the size of a research park and how that size is effected by the presence (or absence) of university involvement. Given the importance of research parks, the issue of their size and of the impact of university involvement on that size is relevant to issues of efficient allocation of economic resources.

2 THE MODEL

The model of the research park developed in this paper is based on the economic theory of clubs. See Sandler and Tschirhart (1980) for a survey of this literature. For members of a private research park, the value of belonging to the park is the opportunity it affords to engage in synergistic R&D activities that can increase the members' profits. There are also, of course, costs of establishing and operating a research park. We assume these costs are shared equally among the members. The objective of a private research park, we assume, is to maximize the average net benefit of the park members. Average net benefit (ANB) is defined to be total R&D benefits to members of the park divided by the number of member firms (AB) minus the average (per firm) cost of establishing and operating the research park (AC). Both the average benefit from joining the park and the average cost of running the park will depend on the number of firms who join the park, N.

For the range of park members around the optimal level, diminishing marginal returns would ensure that the average benefits curve from R&D is declining. Initially, the marginal benefit exceeds the average benefit, causing average benefit to increase with increasing park membership. Each new member's contribution to marginal benefit is lower than that of the previous member, and marginal benefit eventually falls below average benefit, causing the average benefit of adding new members to fall (Figs. 1 and 2). Average benefit may eventually become asymptotic to some value (possibly zero), but this will occur after average benefit is maximized. Average benefit from R&D collaboration is thus assumed to be a strictly quasiconcave function of N. AB reaches a peak value at $N = \hat{N}$ and then steadily diminishes thereafter:

$$AB'(N) > 0 \quad \text{for } N < \hat{N} \tag{1}$$

$$AB'(N) < 0 \quad \text{for } N > \hat{N} \tag{2}$$

The total costs of the research park are composed of a fixed component F, consisting of installation and maintenance of basic infrastructure, administrative overhead, etc., and a variable component VC consisting of the costs of park physical maintenance and joint park

---

[3] Link and Scott (2006), 44–45.

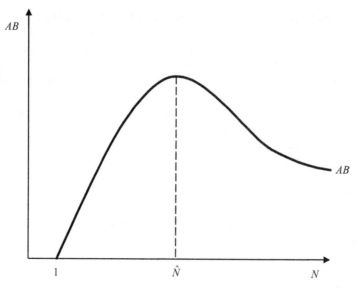

FIGURE 1   Average benefits from R&D collaboration and the number of park members.

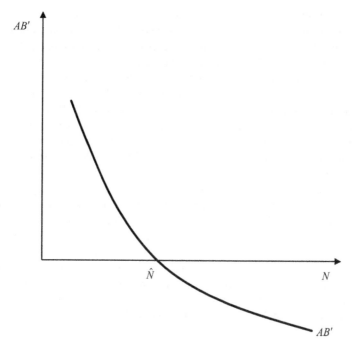

FIGURE 2   Marginal effect on average benefit of admitting a new firm to the park.

activities. Let the total variable cost for a park of a given land size be:

$$VC = c_1 N + c_2 N^2 \quad (c_1, c_2 > 0) \tag{3}$$

The average cost function for the park (Fig. 3) is:

$$AC(N) = \frac{F}{N} + \frac{VC}{N} = \frac{F}{N} + c_1 + c_2 N \tag{4}$$

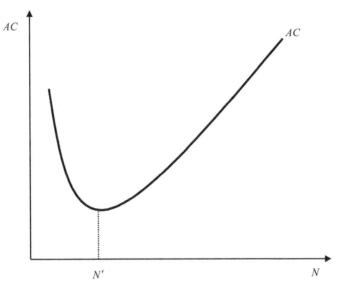

FIGURE 3   Average park costs and the number of park members.

The marginal effect on average cost of admitting a new firm (Fig. 4) into the park is:

$$AC'(N) = -\frac{F}{N^2} + c_2 \tag{5}$$

For small values of N the marginal effect on average cost of admitting a new firm to the park is negative, but for large values of N it will be positive. Decreases in fixed cost cause the AC curve to shift downward, but from Eq. (5) it is clear that decreases in fixed cost cause the AC′

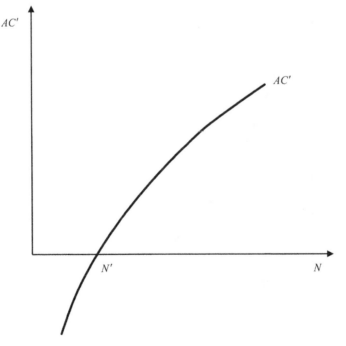

FIGURE 4   The effect of firm entry on AC′.

curve to shift upwards for all values of N. Also note that the AC$'$ curve is always rising with N:

$$AC''(N) = 2\frac{F}{N^3} > 0 \tag{6}$$

For a feasible private research park that has the potential to generate positive average net benefits for the firms, we assume the park's objective function is

$$\text{Max ANB}(N) = \text{AB}(N) - \text{AC}(N) \tag{7}$$

The first-order condition for this optimization problem is:

$$\text{AB}'(N^*) - \text{AC}'(N^*) = 0 \tag{8}$$

As long as the AC$'$ curve intersects the AB$'$ curve from below, as in Figure 5, the value of N that satisfies the first-order condition will maximize the value of average net benefit. If firms were homogeneous in their ability to benefit from R&D collaboration each firm's benefit from joining the park would be the average benefit. With free entry into the park, firms would continue to enter until park members' average net benefit was driven down to zero. Figure 6 illustrates the free entry solution where the average cost curve intersects the average benefit curve from below. The equilibrium number of firms under free entry is denoted by N_e. Because the optimal number of firms (N^*) by assumption generates a positive ANB, $N_e > N^*$. A private research park will always seek to restrict the number of firms in the park below the free entry level.

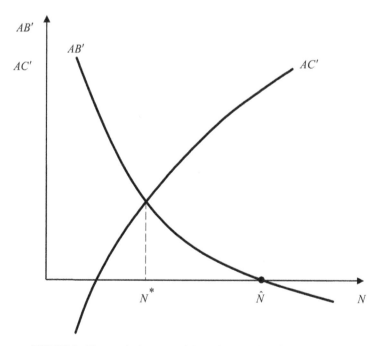

FIGURE 5   The marginal curves and the optimal number of park members.

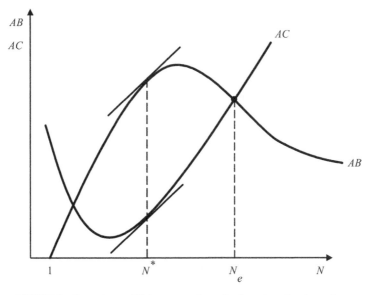

FIGURE 6   Free entry equilibrium versus the optimal number of park members.

3   THE EFFECT OF UNIVERSITY AFFILIATION

Universities provide a wealth of R&D infrastructure, knowledge, ability to synergize, etc. Within the context of the model above, the presence of a university increases the average benefits of R&D collaboration (AB) for any value of N, as shown in Figure 7. We assume it also increases the marginal effect AB′ for every value of N (Fig. 8).

University affiliation is assumed to reduce the fixed costs (F), borne by the research park members by making its infrastructure available to park members. University affiliation may

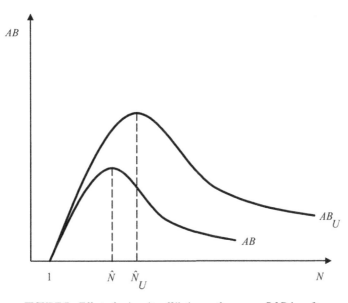

FIGURE 7   Effect of university affiliation on the average R&D benefit.

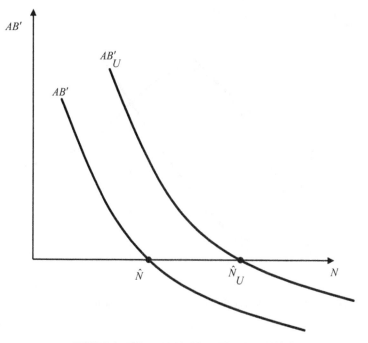

FIGURE 8   Effect of university affiliation on AB′.

also increase variable costs of park operations through agreements it makes with park firms, such as hiring a certain number of University students or graduates per year, etc. For simplicity, we assume that University affiliation may increase the parameter c_1 in the variable cost function, $VC = c_1 N + c_2 N^2$, but has no effect on the parameter c_2. With these assumptions, university affiliation reduces members' average costs for small values of N (less than

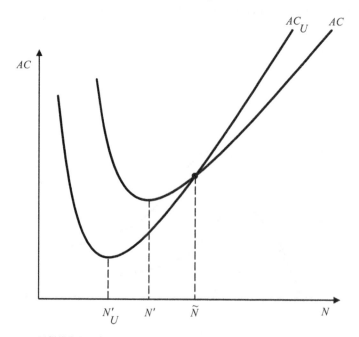

FIGURE 9   Effect of university affiliation on average member cost.

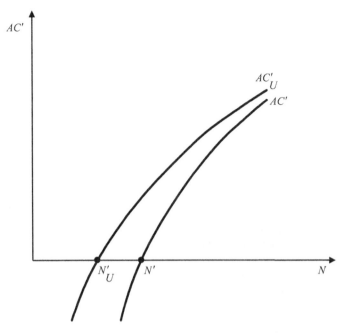

FIGURE 10   Effect of university affiliation on AC'.

$\tilde{N}$), but increases it for larger values, as shown in Figure 9. University affiliation, however, unambiguously shifts the AC' function given by Eq. (5) upward for all values of N, as shown in Figure 10.

Because university affiliation causes both the AB' curve and the AC' curve to shift upward, university affiliation has an ambiguous effect on the optimal number of park firms. Figure 11 illustrates the special case where the optimal number of firms remains unchanged by university

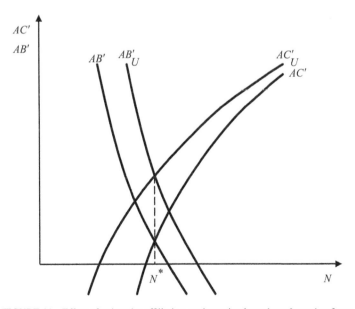

FIGURE 11   Effect of university affiliation on the optimal number of member firms.

affiliation. However, if the AB′ curve (AC′ curve) were to shift up by more than what is indicated in Figure 11, the optimal number of firms would rise (fall).

Up until now we have assumed that the research park is economically feasible without university affiliation. Without university affiliation it is possible that the park's average cost curve lies everywhere above the average benefit curve. Because university affiliation raises the average benefit and lowers the average cost, university affiliation may be necessary for the existence of a research park. Obviously, in this important special case university affiliation increases the optimal park size.

4 CONCLUSION

In a model where the objective of a research park is to maximize the net average benefits of each member firm, the optimum number of firms is determined by the marginal effect that firm entry has on average member benefits and costs. We find that a private research park will always seek to limit the number of firms in the park to a smaller number than would occur if there were free entry into the park. We also find that university affiliation has an ambiguous effect on the optimal number of firms in the park.

Acknowledgement

We wish to thank Matthew Rhodes for his assistance with the figures in this paper.

References

Leyden, D.P. and Link, A.N., and Siegel, D. (2008) A Theoretical and Empirical Analysis of the Decision to Locate on a University Research Park. *IEEE Transactions on Engineering Management*, forthcoming.

Link, A.N. and Scott, J.T. (2003) U.S. Science Parks: The Diffusion of an Innovation and Its Effects on the Academic Missions of Universities. *International Journal of Industrial Organization*, **21**, 1323–1356.

Link, A.N. and Scott, J.T. (2006) U.S. University Research Parks. *Journal of Productivity Analysis*, **25**, 43–55.

Link, A.N. and Scott, J.T. (2007) *The Economics of University Research Parks*. Mimeograph.

Sandler, T. and Tschirhart, J.T. (1980) The Economic Theory of Clubs: An Evaluative Survey. *Journal of Economic Literature*, **18**, 1481–1521.

INNOVATION PLATFORMS AND THE GOVERNANCE OF KNOWLEDGE: EVIDENCE FROM ITALY AND THE UK

DAVIDE CONSOLI[a] and PIER PAOLO PATRUCCO[b,c]

[a]*Manchester Institute of Innovation Research, University of Manchester, UK;* [b]*Department of Economics, University of Turin, Italy;* [c]*BRICK - Bureau of Research on Innovation, Complexity and Knowledge, Collegio Carlo Alberto, Moncalieri (TO).*

1   INTRODUCTION

The objective of this paper is to analyse the role of technology infrastructure in the innovation process. Conceptually this work connects with empirical studies indicating that innovation is a distributed process generated through interactions among heterogeneous agents. In such a perspective, economic development is driven by the interplay between the individual initiatives of specialized actors and the collective processes that are created to harmonize their tasks and align their incentives. In fact as knowledge is dispersed, fragmented and incomplete, the operation of evolving economies requires dedicated coordination activities to generate complementarities across otherwise dispersed competences (Richardson, 1972; Loasby, 1991; Metcalfe, 1995; Antonelli, 2001). The notion of 'technology infrastructure' embodies a wide class of collective processes which respond to the need of creating and coordinating knowledge in such circumstances.

Technology infrastructures are strategic activities generated through large-scale investments to foster connections across specialized actors either within the public or the private sectors, or at their interface (Smith, 1997). The operation of such infrastructures often relies on generic and non-proprietary technologies which are widely available and, thus, bear upon R&D policy and management as well as on incentives and attitudes to invest. In the form of physical artefacts, such as standards or technological platforms, infrastructures facilitate market transactions for technology-based goods and generate benefits on both the supply and demand side (Tassey, 2000; 2005). The paper presents the case of innovation platforms as a particular instantiation of technology infrastructure with a view to articulate key organizational processes underpinning collective innovation, namely the orchestration of supplier networks, outsourcing and user–producer relations (Garicano, 2000; Crémér *et al.*, 2007).

The paper is structured as follows. Section 2 overviews the literature on innovation and technical change and especially the localized technological change (LTC) approach, which is relevant in view of the centrality that knowledge dynamics and the associated governance mechanisms play in our analysis of technology infrastructure. Section 3 presents two case studies on innovation platforms in the automotive sector in Italy and the health-care sector in the UK. Section 4 elaborates on these and highlights similarities and differences across paths of sectoral and institutional development. Section 5 concludes and summarizes.

2   LOCALIZED AND COLLECTIVE TECHNOLOGICAL CHANGE

This section will introduce the background for the analysis of technology infrastructure, with particular emphasis on the LTC approach. The central claim is that the thrust of economic development is the combined outcome of increasing variety in the knowledge base and the creation of specific coordination mechanisms. This implies that the dynamics of knowledge growth and the associated governance challenges are central to the analysis. The last subsection brings these themes together and looks at the role of innovation platforms as mechanisms for the coordination of knowledge.

2.1   Time, Space and Knowledge: the Building Blocks

The body of work on economics of innovation focuses on the sources and the effects of technological change. In this view, economic development is an evolutionary process driven by interactions between business firms and their environment. In a nutshell, technological change is understood as outcome of interdependent processes, namely growth of variety in the realm of actors – including firms, regulatory bodies and consumers – and the coordinating effort of institutions (David, 1994; Antonelli, 2001; Metcalfe, 2001; Nelson, 2002). We will focus specifically on the strand of analysis on LTC (see Atkinson and Stiglitz, 1969; David, 1975; Antonelli, 2001; 2008).

The LTC view advocates that technological change is a 'localized' process to stress that its path of development carries the contingencies of historical time, of the geographic space and, *a fortiori*, of the relevant forms of knowledge. Accordingly, the LTC approach articulates economic development as a recursive process where (i) an inducement mechanism, due to mismatch between agents' plans and the actual outcomes, triggers the search for new solutions; (ii) this, subsequently, leads to accumulation of technological knowledge and the development of specific competences to implement necessary changes; and (iii) culminates with the actual introduction of innovations which reflects the interplay between micro-behaviours and the macro-characteristics of the environment.

Seen through these lenses economic development features two important properties. First, it is path-dependent, in the sense that the growth and transformation of firms and industries are cumulative processes that absorb the stimuli of the extant environment (David, 1994). Secondly, its viability depends on the management of positive and negative effects of knowledge growth and information exchange – asymmetries being the most obvious example. Furthermore, in this view sustainable competitiveness depends on deepening specialization and developing coordination activities as opposed to the static allocation of existing resources (Pavitt, 1998; Chesbrough, 2003; Nooteboom, 2003). Let us now combine the ingredients of the LTC approach in a dynamic perspective.

2.2   Collective Knowledge and Governance: the Engine of Development

The notions of learning and localized technological knowledge are central to the LTC tenet. Technological change is never the outcome of isolated action but, rather, of collective learning and cumulative interactions: it builds upon past experience and, at the same time, it is constrained by the specific technical and procedural choices that have been adopted throughout its path. In the LTC approach boundedly rational agents generate and exploit new knowledge only within limited domains and circumstances (Antonelli, 2001; 2008). In fact, they are myopic in a two-fold sense: they cannot fully anticipate the outcomes of their decisions, and they are never completely aware of what other agents do – therein including competitors, suppliers and consumers. Allied to this is the notion that agents need to develop competences to adapt their internal activities but also to generate complementarities and absorb external knowledge. For these reasons, the dynamics of knowledge in the LTC context are characterized by relevant search and information costs (Antonelli, 2006).

The generation of localized technological knowledge is a collective effort aimed at creating and sustaining dynamic complementarities across otherwise dispersed competences. Variety of the knowledge base, however, is not sufficient: in fact, specialization is dynamically effective when specific governance mechanisms facilitate the coordination of variety (Prahalad and Hamel, 1990; Coombs and Metcalfe, 2000).[1] Antonelli (2006) has recently articulated the properties of localized technological knowledge, and connected these with a variety of governance tools for its coordination. In particular, he points out, quasi-hierarchical command is most appropriate when knowledge is tacit and sticky; constructed interactions among learning agents work best with articulable types of knowledge; finally, coordinated transactions are needed when knowledge is highly codified.

2.3   Complexity and Knowledge

The analysis of knowledge as a complex dynamic system represents the third key ingredient of the LTC approach. Complexity theory outlines the structural and dynamic properties of economic systems driven by the emergence of micro-behaviours and of their interactions (Arthur *et al.*, 1997; Foster, 2005). Each agent possesses specific and limited cognitive resources and, thus, commands specialized modules of technology and knowledge (Cohen and Levinthal, 1989; Arthur, 2007; Antonelli, 2008). In dynamic environments characterized by recurrent changes in product characteristics and production technologies, the internal capabilities of individual firms hardly suffice and strategies for the governance of knowledge are critical for survival. To this end firms deepen specialization and establish connections to access and contribute to collective knowledge. New knowledge is facilitated by complementarity, rather than substitutability, between internal and external knowledge: the greater the scale of networking the more intense the internal know-how needed to understand, command and recombine external capabilities (Patrucco, 2008).

On the basis of prospective costs associated to changes in their knowledge base, firms position themselves along a strategic spectrum whose extremes are either vertical integration

---

[1] Such processes are particularly evident in both geographical and sectoral contexts where innovation is the outcome of combined horizontal and vertical indivisibilities across various actors. These include firms specialized in different technologies, as well as firms and Universities, technology transfer centres and knowledge-intensive business services (see Patrucco, 2003; 2005).

or the market. The organization design literature is replete with debates over the virtues and the challenges associated with either, and this is not the place to elaborate at length on this. Suffice it to say that notwithstanding the widespread significance of vertical disintegration, some forms of production and provision cannot be served efficiently by market mechanisms and managed through vertical disintegration and total outsourcing only. Hybrid solutions, like networks, are more appropriate when the design of inter-organizational relationships seeks to minimize costs due to external coordination, and to maximize the creative contribution of individual firms (Langlois, 1992). In turn, complex dynamic systems feature simultaneous availability of the outlined options and cyclical adaptation of strategic designs (Ethiraj and Levinthal, 2004). Put another way, decision-making in such contexts is driven by 'dynamic' coordination, that is, by generative interactions that facilitate changes in production, technologies, networks of suppliers, and in the modules of relevant knowledge (Lane and Maxfield, 1997; Cohen and Axelrod, 1999; Loasby, 1999; Potts, 2000). Let us connect the outlined conceptual framework with the case of innovation platforms, an illustrative example of knowledge governance which has captured the attention of scholars and policy-makers alike.

2.4 Dynamic Coordination and Complex Knowledge: Innovation Platforms

Innovation platforms are systemic infrastructures for the organization and coordination of distributed innovation processes that feature high degrees of complexity. The creation of innovation platforms consists in the design and establishment of architectures for inter-organizational coordination (Sah and Stiglitz, 1986; 1988): these define the levels of engagement of each peripheral units, the characteristics of the flows (i.e. unidirectional or bidirectional) of information and knowledge, and the extent of exchange across organizations.[2] The design of a platform determines *ex-ante* but evaluates (and eventually adapts) *ex-post* the creation and the use of knowledge (Garicano, 2000).

The rationale of innovation platforms is to maximize the variety of contributions stemming from a variegated knowledge base while maintaining coherence though a minimum level of hierarchy. In a platform-type of structure, a variety of agents participates to the production and supply of products and services. Each unit exists independently according to own goals and capacity but, at the same time, responds to a collective goal through shared communication rules. The architectures in which they operate are flexible and can be configured in different ways for different uses, very much akin to computer platforms. Innovation platforms are purposefully open to entry of new actors and, thereby, of new competences: the extent of contribution by each additional unit depends endogenously on the relative value of internal competences measured against the collective goal.

Relevant dynamics within platforms span technological and organizational levels, and bear upon both the static and the dynamic coordination of knowledge. From a static viewpoint, platforms connect and integrate activities and capabilities of relevant agents within an industry, thus supporting specialization and favouring the accumulation of specific knowledge. From a dynamic viewpoint, platforms stimulate changes in both the structure of the network and the mechanisms for the governance of technological knowledge.

---

[2] The notion of innovation platforms elaborated here differs from that of technological platform. The latter accounts for ICT-based innovations like virtual networks, and the associated infrastructures, and interfaces and standards (Gawer and Cusumano, 2002). Technology platforms facilitate interoperability and coordination between different firms and technologies in the context of high-tech industries (see i.e. Consoli, 2005) as well as scientific clusters (Robinson *et al.*, 2007). Innovation platforms are strategic organizational vehicles for coordinating specialized agents. ICTs and virtual networks are thus instrumental and yet subsidiary elements. Common to both technology and innovation platforms is the notion of directed and coordinated organization as opposed to 'spontaneous' organization typical of market processes.

The implementation of innovation platforms engenders a dynamic trade-off between deeper specialization and wider variety of the knowledge base (Kogut, 2000; Crémér *et al.*, 2007). In fact, such a trade-off defines the scope, the boundaries and the forms of inter-organizational relations within a platform. On the one hand specialization favours efficient communication within a narrow set of partners but limits both the scope for coordination and accessibility to innovative opportunities. On the other hand the coordination of a bundle of inter-firms and inter-organizations linkages opens up new opportunities but lowers the scope for specialization and the benefits of communication (see Kogut and Zander, 1992).

The phenomenon of innovation platforms stirs an intense debate across disciplines. Management scholars connect the latter to the challenges and the strategic implications associated to the emergence of open systems for production and exchange (Gerstein, 1992; Garud and Kumaraswamy, 1995; Ciborra, 1996; Ethiraj and Levinthal, 2004). In the policy realm innovation platforms are looked at as a key reference model for the creation and management of mixed (i.e. public and private) coalitions (European Commission, 2004). In the context of innovation studies Antonelli (2006) argues that platforms are especially appropriate when technological knowledge exhibits levels of compositeness and cumulability that imply too high coordination costs for a single firm. Recent contributions by Baumol (2002) and Von Hippel (2005) further stress the incentives of knowledge sharing for firms within a platform. Efficiency in knowledge creation, they observe, stems from both internal investments and external learning and is higher than if it relied exclusively on either internal creation (i.e. vertical integration of R&D) or external acquisition (i.e. outsourcing of R&D and design).

Innovation platforms underpin the development of physical technologies too. These integrate a variety of inputs from a range of industries and firms and include innovations such as Internet services, enhanced broadband fibre optics, Asynchronous Digital Subscriber Lines, and Universal Mobile Telecommunications System. As each allows the integration of a variety of content, services, technologies and applications, platform-based technologies are both composite and fungible (Fransman, 2002; Antonelli, 2006). Let us now look at two case studies to illustrate the empirical connotations of the issues outlined so far.

3 TWO CASE STUDIES

This section presents two empirical studies of collective innovation stirred through the creation of innovation platforms. These cases present interesting commonalities and differences. To recap, the creation of innovation platforms is an emerging phenomenon in the context of innovation systems featuring: large-scale of operations; variety in the forms of relevant knowledge; distributed forms of production and supply; and complementarity between manufacturing and service activities. Besides these commonalities, innovation platforms carry idiosyncratic characteristics of the sectoral, geographical, institutional and historical contexts in which they emerge. To the extent that local and hybrid solutions are able to combine the benefits of hierarchical design with the advantages of a distributed structure, innovation platforms are appropriate tools for the coordination of knowledge. Let us now look at the cases of the health-care sector in the UK and the automotive sector in Italy.

3.1 Innovation Platforms in the Health-care Sector of the UK

After having operated within traditional boundaries for decades, managers and practitioners of health-care have begun to explore new routes in search of a model that stimulates and facilitates the emergence of innovation. Advances in medical knowledge have been traditionally understood as a by-product of basic science, but recent research demonstrates convincingly that effective improvements in the provision of health-care are often attained through the development of practical procedures in patient care (Metcalfe *et al.*, 2005; Nelson, 2005). Modern health-care is no longer limited to individual disciplines and does not feature homogeneous supply of medical devices and clinical services but, rather, thrives on the juxtaposition of scientific knowledge and practical skills from a variety of contexts (Consoli 2007; Ramlogan *et al.*, 2007). Recent evidence further indicates that the potential associated to advances in basic scientific research (such as biochemistry and genetics) is likely to encounter bottlenecks when tried immediately in the diagnostic or therapeutic context. Accordingly, it has been argued, progress in the medical and clinical realms relies heavily on cross-boundary activities like the translation of laboratory research, the integration of patient-care experience into the design of training and the management of relationships between health trusts and other relevant actors, such as universities and firms (Rosenberg *et al.*, 1995; Gelijns *et al.*, 2001).

Patient care presents specific challenges due to the highly fragmented nature of service delivery. In fact, clinical information about patients is highly complex, not easily codified and prone informal transmission (Gittell and Weiss, 2004). Furthermore, administrative information becomes ever more complex due to the proliferation of automated management systems that are designed around unit-specific requirements. This is also aggravated by the resilience of functional boundaries dictated by professional status which undermine the effectiveness of relationships and of communication (Wicks, 1998).

Improving coordination across health-care units has become imperative and, specifically, encouraging innovation in front-line activities and pushing outwards those that prove most effective. Clearly this set of objectives does not imply diminished importance of basic research but, rather, points to the necessity to balance investments in basic scientific research – and the associated expectations – with the goal of improving existing activities and competences. The associated policy design seeks to balance top-down forces and bottom-up processes by encouraging cross-fertilization among research activities, the business conduct and their assessment. The National Health System (NHS) of the United Kingdom (UK) has marked a clear step in this direction by establishing the Institute for Innovation and Improvement to the effect of addressing two key issues highlighted in the context of intense policy debates: the translation of basic research into clinical practice (Cooksey, 2006; UK Evaluation Forum, 2006); and the spreading of improvements in routine patient care beyond the source unit (Department of Health, 2003).

The central purpose of the Institute is to accelerate the diffusion of innovative ideas and new practices as well as facilitating the uptake of proven improvements in health-care delivery models and processes. It is argued that the economic incentives at hand are two-fold. First, lower operating costs will generate direct efficiency gains; second, the creation of new services like intellectual property (IP) management is expected to encourage the growth of new niches in the health-care market (Department of Health, 2003). Being a strategic interface among key stakeholders the Institute enables capacity- and capability-building for individuals, teams and organizations. It is structured in teams that pursue and contribute to specific trajectories of development by managing a range of activities and competences, namely: identifying areas of improvement; assessing existing solutions; looking for best practices in external environments (i.e. other countries, companies); creating solutions for private companies or third parties; and, finally, ensuring equitable rewards for all parties.

A key component of the Institute is the National Innovation Centre (NIC), which operates as a platform to connect inventors and relevant stakeholders. The Institute provides a single point of contact to NHS staff (clinical or administrative) and independent providers who strive to develop new procedures and diagnostic or therapeutic devices. The NIC determines both *ex-ante* and *ex-post* standards. It thus provides guidelines and stimulates the response of NHS trusts to specific problems as well as developing specific formats to facilitate the adoption of new practices throughout the NHS.

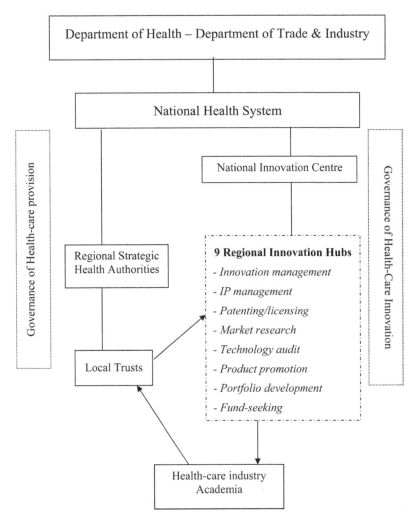

FIGURE 1   Institutional infrastructure for health-care innovation in the UK.

The NIC operates by means of local Innovation Hubs spread throughout the nine jurisdictions of the English Regional Development Agencies.[3] Figure 1 illustrates the multi-layered institutional infrastructure of the health-care system in the UK, and the role of the regional innovation hubs.

Hubs are gatekeepers of local knowledge infrastructures, and foster connections across NHS Trusts, Primary Care units, health authorities and industry players. They do so by providing a range of services to support both local development as well as the diffusion of innovations within the NHS, mainly through the management of IP rights. Most hubs offer two broad typologies of services, either aimed at NHS staff – like training, technology audits, IP management – or at local business – like market research, access to medical staff for exploring innovative ideas, licensing arrangements. Table I provides a further useful indication of cross-regional specialization with a map of the innovations (columns) that have been developed during the last two years with the contribution of the hubs (rows).

---

[3] North (Sunderland); Yorkshire and Humber (Leeds); North West (Manchester); West Midlands (Birmingham); East Midlands (Nottingham); East (Cambridge); London; South East (Egham); South West (Salisbury).

TABLE I   NHS Innovation hubs in the UK and their successes.

	Manufactured products		Services	
	Medical devices	Clinical support	Patient services	Staff services
North (Sunderland) 6	– Pupilometer* – Blood tag reader* – Fluid flood meter – Hand-splint support*		– Drop-off repair system	– Booklet on speech for children with special needs*
Yorkshire (Leeds) 34	– Panoramic test* – Motorized lifting aid* – Sway Pen device – Digital video sleep monitoring system* – Cast battery device* – Snore capture device* – Switch device for disabled children – Patients lifting device* – Hip stick for wheelchair users* – Motorized drip stand*	– Electronic patient questionnaire* – Support arm* – Personnel Management database – Software to assess motor skills* – Test for panoramic dental X-ray – Ultrasound device for blood flow* – Fibre-optic device for tracheal intubations* – Phantom for X-ray bone densitometers* – Visual field analyser – Urological Digital Diary* – High-resolution dose meter* – Software for digital manipulation* – Radiological software package* – Solution for storing transplant organs – Focussed gene array* – Diagnostics for colorectal cancer* – Measurement of gastric acid secretion – DNA/RNA extraction buffer* – Markers of Preeclampsia		– Interactive Radiotherapy training – Fire safety training simulator – Training device for colorectal surgery – Patient safety device – Haematology training aid

Region	Innovations
West Midlands (Birmingham) 5	– Multi-grip walking stick* – Breathing support valve* – Pyjama design for in-patients* – Sensory software*
East Midlands (Nottingham) 2	– Sterilizing sleeve for limb surgery* – Optical coherence tomography probe*
East (Cambridge) 9	– Needle Exchange Cabinet – Pelvic cushion – R&D operating system* – Web database for haematology diseases* – Lifestyle check-up software – Improvements Review Toolkit* – Resource pack to assist patients with learning disabilities
North West (Manchester) 20	– Health Screening Software for GPs – Falls care assessment bundle – Patient observation chart – Diabetes management program – Transcranial magnetic stimulation – Home pulmonary rehabilitation – Prevention for heart diseases – Down-syndrome Children support – Young pregnant support – Breastfeeding support – Nurse intervention for Hypertension due to diabetes – Diagnostics for mental health – Assistance for nebulized medication – Information Governance Booklet – Smoking cessation service – Protocol for patient constipation – Buildings design project – Secretarial services improvement program – Management of needle stick injuries

(continued)

TABLE I   Continued.

| | Manufactured products | | Services | |
	Medical devices	Clinical support	Patient services	Staff services
			– Screening program for Gonorrhoea – Health awareness development program – Prescription support practice – Fear of falling booklet	
London 10	– Aid for Parkinson's patients – Falls mat	– Multi-purpose sensors – Fibre-optic oximeter – Airway inspection device – Anti-coagulant for blood collection* – Support for fractured arms – Laparoscopic tool – Collapsible bed tray		
South East (Egham) 5	– GPS tracker for patient w/ dementia*	– Slide comparator for histological exams – Dosimeter for nuclear medicine* – Electronic quality Audit for trials		Training courses: – Defibrillation; – Primary-care skills;
South West (Salisbury) 3	– Electronic muscular stimulators*			– Functional electric stimulation courses* – Infection control training package

*Commercialization licensed to third party/spin-out or developed in partnership.

These innovations fall into two macro-categories (manufactured products or services) which are further classified in: medical devices; tools for support of clinical activities; services for patients and NHS staff services. The cross-hubs innovative performance features a great degree of variety with respect to several dimensions. First, the number of entries in the table indicates more intense activity taking place in Yorkshire, Manchester, London and Cambridge; second, it reveals a bias towards novel clinical and medical product, as opposed to patient services, in all the hubs with the exception of Manchester; third the table highlights variety in terms of product and service developments, whereby some are managed carried out in-house by the trusts and some entail the involvement of third parties either through partnerships or spin-outs.

The platform structure underlying the NIC provides coherence to an otherwise dispersed network of health-care professionals and, in so doing, it facilitates the translation of feedback from front-line care into systematic innovation. The integration of health-care provision and innovative activities generate benefits that stretch beyond the life cycle of individual solutions, be they medical products or clinical services. Each hub filters the bottom-up inputs of local innovators according to top-down specifications on policy and funding priorities. The conduct of hubs is only restrained by geographical location and, accordingly, by region-specific priorities and technical and procedural strategies can be adjusted to accommodate the strengths and the limitations of the collaborative relationships at hand. Accordingly, the relative contribution of each unit to the platform is endogenously determined by the impact of localized incentives. Therefore, clinical staff seeks professional recognition as well as monetary returns from IPs; local business firms on the other hand will prefer flexible strategies outside the remit of traditional procurement contracts. In such a context research capacity and the ability to carry over activities promoted locally by local hubs to national scale, is also likely to be endogenous.

3.2 Innovation Platforms in the Automotive Sector of Piedmont

The role of innovation platforms as vehicles for strategic coordination is relevant also for the analysis of the evolution of the automotive industry. The case of Piedmont is interesting in view of the following: (i) the difficulties of a traditional big player, i.e. FIAT, as inducement factor for the ongoing structural and organizational change in the automotive production system; (ii) the increasing complexity of the knowledge and technological base; (iii) the intensification of technical and managerial specialization; and (iv) the progressive importance of coordination mechanisms. Successful product innovation nowadays rests upon the orchestration of a wide network of suppliers to adapt the organization of production.

A dominant characteristic of car production is the complexity of the knowledge base, due to both static and dynamic aspects. On the one hand car production relies on complementarities across a wide range of technologies and materials which, in turn, imply the combination of knowledge from engineering, electronics, chemistry, plastics technology, robotics, informatics and telecommunications. On the other hand no single firm can command all of these, thus making knowledge complex in that it requires the integration and recombination of external and internal expertise by means of supply and demand of products, components and process technologies. As a result the coordination of components, technologies and modules of knowledge requires a mix of internal specialization and outsourcing.

In the last three decades the intertwining effects of market saturation, product differentiation, variations in demand and financial pressures have triggered significant changes in the automotive sector. Increasing specialization and fragmentation stimulated greater availability of business options for original equipment manufacturers (OEMs, i.e. car-makers), especially in relation to outsourcing-based production. On the one hand know-how and capabilities are highly specific and thus widely distributed across OEMs and suppliers. On the other hand product architectures tend to differ substantially across models. Therefore, interchangeability and reversibility across modules, components and activities are restrained by such significant variations. By the same token, OEMs confront high switching costs associated to shifting suppliers, and costs due to changes in the technology modules and in the design of the system. Over the years the combination of such circumstances has encouraged preferential interactions between OEMs and suppliers (Sako, 2003).

The evolution of car production in Piedmont reflects in many ways the vicissitudes that FIAT, its most representative actor, experienced during the 1990s. The combined effect of increased complexity in the knowledge base together with a managerial crisis within FIAT stimulated a turn towards vertical disintegration and intense externalization. However, the creation of such partnerships undermined FIAT's traditional stronghold in the local network of small and large firms. The crisis of FIAT was also an important catalyst for the growth of a sophisticated network of highly specialized supplier which is at the core of radical transformations in car production. This growing network targets international markets, co-operates with leading design firms (such as Pininfarina and Giugiaro), machine tool firms, research and training organizations (CRF and ISVOR), and collaborates with universities and research centres through sponsorships (Enrietti and Bianchi, 2003).

In this evolving technological and competitive context, FIAT has undergone significant changes. First, it moved away from its traditional vertically integrated structure to endorse a model of distributed production. In concomitance to this, it has systematically adopted outsourcing of both components and strategic and high-value activities (such as design and R&D) to local small suppliers. Finally, to accommodate modular product design it has engaged systematically with suppliers for co-innovation and co-design. Table II highlights parallels between the evolution of FIAT and of the automotive sector in Piedmont:

1. Coordination through vertical integration was typical in the 1970s: coordination of innovative and productive activities takes place through a Fordist-type organization and is based upon internal accumulation of R&D, capabilities in the design of cars models, and capabilities in technology design. In this phase, innovation is observed exclusively within FIAT and in isolation.

2. Coordination through centralized networks of local suppliers progressively takes place during the 1980s: as a reaction to changes in consumers' needs and uncertainty in the supply strategies to meet them, FIAT changes its structure to embrace outsourcing of components to local small suppliers. In doing so it also contributes to the creation of a local – and closed – network of suppliers coordinated centrally: R&D and design are thus defined *ex-ante* by FIAT and transmitted top-down to suppliers.

3. Coordination through decomposed and decentralized network in the 1990s: initially peripheral firms become first-tier suppliers and, after having developed significant competences, can reap economies of specialization and learning. Such firms are part of an international network of producers which target external markets and provide product-design services. At this point FIAT outsources strategic activities such as design, and gives over activities, autonomy and key decision processes concerning design. Innovation therefore occurs in a bottom-up fashion, and is triggered by the activity of first-tier suppliers, at the same time undermining the OEM's ability to innovate as well as to coordinate the network.

4. Coordination through innovation platforms: in the last phase FIAT brings back R&D and design in-house as a reaction to the recent loss of innovative capacity. The firm's strategy combines internal know-how with the competences of first-tier suppliers on R&D and design to create and exploit synergies. Accordingly, coordination rests on a variety of 'de-layered' organizational relations benefiting from a wide pool of resources and knowledge. Herein technological cooperation takes place vertically (i.e. within the supply

TABLE II   The phases of institutional change in the coordination of car production in Turin.

Phase	Coordination structure	Organization mode	Innovation
I Phase: '1970s	The firm	– Vertical integration of production – Internal accumulation of R&D – Internal accumulation of capabilities in the design of cars models – Internal accumulation of capabilities in technology design	– Innovation in isolation
II Phase: '1980s	The centralized network	– Outsourcing of components production – Central coordination of suppliers by the OEM – Exclusive supply from small suppliers to the OEM	– *Ex-ante* and top-down design of both cars models and components – Innovation undertaken internally by the OEM
III Phase: '1990s	The decomposed network	– Suppliers benefit from economies of specialization and learning – First-tier suppliers emerge as innovators at the local and international levels – Outsourcing of components production – Outsourcing of design in both components and modules – Modular product and system architecture design	– Outsourcing of R&D and design – Bottom-up (first-tier suppliers driven) innovative process
IV Phase: ongoing	The innovation platforms	– In-sourcing of innovative and value adding activities – Acquisition of external resources built in phase III – Vertical cooperation between OEM and FTSs – Horizontal cooperation between OEMs and between FTSs – Internal to the OEM product and system architecture design	– Integration of top-down (OEM) and bottom-up (first-tier suppliers) innovative process – Co-design – Co-innovation

chain of FIAT), horizontally (i.e. between FIAT and different OEMs) and diagonally (i.e. through different supply chains through the cooperation of first-tier suppliers with different OEMs). Innovation in this phase reflects the integration of top down and bottom-up processes, and takes place in a distributed fashion, through bidirectional exchanges of technical information on shared R&D and design activities, mainly between FIAT and first-tier suppliers.

Important changes involved not only the choice between make and buy, between internal production and external provision, but also the way in which FIAT coordinates and manages external supply. A straightforward example of these is the adoption of the so-called advanced product quality planning (APQP)[4] method to manage the network of suppliers and their activities. Prior to the adoption of APQP the definition of new cars and component characteristics and their acquisition from suppliers was defined *ex-ante* and designed centrally by FIAT: given

---

[4] The APQP (Advanced Product Quality Planning) has been adopted by Fiat in the context of the partnership with GM, established in 2000 and failed in 2005. The APQP method is a structured system for the control of the different phases of new products development, from early conception to design and to production. The method is part of quality standard QS-9000 and ISO-TS 16949.

ex-ante characteristics of the components, FIAT set prices and identified appropriate suppliers. After the adoption of APQP and as a result of higher decentralization due to suppliers' acquired competences, the process has reverted. Now FIAT defines the general design and characteristics of new models and transmits such information to the network of suppliers. Accordingly, each supplier proposes a project for the production of the given component or system following technical specifications and price/quality requirements provided by FIAT. The selection of the most appropriate project is then followed by a negotiation between FIAT and the suppliers in order to specify the fine details concerning the characteristics and the prices of the component or system.

The structure of the innovation platform operating in the automotive sector of Piedmont is shown in Figure 2 where we observe medium-sized suppliers featuring as central nodes in the network of distributed producers.

Interestingly enough, the progressive transfer of upstream strategic activities and autonomy from FIAT to suppliers initiated in the 1990s has recently triggered the participation of second-tier suppliers (Whitford and Enrietti, 2005). This process is especially important for standards concerning production efficiency, quality of components and modules and selection of innovative capabilities to be integrated. Although the platform stems mainly from efforts made by FIAT to restore its own centrality in the sector, the innovative performance of the distributed network now hinges on the coordination of top-down management by FIAT (i.e. the general and macro template of a new car) with bottom-up activities by specialized suppliers (i.e. the actual implementation of modules and components with new features and performances). Product innovation in the automotive sector has thus become an emergent property defined by the cooperative relationship between FIAT and suppliers along the production chain, a cooperation aided by complementarities across different activities, technologies and spaces of competences.

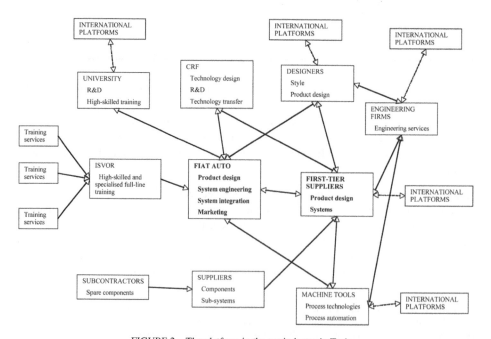

FIGURE 2   The platform in the car industry in Turin.

4 DISCUSSION

Innovation platforms favour the exploitation of collective and heterogeneous pools of competences that are embedded in the connective structure of the system. Their chief task, the coordination of different capabilities, is achieved through the establishment of qualified nodes of interaction. Such infrastructures operate in a semi-hierarchical fashion to reap the benefits of diffuse participation while preserving coherence of the collective goal. The distributed and open mode of operation of innovation platforms stimulates the introduction and integration of new products and services through dynamic complementarities both within and across industries and sectors. They favour both user–producer collaboration and rapid trial-and-error learning for the design of new products, components and services. Clearly from time-to-time redundancies, networking costs and governance issues limit the scope and the advantages of such solutions and stimulate the search for new configurations.

Knowledge governance by means of platforms is most appropriate in environments that either undergo frequent changes or feature a degree of variety which would result in untapped potential in the absence of appropriate coordination (Antonelli, 2006). The collective knowledge generated in such a context is complex – in that it relies on the dynamic interactions and learning among actors – as well as open – in that it draws on shared competences and technologies as opposed to exclusive protection and appropriation of R&D activities (see Chesbrough; 2003; Chesbrough et al., 2006). Accordingly, the interaction between internal and external learning opportunities based, for instance, on technological partnerships, R&D alliances and technology transfer mechanisms, defines a path of dynamic adaptation between specialization and variety of the knowledge base in a system of innovation.

Levels of strategic decisions in a platform are established without ambiguities, as well as the degree of participation in each task. Accordingly, the central node filters the inclusion of new members and, thus, commands strategic knowledge about the platform design; at another level coherent rules of engagement favour the entry of new participants, together with their technology and competences. Clearly this route implies a flexible approach to the establishment of bargaining power and power relations across actors (Baldwin and Clark, 2000; Volpato and Stocchetti, 2002; Steinmueller, 2003).

The two illustrative examples discussed above provide interesting indications on innovation platforms. In the case of health-care the central hub, the Innovation Institute, determines the goals and the standards of operation (i.e. for the management of IP rights) which are subsequently implemented on a local basis by the regional hubs. This ensures lower set-up and transaction costs compared to strongly decentralized organizations, which operate on the basis of outsourcing and distributed networking. Likewise, in the case of car production centralized decision-making is necessary due to partial reversibility and interchangeability across models. Thereby, cooperation between OEMs and suppliers entails the adaptation of the latter's capabilities around the specifications established by the former. This, in turn, provides suppliers with incentives to develop transferable know-how and competences. Both case studies feature co-investments and co-design as distinguishing outcomes of the organization of components and subsystems within innovation platforms. This is evident also in the characteristics of the by-products: digital platforms, for instance, are purposefully designed to function as open products to allow flexible adoption by small suppliers and knowledge services firms. In doing so software acquire coherence and, thus, fungibility of use in the system.

5 CONCLUDING REMARKS

The paper has looked at the generation and diffusion of technological knowledge in the context of systems of innovation. The main argument proposed here is two-fold: first, technological change is a collective process generated by the coordination of dispersed capabilities across a variety of agents; second, the viability of the process relies on the creation of infrastructures that facilitate the emergence of dynamics interrelationships within and across activities, and the forms of specialization embedded.

Technology infrastructures are strategic tools to orchestrate inter-organizational coordination within systems of innovation. The paper has argued that innovation platforms are a particular instantiation of technology infrastructure. Their creation entails the search for and the development of complementarities – as opposed to mere agglomeration – among a variety of activities. Innovation platforms are designed and implemented purposefully, as opposed to 'spontaneous' phenomena like networks are often referred to in economics; more in general, the concept of innovation platforms subordinates the role of network-type of activities to the relational structures that contribute to their generation and mode of operation.

The paper has presented two illustrative examples of innovation platforms. The first looks at recent changes in the UK health-care system and, in particular, at the creation of a national innovation platform for innovation. This operates locally through nine regional hubs with the aim of spreading successful but episodic improvements beyond individual health-care units. The second example of the automotive industry in Piedmont shows that the shift from vertically integrated production to a distributed platform stems from and reinforces the ethos of cooperation between large firms and specialized suppliers for the design of a complex product. Both cases highlight interesting patterns of innovation and change in the context of systems characterized by growing variety in the knowledge base and the stabilizing effects of governance mechanisms. It is hoped that future research will assess systematically the trade-offs entailed by the adoption of distributed innovation to better understand the challenges that emerge in dynamically unstable competitive environments.

Acknowledgements

Authorship is alphabetical and both authors contributed equally. We are grateful to two anonymous referees and to the guest editors for helpful comments on an earlier draft of the paper. The financial support of CSI Piemonte through the project 'Analisi Economica dell'Innovazione nei Servizi di Rete in Piemonte' is gratefully acknowledged.

References

Antonelli, C. (2001) *The Microeconomics of Technological Systems*. Oxford: Oxford University Press.
Antonelli, C. (2006) The Business Governance of Localized Knowledge: An Information Economics Approach to the Economics of Knowledge. *Industry and Innovation,* **13**(2), 227–261.
Antonelli, C. (2008) *Localized Technological Change: Towards the Economics of Complexity*. London: Routledge (Forthcoming).
Arthur, B., Durlauf, S. and Lane, D. (eds.) (1997) *Economy as an Evolving Complex System II*. Reader, Mass.: Addison-Wesley.
Arthur, W.B. (2007) The Structure of Invention. *Research Policy,* **36**(2), 274–287.
Atkinson, A.B. and Stiglitz, J.E. (1969) A New View of Technological Change. *Economic Journal,* **79**, 573–578.
Baldwin, C.I. and Clark, K.B. (2000) *Design Rules: The Power of Modularity*. Cambridge: MIT Press.
Baumol, W.J. (2002) *The Free-Market Innovation Machine. Analyzing the Growth Miracle of Capitalism*. Princeton: Princeton University Press.
Chesbrough, H.W., Vanhaverbeke, W. and West, J. (eds.) (2006) *Open Innovation: Researching a New Paradigm*. Oxford: Oxford University Press.
Chesbrough, H. (2003) *Open Innovation. The New Imperative for Creating and Profiting from Technology*. Boston: Harvard Business School Press.
Ciborra, C. (1996) The Platform Organization: Recombining Strategies, Structures and Surprises. *Organizational Science,* **7**, 103–118.
Cohen, W. and Levinthal, D. (1989) Innovation and Learning: The Two Faces of R&D. *Economic Journal,* **99**, 569–596.

Cohen, M. and Axelrod, R. (1999) *Harnessing Complexity: Organizational Implications of a Scientific Frontier*. Free Press: New York.

Consoli, D. (2005) The Dynamics of Technological Change in UK Retail Banking Services: An Evolutionary Perspective. *Research Policy, 34*, 461–480.

Consoli, D. (2007) Services and Systemic Innovation: A Cross-Sectoral Analysis. *Journal of Institutional Economics, 3*, 71–89.

Cooksey, D. (2006) *A Review of UK Health Research Funding*. Report to HM Treasury.

Coombs, R. and Metcalfe, J.S. (2000) Organizing for Innovation: Co-Ordinating Distributed Innovation Capabilities. In Foss, N. and Mahnke, V. (eds.) *Competence, Governance and Entrepreneurship*. Oxford: Oxford University Press.

Crémér, J., Garicano, L. and Prat, A. (2007) Language and the Theory of the Firm. *Quarterly Journal of Economics, 122*(1), 373–407.

David, P.A. (1975) *Technical Choice, Innovation and Economic Growth*. Cambridge: Cambridge University Press.

David, P.A. (1994) Why Are Institutions the 'Carriers of History'? Path Dependence and the Evolution of Conventions, Organizations and Institutions. *Economic Dynamics and Structural Change, 5*, 205–220.

Department of Health (2003) The NHS as an Innovative Organisation: a Framework and Guidance on the Management of Intellectual Property in the NHS.

Enrietti, A. and Bianchi, R. (2003) Is a District Possible in the Car Industry? The Case of the Turin Area. In Belussi, F., Gottardi, G. and Rullani, E. (eds.) *The Technological Evolution of Industrial Districts*. Boston: Kluwer.

European Commission (2004) *Technology Platforms: from Definition to Implementation of a Common Research Agenda*. Director-General for Research.

Foster, J. (2005) From Simplistic to Complex Systems in Economics. *Cambridge Journal of Economics, 29*(6), 873–892.

Fransman, M. (2002) *Telecoms in the Internet Age: From Boom to Bust to ....?*. Oxford: Oxford University Press.

Ethiraj, S.K. and Levinthal, D.A. (2004) Modularity and Innovation in Complex Systems. *Management Science, 50*(2), 159–173.

Garicano, L. (2000) Hierarchies and the Organization of Knowledge in Production. *Journal of Political Economy, 208*(5), 874–904.

Garud, R. and Kumaraswamy, A. (1995) Technological and Organizational Designs for realizing Economies of Substitution. *Strategic Management Journal, 16*, 93–109.

Gawer, A. and Cusumano, M.A. (2002) *Platform Leadership: How Intel, Microsoft, and Cisco Drive Industry Innovation*. Cambridge, MA: Harvard Business School Press.

Gelijns A.C., Zivin, J. and Nelson, R.R. (2001) Uncertainty and Technological Change in Medicine. *Journal of Health Politics, Policy and Law, 26*, 913–924.

Gerstein, S. (1992) From Machine Bureaucracies to Networked Organizations: An Architectural Journey. In Nadler, D.A., Gerstein, M.A. and Shaw, R.B. (eds.) *Organizational Architecture: Designs for Changing Organizations*. San Francisco: Jossey-Bass.

Gittell, J.H. and Weiss, L. (2004) Coordination Networks within and across Organizations: A Multi-Level Framework. *Journal of Management Studies, 41*(1), 127–153.

Kogut, B. (2000) The Network as Knowledge: Generative Rules and the Emergence of Structure. *Strategic Management Journal, 21*(3), 405–425.

Kogut, B. and Zander, U. (1992) Knowledge of the Firm, Combinative Capabilities, and the Replication of Technology. *Organization Science, 3*(3), 383–397.

Lane, D.A. and Maxfield, R. (1997) Strategy Under Complexity: Fostering Generative Relationships. In Arthur, B., Durlauf, S. and Lane, D. (eds.) *Economy as an Evolving Complex System II*. Reader, Mass.: Addison-Wesley.

Langlois, R.N. (1992) Transaction Costs in Real Time. *Industrial and Corporate Change, 1*, 99–127.

Loasby, B.J. (1991) *Equilibrium and Evolution. An Exploration of Connecting Principles in Economics*. Manchester: Manchester University Press.

Loasby, B.J. (1999) *Knowledge, Institutions and Evolution in Economics*. London: Routledge.

Metcalfe, J.S. (1995) Technology Systems and Technology Policy in an Evolutionary Framework. *Cambridge Journal of Economics, 19*, 25–46.

Metcalfe, J.S. (2001) Institutions and Progress. *Industrial and Corporate Change, 10*, 561–586.

Metcalfe, J.S., James, A. and Mina, A. (2005) Emergent Innovation Systems and the Delivery of Clinical Services: The Case of Intra-Ocular Lenses. *Research Policy, 34*(9), 1283–1304.

Nelson, R.R. (2002) Bringing Institutions into Evolutionary Growth Theory. *Journal of Evolutionary Economics, 12*, 17–28.

Nelson, R.R. (2005) Physical and Social Technologies, and their Evolution. In Nelson, R.R. *Technology, Institutions, and Economic Growth*. Boston: Harvard University Press.

Nooteboom, B. (2003) Managing Exploration and Exploitation. In Rizzello, S. (ed.) *Cognitive Developments in Economics*. London: Routledge.

Patrucco, P.P. (2003) Institutional Variety, Networking and Knowledge Exchange: Communication and Innovation in the Case of the Brianza Technological District. *Regional Studies, 37*(2), 159–172.

Patrucco, P.P. (2005) The Emergence of Technology Systems: Knowledge Production and Distribution in the Case of the Emilian Plastics District. *Cambridge Journal of Economics, 29*(1), 37–56.

Patrucco, P.P. (2009) Collective Knowledge Production Costs and the Dynamics of Technological Systems. *Economics of Innovation and New Technology,* forthcoming.

Pavitt, K. (1998) Technologies, Products and Organization in the Innovating Firm: What Adam Smith Tells Us and Joseph Schumpeter Doesn't. *Industrial and Corporate Change,* **7**(3), 433–452.

Potts, J. (2000) *The New Evolutionary Microeconomics: Complexity, Competence and Adaptive Behaviour.* Cheltenham: Edward Elgar.

Prahalad, C.K. and Hamel, G. (1990) The Core Competence of the Corporation. *Harvard Business Review,* **68**(3), 79–91.

Ramlogan, R., Mina, A., Tampubolon, G. and Metcalfe, J.S. (2007) Networks of Knowledge: The Distributed Nature of Medical Innovation. *Scientometrics,* **70**(2), 459–489.

Richardson, G.B. (1972) The Organization of Industry. *Economic Journal,* **82**, 883–897.

Robinson, D.K.R., Rip, A. and Mangematin, V. (2007) Technological Agglomeration and the Emergence of Clusters and Networks in Nanotechnology. *Research Policy,* **36**(6), 871–879.

Rosenberg, N., Gelijns, A.C. and Dawkins, H. (eds.) (1995) *Sources of Medical Technology: Universities and Industry.* Washington DC: National Academy of Sciences Press.

Sah, R.K. and Stiglitz, J.E. (1986) The Architecture of Economic Systems: Hierarchies and Polyarchies. *American Economic Review,* **76**(4), 716–727.

Sah, R.K. and Stiglitz, J.E. (1988) Committees, Hierarchies and Polyarchies. *Economic Journal,* **98**(391), 451–470.

Sako, M. (2003) Modularity and Outsourcing: The Nature of Co-Evolution of Product Architecture and Organization Architecture in the Global Automotive Industry. In Prencipe, A., Davies, A. and Hobday, M. (eds.) *The Business of System Integration.* Oxford: Oxford University Press.

Smith, K. (1997) Economic Infrastructures and Innovation Systems. In Edquist, C. (ed.) *Innovation Systems: Institutions, Organisations and Dynamics.* London: Pinter.

Steinmueller, W.E. (2003) The Role of Technical Standards in Coordinating the Division of Labour in Complex Systems Industries. In Prencipe, A., Davies, A. and Hobday, M. (eds.) *The Business of System Integration.* Oxford: Oxford University Press.

Tassey, G. (2000) Standardization in Technology-Based Markets. *Research Policy,* **29**(4–5), 587–602.

Tassey, G. (2005) Underinvestment in Public Good Technologies. *Journal of Technology Transfer,* **30**(1–2), 89–113.

UK Evaluation Forum (2006) *Medical Research: Assessing the Benefits to Society.* Report by Academy of Medical Sciences, Medical Research Council and Wellcome Trust.

Volpato, G. and Stocchetti, A. (2002) Managing Information Flows in Supplier–Customer Relationships: Issues, Methods and Emerging Problems. *Actes du GERPISA,* **33**, 7–27.

Von Hippel, E. (2005) *Democratizing Innovation.* Cambridge, MA: MIT Press.

Whitford, J. and Enrietti, A. (2005) Surviving the Fall of a King: The Regional Institutional Implications of Crisis at Fiat Auto. *International Journal of Urban and Regional Research,* **29**(4), 771–795.

Wicks, D. (1998) *Nurses and Doctors at Work: Rethinking Professional Boundaries.* Philadelphia, PA: Taylor and Francis.

ASSESSING THE RELATIVE PERFORMANCE OF UNIVERSITY TECHNOLOGY TRANSFER IN THE US AND UK: A STOCHASTIC DISTANCE FUNCTION APPROACH

DONALD SIEGEL[a], MIKE WRIGHT[b], WENDY CHAPPLE[b] and ANDY LOCKETT[b]

[a]*Department of Management and Marketing, A. Gary Anderson Graduate School of Management, University of California at Riverside, Riverside, CA 92521, USA*
[b]*Nottingham University Business School, University of Nottingham, Jubilee Campus, Nottingham NG8 1BB, UK*

1   INTRODUCTION

In recent years, there has been a substantial increase in the rate of commercialization of intellectual property at US and UK universities. More specifically, universities have attempted to formalize technology transfer and capture a larger share of the economic rents associated with technological innovation by establishing technology transfer offices (henceforth, TTOs). TTOs facilitate technological diffusion through the licensing of a university-based technology to an existing firm or new venture. Thus, they contribute to the development of new technology infrastructure. University technology transfer can also potentially yield economic benefits to the local region, through job and new firm creation or the stimulation of additional research activity in nearby firms.

Given the critical managerial and policy implications of university technology transfer, there is considerable interest in assessing and 'explaining' relative performance. Licensing has traditionally been the most popular mode of university technology transfer (Jensen and Thursby, 2001). As a result, several studies have used either the number of licenses or licensing income as the single output.

From the university's perspective, an advantage of licensing as a mechanism for technology transfer is that it allows academics to continue their pursuit of research, without devoting effort to commercialization. However, for certain technologies, patenting and licensing is difficult or infeasible. Thus, an exclusive focus on licensing might prevent universities from reaping a substantial return on their intellectual property portfolio.

Therefore, universities might seek more direct involvement in the commercialization of new technology by 'spinning off' a company (Shane, 2002; Shane and Stuart, 2002). Typically, the university assumes equity in the start-up, and thus, owns a percentage of the company. Siegel *et al.* (2003b) report that universities are increasingly focusing greater attention on the entrepreneurial dimension of technology transfer. As a result, there has been growing interest in the role of university spin-offs (DiGregorio and Shane, 2003).

With respect to cross-country comparisons, there is a general sense that the UK is not as advanced as the US in university technology transfer. In the UK, this has engendered a policy debate concerning the nature of outputs resulting from university technology transfer. The UK Treasury-sponsored Lambert Review of business–university collaboration (Lambert, 2003) asserted that British universities needed to determine the optimal mix of licensing and spin-off or licensing activity.

This paper takes an account of these two important trends in university technology transfer: (1) the tendency of universities to benchmark their performance against domestic and foreign rivals and (2) the growing emphasis on the entrepreneurial dimension of technology commercialization at universities. More specifically, the study potentially makes two contributions to the literature. The paper contains the first econometric evidence on the relative efficiency of university TTOs that is based on multiple outputs. Specifically, we outline and estimate a stochastic, multiple-output distance function to capture the efficiency of both university licensing and spin-off generation. We also present the first cross-country comparison of the relative performance of university TTOs.

The remainder of this paper is organized as follows. Section 2 outlines our specification of the technology transfer production function and factors that may explain some of the variation in relative performance across universities. Section 3 presents the econometric model, which is based on the specification of a stochastic distance function. Section 4 describes the data and Sec. 5 presents empirical results. Preliminary conclusions and suggestions for additional research are presented in the final section.

2   INPUTS, OUTPUTS, AND DETERMINANTS OF RELATIVE 'EFFICIENCY' IN UNIVERSITY TECHNOLOGY TRANSFER

Studies of the effectiveness of university technology transfer of US universities (e.g., Thursby and Kemp, 2002; Thursby and Thursby, 2002; Siegel *et al.*, 2003a) have been based on a production function framework. Several key stylized facts have emerged from field and survey research on TTOs (e.g., Thursby *et al.*, 2001; Siegel *et al.*, 2003a), which are relevant to the specification of this production function. The first is that although faculty members working on a federal research grant are required to disclose inventions to the university TTO, some researchers do not comply with this regulation and the rule is rarely enforced. This aberrant behavior highlights the critical task of TTO staff in simply eliciting disclosures from faculty members and thus, increasing the potential pool of potential technologies for licensing. Technology licensing officers can potentially play an important role by providing 'business coaching' and encouraging faculty members to engage in entrepreneurial and licensing activity.

Field research has also revealed that the importance of patents in this process is often overstated. That is, many firms license technologies long before the university patents them, if they are patented at all. This occurs for several reasons. First, patent protection may not be viable or critical for a particular type of technology. For instance, patents are not important in the computer software industry or in the design of integrated circuits. Second, firms may have considerable faith in the scientist's ability or reputation, or because the inventor has a long-standing financial relationship with the firm.[1] Finally, some firms (especially younger, more entrepreneurial companies) are anxious to lock-in promising embryonic technologies at a low price.

Another stylized fact culled from interviews of licensing officers is the importance of (external) intellectual property lawyers in the process of technology transfer. Some institutions use these lawyers to help them obtain copyrights and in various aspects of patenting and licensing, especially in support of prosecution, maintenance, litigation, and interference. Indeed, it is quite common for universities to devote substantial resources to the maintenance and re-negotiation of licensing agreements, due to the embryonic nature (e.g., uncertainty) of the technologies and to the fledgling nature of many of the firms that license university-based technologies. Therefore, we use legal expenditures as an input into the creation of licenses, licensing income, and university spinouts.

A key difference between the two countries should be noted. In the US, the Bayh–Dole Act stipulates that scientists must disclose inventions arising from federally funded research to the university TTO. There is no such legislation in the UK. The 1997 UK Patent Act states that inventions of employees who may reasonably expect to make inventions are clearly owned by the employer, so long as it is stated in the employment contract. If ownership is not stated in an employment contract then the intellectual property right (IPR) belongs to the inventor. Universities are increasingly exercising their property rights over inventions.

As alluded to earlier, even the presence of the Bayh–Dole Act, Thursby and Kemp (2002) found typically less than half of faculty inventions with commercial disclosure are disclosed to TTOs. Furthermore, the use of an invention disclosure as a proxy for the stock of technology is context specific. The fact that the UK academics are not required to disclose scientific discoveries implies that the true quantity of a university's pool of available technologies for commercialization is unobservable. The use of patents as an indicator of technological input is also problematic because there is substantial variation in quality and in patenting strategies across universities. Some universities generate numerous patents because start-up costs are relatively small. However, they also find that cost of enforcing patents is high and sometimes not worth the effort. In light of the shortcomings of invention disclosures and patents as indicators, we use research expenditure as our measure of technological input.

There is a perception in the academic literature that equity ownership in a university spinout might increase the potential upside gain, which appears to be an attractive option to universities. Evidence from a small set of universities suggests that assuming an equity position in spinout company yields a higher average long-run than the average return on a license (Bray and Lee, 2000). The UK treasury-sponsored Lambert review of business–university collaboration (2003) concluded that British universities were also beginning to emphasize spinout creation.

---

[1] Inventors often use such funds to support graduate students, post-doctoral fellows, and other laboratory costs.

Thus, in order to evaluate technology transfer performance, we need to assess both licensing and spinout activity.

Relative efficiency in university technology transfer is also likely to be related to environmental and organizational factors, such as the presence of a medical school on campus and proxies for the extent to which there is a supportive culture for technology commercialization. A recent study reports that over 60% of MIT's university licenses result from a biomedical invention.[2] Bulut and Moschini (2007) conducted an econometric analysis of university licensing income and found that most of the revenue gains were concentrated in private universities with medical schools.

Experience in spinning out companies and licensing may increase the efficiency of a university, as universities 'learn' how to become better at creating spinouts and licenses. Our proxy for experience is the length of time a university has had a TTO. Thus, in our equation 'explaining' relative performance, we include a dummy variable denoting whether the university has a medical school and a measure of the age of the TTO.

Other institutional factors that might explain variation in relative performance are the existence of a university science park or incubator. Science parks are designed to foster the formation and growth of innovative firms, provide an environment which enables large companies to develop relationships with small, innovative firms and promote formal and operational links with universities and other research institutions (Phan *et al.*, 2005). Incubators, on the other hand, are focused on the creation and development of new firms (start ups), which are also concentrated in a limited space.

Finally, regional factors may also be important, such as the R&D intensity of local firms, the availability of venture capital, and proxies for economic performance. Whether the university is located in a 'research active' region has implications for quality of staff/ agglomeration effects between business and university.

3   ECONOMETRIC MODEL

Our framework for constructing measures of relative productivity is stochastic frontier estimation, which was developed independently by Aigner *et al.* (1977) and Meeusen and van den Broeck (1977). This method generates a production (or cost) frontier with a stochastic error term that consists of two components: a conventional random error ('white noise') and a term that represents deviations from the frontier, or relative inefficiency.

Assume that the production function can be characterized as:

$$y_i = X_i \beta + \epsilon_i \tag{1}$$

where the subscript i refers to the ith university, y represents technology transfer output, X denotes a vector of inputs, β is the unknown parameter vector, and ϵ an error term that consists of two components, $\epsilon_i = (V_i - U_i)$, where U_i is a non-negative error term representing technical inefficiency, or failure to produce maximal output given the set of inputs used, and V_i is a symmetric error term that accounts for random effects. Thus, we can rewrite Eq. (1) as:

$$y_i = X_i \beta + V_i - U_i \tag{2}$$

---

[2] See Pressman *et al.* (1995).

Consistent with Aigner *et al.* (1977), we assume that the U_i and V_i have the following distributions:

$$V_i \sim \text{i.i.d.} \; N\left(0, \sigma_v^2\right)$$

$$U_i \sim \text{i.i.d.} \; N^+\left(0, \sigma_u^2\right), \quad U_i \geq 0 \sim \sigma$$

That is, the inefficiency term, U_i, is assumed to have a half-normal distribution; i.e., universities are either 'on the frontier' or below it.[3] Jondrow *et al.* (1982) specify a functional form for the conditional distribution of $[U_i/(V_i - U_i)]$, the mean (or mode) of which provides a point estimate of U_i.

An important parameter in stochastic frontier models is $\gamma = \sigma_u^2/(\sigma_v^2 + \sigma_u^2)\gamma\sigma$, the ratio of the standard error of technical inefficiency to the standard error of statistical noise, which is bounded between 0 and 1. Note that $\gamma = 0$ under the null hypothesis of an absence of inefficiency, which would imply that all of the variance in the observed error term can be attributed to statistical noise. In our empirical analysis, we will formally test this null hypothesis for each variation of the econometric model.

An important extension of the stochastic frontier literature (see Pitt and Lee, 1981) has been the ability to incorporate determinants of technical inefficiency into these models. This extension is crucial to our analysis, since a chief goal of our study is 'explain' deviations from the frontier (i.e., relative inefficiency in university-industry technology transfer (UITT)). Consistent with Kumbhakar *et al.* (1991) and Reifschneider and Stevenson (1991), we conjecture that the U_i are independently distributed as truncations at zero of the $N(m_i, \sigma_u^2)\sigma$ istribution with:

$$m_i = \mathbf{Z}_i\theta \tag{3}$$

where $\mathbf{Z}$ is a vector of environmental, institutional, and organizational variables that are hypothesized to influence relative efficiency and θ is a parameter vector.[4]

As shown in Battese and Coelli (1995), simultaneous estimation of the production frontier and inefficiency equations [Eqs. (1) and (2)] by maximum likelihood methods generates estimates of the parameter vectors β and θ, which we can use to compute estimates of relative productivity. The authors also note that this method is preferable to a two-stage approach, which involves computing estimates of relative productivity and then running ordinary least squares (OLS) regressions on a set of determinants of establishment-level relative inefficiency. The problem with the two-stage approach is that it yields inconsistent estimates, since the inefficiency effects in the first stage of the model are assumed to i.i.d., while in the second stage they are hypothesized to be a function of university-specific factors.

In Sec. 2, we argued that the process of technology transfer is characterized by multiple outputs: licensing and start-up activity. With multiple outputs, it is appropriate to employ a 'distance' function approach, which can be considered as a generalization of the single output production (or cost) frontier (Fare and Primont, 1990). Distance functions can be estimated using non-parametric or parametric methods. We choose to estimate the frontier parametrically, since our intention is to conduct statistical inference.

The distance function can be expressed as:

$$\ln D_o = \alpha_0 + \sum_{m=1}^{M-1} \alpha_m \ln y_m + \sum_{k=1}^{K} \beta \ln x_k + \ln \varepsilon \tag{4}$$

---

[3] Other distributional assumptions for the inefficiency disturbance that have been invoked are truncated normal and exponential (see Sena, 1999).

[4] As discussed in Battese and Coelli (1995), this model can also incorporate panel data.

Noting that homogeneity implies that:

$$D_o(x, \omega y) = \omega D_o(x, y) \tag{5}$$

Hence, if we arbitrarily choose one of the outputs, such as the Mth output, and set $\omega = 1/y_M$, we obtain:

$$D_o\left(\frac{x, y}{y_M}\right) = D_o\frac{(x, y)}{y_M} \tag{6}$$

For the Cobb–Douglas case, this yields:

$$\ln(D_o/y_m) = \alpha_0 + \sum_{m=1}^{M-1} \alpha_m \ln y^* + \sum_{K=1}^{k} \beta_K \ln x_k + \ln \varepsilon \tag{7}$$

where $y* = y_m/y_M$, and can rewrite the distance function more concisely as:

$$-\ln(D_o) - \ln(y_M) = CD\left(\frac{x, y}{y_M, \alpha, \beta}\right) \tag{8}$$

and hence:

$$-\ln(y_M) = CD\left(\frac{x, y}{y_M, \alpha, \beta}\right) + \ln(D_o) \tag{9}$$

Hence if we append a symmetric error term v to account for statistical noise and re-write ln (D_o) as μ, we can obtain the stochastic output distance function, with the usual composite error term $\varepsilon = v + \mu$. We make the standard assumptions that the v are normally distributed random variables, while the μ are assumed to have a truncated normal distribution:

$$-\ln(y_M) = CD\left(\frac{x, y}{y_M, \alpha, \beta}\right) + v - \mu \tag{10}$$

In the stochastic frontier approach, the predicted value of the output distance function for the ith firm, $D_{oi} = \exp(-\mu)$ is not directly observable but must be derived from the composed error term, ε_i. Hence, predictions for D_o are obtained using Coelli's Frontier 4.1 program, based on the conditional expectation $D_{oi} = E[(-\mu)\varepsilon_i]$.

The second equation we estimate is the one, which 'explains' technical inefficiency for the ith university (U_i):

$$U_i = \delta_0 + \delta_M \text{ MED}_i + \delta_{\text{INC}} \text{ INCUB}_i + \delta_{\text{SCI}} \text{ SCI}_i + \delta_A \text{ AGE}_i + \delta_{\text{GDP}} \text{ REGGDP}_{ij}$$
$$+ \delta_{\text{RD}} \text{ REGRD}_{ij} + \delta_{\text{VC}} \text{ REGVC}_{ij} + \mu_i$$

where MED, INCUB, and SCI are dummy variables that are equal to 1 if the university has a medical school, an incubator, or a science park; 0 otherwise, respectively; AGE is the age of the TTO and REGGDP, REGRD, and REGVC are regional industry GDP, R&D intensity, and venture capital, respectively, where j denotes the region surrounding the university.

4 DATA

Our primary data source for US universities is the comprehensive survey conducted by the Association of University Technology Managers (AUTM, 2001). The AUTM file contains annual data on the number of licensing agreements (NOLIC), royalty income generated by licenses (LICINC), university startups generated (USO), research income (RESINC), number of full-time-equivalent employees in the TTO (STAFF), and (external) legal expenditures on technology transfer (LEGAL). We also include controls for faculty quality (FACQUAL), which is proxied in the US by the average ranking of a university's doctoral programs and in the UK by the university's average research assessment exercise score.[5]

Corresponding data from the UK were derived from a survey conducted in March 2002, which was then repeated in March 2003. This survey consisted of quantitative and qualitative questions. Given that this is a somewhat new database, we describe it some detail. The survey was mailed to the top 122 UK universities, as ranked by research income. These institutions were identified using the Higher Education Statistics agency (HESA, 2001) publication 'Resources of Higher Education Institutions (2000/2001)'. The remaining 45 universities accounted for only 0.2% of UK universities' total research grants and contract expenditures in 2001. We received information for 98 of these top 122 universities. Several institutions reported numerous zeros. This indicates that the university was not very active in technology transfer and thus, provided us with only very limited information on this activity. Our final sample consists of only those institutions that provided complete information in both rounds of surveys, as we used lagged inputs and determinants of technical inefficiency.

To test whether our sample is representative, we examined the differences between the universities in our sample of full respondents against the remaining universities. This analysis indicates that our sample of universities relates to those that are more active in technology transfer activities.

5   EMPIRICAL RESULTS

Descriptive statistics for the inputs and outputs and determinants of relative efficiency are presented in Table I. Columns 2–4 in Table I present results for the pooled sample. Columns 5–7 and 8–10 contain separate results for the US and the UK, respectively. The representative university in our sample consummated 29 licensing agreements in 2001, earns $8.4 million

TABLE I   Summary statistics for outputs, inputs, and determinants of relative efficiency for 120 US and UK universities.

Variable	Pooled			US			UK		
	N	Mean	Standard deviation	N	Mean	Standard deviation	N	Mean	Standard deviation
Number of university spinouts	120	3.88	4.15	83	4.27	4.71	37	3	2.31
Number of licenses	120	30.4	44.63	83	39.25	50.6	37	11	13.33
Licensing income ($ mil)	120	8.9	29.4	83	12.6	34.8	37	0.6	1.01
Total research income ($ mil)	120	193	247	83	258	270	37	47.1	69.7
External legal IP expense ($ mil)	120	0.96	1.64	83	1.26	1.9	37	0.30	0.46
Number of TTO staff	120	5.41	6.13	83	4.37	5.25	37	6.85	7.65
Medical school	120	0.62	0.49	83	0.64	0.48	37	0.57	0.50
Science park	120	0.43	0.50	83	0.45	0.50	37	0.38	0.49
Age of TTO	120	14.88	12.07	83	17.10	13.0	37	9.24	7.24
Proportion of research income from business	120	26.86	191.53	83	32.07	229.81	37	15.16	27.48
Faculty quality	120	3.48	0.86	83	3.15	0.70	37	4.22	0.72
Incubator	120	0.45	0.50	83	0.43	0.50	37	0.49	0.51
GDP per capita ($ mil)	120	28.6	5.9	83	30.4	4.3	37	24.6	7.05
R&D as a % of GDP	120	2.18	1.40	83	2.57	1.42	37	1.30	0.86
Regional VC	120	6.08	8.53	83	4.17	8.70	37	10.38	6.37

[5] Both quality indicators are based on the scale: 1–5, where 5 is the highest score.

in licensing income, spends \$176 million on research, employs over five full time workers in the TTO, and spends \$860,000 on external legal fees to protect its intellectual property. Not surprisingly, US universities have higher levels of outputs and inputs, expect that UK universities appear to hire more TTO staff. The UK figures are somewhat skewed universities with zero values for outputs (and thus, many smaller universities) have been excluded from the analysis.

Table II summarizes the specifications of the technology transfer production functions and determinants of relative efficiency equations that we estimated. There are three output specifications: In Model 1, the outputs are the number of USOs and the number of licenses. Model 2 has the number of USOs and licensing income are the two outputs. Model 3 has three outputs: the number of licenses, licensing income, and the number of USOs. For each of these output specifications, we deal with the cross-country analysis in three ways. In version A, we pool the data. In version B, we have a dummy variable for US universities, while in version C, we interact the US university dummy with the production function parameters.

Table III presents the results of two key hypothesis tests. The findings indicate that we can decisively reject the absence of inefficiency. More importantly, the tests reveal that for each output measure, we should have separate production function parameters for US and UK universities. This provides strong support for version C. For simplicity, we present the results for the distance functions using the Cobb–Douglas functional form. More importantly, the findings in Table III provide strong support for the conjecture that US universities are more efficient at technology transfer than UK universities.

TABLE II Specifications of university technology transfer production functions and determinants of relative efficiency.

	1A	1B	1C	1D	1E	2A	2B	2C	2D	2E	3A	3B	3C	3D	3E
Outputs															
USOs	✓	✓	✓	✓	✓	✓	✓	✓	✓	✓	✓	✓	✓	✓	✓
Number of licenses	✓	✓	✓	✓	✓						✓	✓	✓	✓	✓
Licensing income						✓	✓	✓	✓	✓	✓	✓	✓	✓	✓
Inputs															
Total research income	✓	✓	✓	✓	✓	✓	✓	✓	✓	✓	✓	✓	✓	✓	✓
External legal IP expenditure	✓	✓	✓	✓	✓	✓	✓	✓	✓	✓	✓	✓	✓	✓	✓
Number of TTO staff	✓	✓	✓	✓	✓	✓	✓	✓	✓	✓	✓	✓	✓	✓	✓
US × total research income		✓	✓				✓	✓				✓	✓		
US × external legal IP expenditure			✓	✓				✓	✓				✓	✓	
US × number of TTO staff			✓	✓				✓	✓				✓	✓	
Faculty quality × total research income				✓					✓					✓	✓
Faculty quality × external IP expenditure				✓					✓					✓	✓
Faculty quality × number of TTO staff				✓					✓					✓	✓
Inefficiency models															
Dummy for medical school	✓	✓	✓	✓	✓	✓	✓	✓	✓	✓	✓	✓	✓	✓	✓
Dummy for incubator	✓	✓	✓	✓	✓	✓	✓	✓	✓	✓	✓	✓	✓	✓	✓
Dummy for science park	✓	✓	✓	✓	✓	✓	✓	✓	✓	✓	✓	✓	✓	✓	✓
Age of TTO	✓	✓	✓	✓	✓	✓	✓	✓	✓	✓	✓	✓	✓	✓	✓
Proportion of research income from business	✓	✓	✓	✓	✓	✓	✓	✓	✓	✓	✓	✓	✓	✓	✓
Regional GDP per capita	✓	✓	✓	✓	✓	✓	✓	✓	✓	✓	✓	✓	✓	✓	✓
Regional R&D	✓	✓	✓	✓	✓	✓	✓	✓	✓	✓	✓	✓	✓	✓	✓
Regional VC	✓	✓	✓	✓	✓	✓	✓	✓	✓	✓	✓	✓	✓	✓	✓
Faculty quality				✓	✓				✓					✓	
US university dummy		✓					✓		✓				✓		✓

TABLE III   Hypothesis tests (nested models).

Null hypothesis	λ	Critical $\chi^2_{0.95}$ value†	Decision
Output is number of USOs and number of licenses (Model 1)			
There is no significant difference between US production parameters and UK production parameters	$H_0: \beta_{iUS} = 0, i = 1, \ldots, 3$	15.44	7.81	Reject H_0; 1B preferred
There is no technical inefficiency	$H_0: \gamma = 0$	23.69	11.38	Reject H_0
Output is number of USOs and licensing income (Model 2)			
There is no significant difference between US production parameters and UK production parameters	$H_0: \beta_{iUS} = 0, i = 1, \ldots, 3$	14.48	7.81	Reject H_0; 2B preferred
There is no technical inefficiency	$H_0: \gamma = 0$	12.86	11.38	Reject H_0
Output is number of USOs, licensing income and licensing revenue (Model 3)			
There is no significant difference between US production parameters and UK production parameters	$H_0: \beta_{iUS} = 0, i = 1, \ldots, 3$	15.72	7.81	Reject H_0; 3C preferred
There is no technical inefficiency	$H_0: \gamma = 0$	14.49	11.38	Reject H_0

†The critical values for $\gamma = 0$ are obtained from table I of Kodde and Palm (1986) due to the mixed χ^2 distribution. All other tests use regular χ^2 distributions. The degrees of freedom are $q + 1$, where q is the number of parameters which are specified to be 0.

Table IV contains maximum likelihood estimates of the output elasticities of the distance function. The coefficients on STAFF and LEGAL are, for the most part, positive and highly statistically significant. Research income does not appear to be the critical input in this process. The magnitudes of the estimated coefficients are consistent with previous US studies (Siegel *et al.*, 2003a). We also find evidence of constant or decreasing returns to scale. This represents the increase in the normalized output, holding all output ratios constant, since outputs are on the right hand side of the equation. Therefore, in essence it represents increases in all outputs keeping output composition constant, i.e., larger TTOs generate less licenses, income, and spinouts. This is consistent with our previous UK findings (Chapple *et al.*, 2005), which was based on a single output (either number of licenses or licensing income). In the single output case, we found decreasing returns to scale, which we attributed to either 'x inefficiency' in

TABLE IV   Output elasticities of technology transfer inputs.

Input	Model 1C USO + NUMLIC	Model 2C USO and LICINC	Model 3C USO, NUMLIC, LICINC
ε RESINC	0.01 (0.04)	0.07 (0.06)	−0.02 (0.05)
ε STAFF	0.47*** (0.09)	0.38*** (0.11)	0.50*** (0.09)
ε LEGAL	0.44*** (0.12)	0.23 (0.16)	0.44*** (0.11)
Returns to scale parameter	0.92	0.68	0.92

Standard errors are in parentheses.
Significance: *$p < 0.1$; **$p < 0.05$; ***$p < 0.01$.

TABLE V   Estimated average technical efficiency: parsimonious model.

Output	USO, NUMLIC	USO, LICINC	USO, NUMLIC, LICINC
Model	Model 1C	Model 2C	Model 3C
Estimated technical efficiency	0.73	0.80	0.59

larger TTOs or strategies employed by the TTOs being different, whereby licensing was only undertaken for lucrative inventions.

Turning to the technical inefficiency scores, Table V reveals that the average efficiency scores are 0.73, 0.80, and 0.59, using the three different sets of outputs. Computing the average of these three values, which is 70.7, the results suggest that representative institutions could increase technology output by approximately 30%. The results for multiple outputs demonstrate substantially higher levels of efficiency than reported previously for UK universities, where technical efficiency scores were reported as 0.26 (for number of licenses) and 0.29 (licensing income) in single output models (Chapple *et al.*, 2005).

Table VI presents our empirical results relating to the determinants of technical inefficiency. A strong result is that universities with a medical school are more efficient. In contrast, the existence of a university science park does not appear to have an impact on relative efficiency in technology transfer. On the other hand, universities with an incubator appear to be closer to the frontier. This finding is perhaps not surprising, since the stated objective of university incubators is to aid the creation of new firms, typically based on university-owned technologies. However, the age of the university TTO appears to have the opposite effect from that which we proposed. That is, we find that older TTOs are less efficient. One interpretation of this result is that older TTOs are less focused on licensing and, instead, place greater emphasis on alternative mechanisms of technology transfer, such as placement of students and sponsored research.[6]

Direct connections with industry are also important. Universities receiving a higher proportion of their research income from industry are closer to the frontier, although this finding holds only for the three output specifications. Indirect connections between universities and local firms in the region appear to be less important, in terms of explaining the relative efficiency of university technology transfer. Of the regional variables, only R&D activity appears to have significant explanatory power. Contrary to expectations, the availability of venture

TABLE VI   Determinants of technical efficiency: parsimonious model

Inefficiency model: outputs	USO, NUMLIC	USO, LICINC	USO, NUMLIC, LICINC
Model	Model 1C	Model 2C	Model 3C
MED	-0.08^* (0.02)	-0.04^* (0.01)	-0.03^{**} (0.01)
INCUB	-0.02^{**} (0.009)	-0.02 (0.02)	-0.01^{**} (0.005)
SCI	0.13 (0.12)	0.05 (0.10)	0.16 (0.12)
AGE	0.01 (0.06)	0.01^{**} (0.005)	0.02^{**} (0.007)
PROPBUS	-0.02 (0.02)	-0.01 (0.01)	-0.02^{**} (0.008)
REGGDP	0.03 (002)	0.00 (0.01)	-0.01 (0.01)
REGRD	-0.02^{**} (0.01)	0.01 (0.02)	-0.01^{**} (0.004)
REGVC	-0.01 (0.01)	0.01 (0.03)	-0.03 (0.04)

Standard errors are in parentheses. As US dummies are contained in frontier, these are not estimated in the efficiency model.
Significance: $^*p < 0.1$; $^{**}p < 0.05$; $^{***}p < 0.01$.

---

[6] We are indebted to an anonymous referee for raising this issue.

capital within the university's local region does not appear to have any effect on relative performance.

In future research, we intend to include each university's royalty distribution formula (Link and Siegel, 2005), which measures the fraction of the licensing revenue that accrues to the faculty inventor. It might also be useful to separate private and public US universities.

6 DISCUSSION AND CONCLUSIONS

This paper makes two potential contributions to the literature. It is the first cross-country comparison of the relative technology transfer performance of universities. We also extend previous studies by constructing a multiple output distance function, which includes number of licenses, licensing income, and new USOs and equity backed USOs. Previous studies have focused on the number of licenses, licensing income, and university spinout companies in isolation. A key finding is that US universities are more productive than UK universities in technology commercialization.

Our finding that there are constant and possibly, decreasing returns to scale in university technology transfer may reflect the broader-based nature of research disciplines in larger universities. Recent studies suggest that different scientific disciplines require diverse approaches to technology transfer (Owen Smith and Powell, 2001). This could influence the relative importance and feasibility of licensing versus spin-offs between different scientific fields (e.g., life sciences and engineering). Universities may not have the requisite expertise to identify and implement the most appropriate mode of commercialization of inventions across the range of disciplines. This suggests that if universities are to increase the size of their TTOs, they may need to achieve a match between their range of scientific research disciplines and the subject backgrounds of their recruits. Still, based on the evidence presented, we must conclude that there is no evidence to support the assertion that large universities have systematic advantages, relative to smaller institutions.

The finding of the importance of the availability of early stage venture capital, but not venture capital in general, is interesting. Problems associated with UK venture capitalists' investment in early stage high-tech firms are well known (Lockett et al., 2002). There is a need for universities to develop closer links with those venture capital firms that are interested in early stage ventures that are emanating from these research institutions. Not all venture capital firms interested in early stage technology ventures are interested in those created by universities (Wright et al., 2006). Universities need the expertise to recognize and develop strong links with venture capitalists who are interested in investing in spin-offs (so-called 'surrogate' entrepreneurs). An important part of this process may be to ensure that spin-offs are 'investor ready', which may include addressing concerns about the ownership and control of the IP to be incorporated into spin-offs. This lends support to the notion of recruiting more technology transfer officer skills from the private sector and/or attracting business developers from the private sector that want to step into the spin-off during the pre seed phase and develop the business plan.

The analysis suggests implications for policy relating to the balance between spin-offs and licensing in university technology transfer (see e.g., Lambert, 2003; HM Treasury, 2004). The lower TTO efficiency we identify for multiple outputs than for licensing alone emphasizes the need for the development of skills that enable TTOs to select between licensing and spin-off as the most appropriate mode for the commercialization of a particular invention and that there is scope for achieving an appropriate mix of licensing and spin-offs.

It is debatable whether the skills relevant for licensing are synonymous with those required for the development of spin-offs. TTOs' recruitment policies may need to be mindful of the need to identify a range of individuals with different skills. For example, developing links with surrogate entrepreneurs may be appropriate for spin-off activity (Franklin *et al.*, 2001), while establishing and strengthening links with suitable industry partners may be more appropriate for licensing activities. Our measure of human capital relates to the number of TTO staff, without controlling for their expertise or quality. Additional research is needed to explore the importance of these human capital characteristics, in terms of 'explaining' relative performance.

Acknowledgements

We thank Gregory Graff, Catherine Morrison Paul, Matthias Staat, David Zilberman, two anonymous reviewers, and seminar participants at the January 2004 AEA meetings, the June 2004 North American productivity workshop at the University of Toronto, the 2005 second ZEW conference on the economics of innovation and patenting, the March 2007 USDA NC-1034 symposium at the University of California, Berkeley, and the University of California at Riverside for insightful comments and suggestions. The first author gratefully acknowledges financial support from the Alfred P. Sloan Foundation through the NBER project on industrial technology and productivity.

References

Aigner, D., Lovell, C.A.K. and Schmidt, P. (1977) Formulation and Estimation of Stochastic Frontier Production Function Models. *Journal of Econometrics*, **6**(1), 21–37.

Association of University Technology Managers (AUTM) (2001) *The AUTM Licensing Survey*, Fiscal Year 2000.

Battese, G. and Coelli, T. (1995) A Model for Technical Inefficiency Effects in a Stochastic Frontier Production Function for Panel Data. *Empirical Economics*, **20**, 325–332.

Bray, M.J. and Lee, J.N. (2000) University Revenues from Technology Transfer: Licensing Fees vs Equity Positions. *Journal of Business Venturing*, **15**(5/6), 385–392.

Bulut, H., Moschini, G. (2008) US Universities' Net Returns from Patenting and Licensing: A Quantile Regression Analysis. *Economics of Innovation and New Technology*, **18**(2), in press.

Chapple, W., Lockett, A., Siegel, D. and Wright, M. (2005) Assessing the Relative Performance of U.K. University Technology Transfer Offices: Parametric and Non-parametric Evidence. *Research Policy* **34**, 369–384.

DiGregorio, D. and Shane, S. (2003) Why Do Some Universities Generate More Start-ups Than Others? *Research Policy*, **32**(2), 209–227.

Fare, R. and Primont, D. (1995) *Multi-output Production and Duality: Theory and Applications*. Boston, MA: Kluwer Academic Publishers.

Franklin, S., Wright, M. and Lockett, A. (2001) Academic and Surrogate Entrepreneurs in University Spin-out Companies. *Journal of Technology Transfer*, **26**(1–2), 127–141.

Higher Education Statistics Agency (HESA) (2001) *Resources of Higher Education Institutions* (2000/2001). London: Stationery Office.

HM Treasury (2004) *Science and Innovation Investment Framework 2004–2014*. London: HM Treasury/DTIi/ Department for Education and Skills.

Jensen, R. and Thursby, M. (2001) Proofs and Prototypes for Sale: The Licensing of University Inventions. *American Economic Review*, **91**(1), 240–259.

Jondrow, J., Lovell, C.A.K., Materov, I.S. and Schmidt, P. (1982) On the Estimation of Technical Inefficiency in the Stochastic Frontier Production Function Modal. *Journal of Econometrics*, **19**, 233–38.

Kodde, D. and Palm, F. (1986) Wald Criteria for Jointly Testing Equality and Inequality Restrictions. *Econometrica*, **54**, 1243–1248.

Kumbhakar, S.C., Ghosh, S. and McGuckin, J.T. (1991) A Generalized Production Frontier Approach for Estimating Determinants of Inefficiency in US Dairy Farms. *Journal of Business and Economic Statistics*, **9**, 279–286.

Lambert, R. (2003) *Lambert Review of Business–University Collaboration*. London: HMSO.

Link, A.N. and Siegel, D.S. (2005) Generating Science-based Growth: An Econometric Analysis of the Impact of Organizational Incentives on University-Industry Technology Transfer. *European Journal of Finance*, **11**(3), 169–182.

Lockett, A., Murray, G. and Wright, M. (2002) Do UK Venture Capitalists still have a Bias against Technology Investments? *Research Policy*, **31**, 1009–1030.

Meeusen, W. and van den Broeck, J. (1977) Efficiency Estimation from Cobb–Douglas Production Functions with Composed Error. *International Economic Review*, **18**, 435–444.

Owen Smith, J. and Powell, W.W. (2001) To Patent or Not: Faculty Decisions and Institutional Success in Technology Transfer. *Journal of Technology Transfer*, **26**(1–2), 99–114.

Phan, P., Siegel, D. and Wright, M. (2005) Science Parks and Incubators: Observations, Synthesis and Future Research. *Journal of Business Venturing*, **20**(2), 165–182.

Pitt, M.M. and Lee, L. (1981) The Measurement and Sources of Technical Inefficiency in the Indonesian Weaving Industry. *Journal of Development Economics*, **9**, 43–64.

Pressman, L., Guterman, S., Abrams, I., Geist, D. and Nelsen, L. (1995) Pre-production Investment and Jobs Induced by MIT Exclusive Patent Licenses: A Preliminary Model to Measure the Economic Impact of University Licensing. *Journal of the Association of University Technology Managers*, **7**, 77–90.

Reifschneider, D. and Stevenson, R. (1991) Systematic Departures from the Frontier: A Framework for the Analysis of Firm Inefficiency. *International Economic Review*, **32**(3), 715–723.

Sena, V. (1999) Stochastic Frontier Estimation: A Review of the Software Options. *Journal of Applied Econometrics*, **14**(5), 579–586.

Shane, S. (2002) Selling University Technology: Patterns From MIT. *Management Science*, **48**(1), 122–138.

Shane, S. and Stuart, T. (2002) Organizational Endowments and the Performance of University Start-ups. *Management Science*, **48**(1), 154–171.

Siegel, D.S., Waldman, D. and Link, A. (2003a) Assessing the Impact of Organizational Practices on the Relative Productivity of University Technology Transfer Offices: An Exploratory Study. *Research Policy*, **32**(1), 27–48.

Siegel, D.S., Waldman, D., Atwater, L. and Link, A. (2003b) Commercial Knowledge Transfers from Universities to Firms: Improving the Effectiveness of University–Industry Collaboration. *Journal of High Technology Management Research*, **14**, 111–133.

Simar, L. and Wilson, P. (2004) *Estimation and Inference in Two Stage, Semi-parametric Models of Production Processes*. Mimeo, Department of Economics, University of Texas.

Thursby, J.G., Kemp, S. (2002) Growth and Productive Efficiency of University Intellectual Property Licensing. *Research Policy*, **31**, 109–124.

Thursby, J.G. and Thursby, M. (2002) Who is Selling the Ivory Tower? Sources of Growth in University Licensing. *Management Science*, **48**(1), 90–104.

Thursby, J.G., Jensen, R. and Thursby, M.C. (2001) Objectives, Characteristics and Outcomes of University Licensing: A Survey of Major US Universities. *Journal of Technology Transfer*, **26**, 59–72.

Wright, M., Clarysse, B., Lockett, A. and Binks, M. (2006) University Spin-out Companies and Venture Capital. *Research Policy*, **35**(4), 481–501.

PLACING INNOVATION: AN APPROACH TO IDENTIFYING EMERGENT TECHNOLOGICAL ACTIVITY

PHILIP AUERSWALD and RAJENDRA KULKARNI

School of Public Policy, George Mason University, Fairfax, VA, USA

1 INTRODUCTION

Identifying the elements of physical and organizational infrastructure most important for technological innovation is difficult for at least two reasons. The first is that measuring technological innovation is itself difficult. Patents are most often used as an innovation indicator. However, as is well known, patents measure invention (a novel technical idea with market potential) not innovation (the successful application of that idea in markets). Furthermore, significant differences in the propensity to patent exist among different industries, and may also exist between process and product patents. Many innovations are not patented at all.[1] The second reason is that establishing causality is difficult. Hypotheses regarding the drivers of regional innovation are numerous and diverse, making it a challenge to test rigorously the relative impact of each. Furthermore, the identification of innovation determinants is subject generically to an endogeneity problem, as most of the drivers of regional innovative capacity are also affected by regional innovative capacity.

In this paper, we partially address the challenges involved in identifying the elements of physical and organizational infrastructure most important for technological innovation: (1) we describe a new approach to measuring innovation; and (2) we employ this approach both to compare established technology regions with emerging ones and to describe how technologies

---

[1] Alternatives include intellectual property protection through copyright law or trade secret law, or development through an open source model.

migrate as they develop. We do not take on the most difficult challenge: going beyond the identification of correlations to establish causality.

Section 2 describes data and methods. Section 3 presents results. Section 4 concludes.

2 DATA AND METHODS

2.1 Measuring Innovation

Unlike the cross-country study of economic growth that straightforwardly seeks to explain variations in conventionally measured GDP, the study of regional innovation is complicated by the absence of reliable outcome measures. Patents are the most frequently utilized proxy for innovation outcomes.[2] The literature contains numerous approaches to dealing with the variability of patent quality. One approach the focuses on the references to prior art in the patents themselves. The number of references to prior art, also known as 'backward citations', has been argued by some to be an indication of the potential value of a patent. Refinements of this approach have measured the dispersion of citations made across patent classes. The number of claims made in the patent – the manner in which an invention is defined – provides another approach. Both of these approaches (counts of backward citations and counts of claims) have the benefit of being applicable to current patents, but they also have the deficiency of being, in some sense, self-reported. Furthermore, it is not clear *a priori* whether large numbers of backward citations or claims are indicative of a patent that is exceptionally novel, or rather one that is exceptionally derivative and incremental.[3]

It is clear that the quality of an academic article is better measured by the number of references the article receives in the subsequent literature than it might be by, say, counting the number of theorems it proves, or even the number of references it itself contains. It is not surprising, then, to find that a preferred indicator of patent quality is the number of times that the patent is referred to by other patents, known as 'forward citations'. Forward citations link a particular patent to future inventions to which it has in some way contributed. Large numbers of forward citations indicate that a patent has had an impact on the emergence of new technical ideas.

For policy purposes, however, forward citations have a significant drawback: they take many years to accumulate. We can today readily identify the seminal patents that enabled electronic fuel injection systems or combinatorial chemistry. However, those inventions are decades old. Identifying such highly cited patents thus does not directly assist in the task of contemporane-ously identifying emerging technology regions. A method developed by Anthony Breitzman, Diana Hicks, and Patrick Thomas (see Breitzman, 2005 and Thomas and Breitzman, 2006, formerly associated with CHI research) represents an approach to addressing this shortcoming by making use of both backward citations (citations contained within a patent) and forward citations (citations received by a patent) to identify 'emerging technology patents'.

Intuitively, the algorithm is analogous to the ones used by online booksellers to come up with book titles listed under the banner 'Buyers like you also bought these books'. In this case, each purchase is like a backward citation: Buyer A reveals something about his interests by buying a certain book, just as an inventor reveals something about her interests by citing a

---

[2] Acs *et al.* (2002) summarize the problems with using patents as a measure of innovation outcomes: 'Although patents are good indicators of new technology creation, they do not measure the economic value of these technologies (Hall *et al.* 2001). According to Griliches (1979) and Pakes and Griliches (1980, p. 378), "patents are a flawed measure (of innovative output) particularly since not all new innovations are patented and since patents differ greatly in their economic impact."' See also Griliches (1990).

[3] See Lanjouw and Shankerman (1999), Allison *et al.* (2003), and references therein.

previous patent. Furthermore, the fact that Buyer A and Buyer B both bought the same book indicates that the two have something in common; the same holds for Inventor A and Inventor B both citing the same prior patent. If it turns out that six out of seven books purchased in a given month by Buyer A were also among those purchased by Buyer B, we would have a very strong reason to believe both that: (1) Buyers A and B share interests, defining a 'virtual cluster' of book buyers; and (2) the books purchased by both buyers are potentially 'hot' items.

Figure 1(a) and (b) illustrate the manner in which frequently- and recently-cited 'hot' patents define 'virtual clusters' of core technologies (in our analogy, the books purchased),

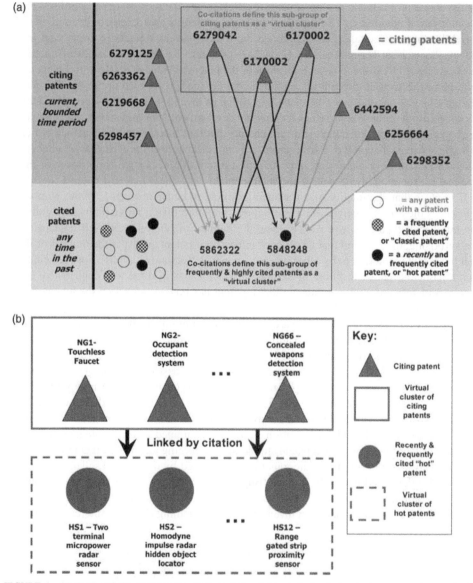

FIGURE 1 (a) (top) and (b) (bottom) Co-citations define 'virtual clusters' of patents, representing particular 'emerging technology patents' (triangles). The frequently- and recently-cited patents we term 'hot patents' (solid circles).

just as the same citations reveal relationships among current patents (in our analogy, the buyers) that are their own 'virtual clusters'. (In the application, it is possible for a 'cluster' to have only one element, and for that single patent to be considered nonetheless an emerging technology patent.)

In more precise terms, then, the Breitzman *et al.* method is in three parts:

Step 1: Select a time period.   The first step is to select one or more time periods for use in the study; in this paper, the time period is January 2001–August 2002. The domain of analysis begins as all utility patents granted between January 2001 and August 2002. We can refer to this set of patents as the '2002 cohort'.

Step 2: Identify a subset of all patents that are both frequently- and recently-cited.   The second step is to look at the citations received by all patents in the domain of study. Note that the citations will include patents not in the 2002 cohort. That is to say that a 2002 patent may cite a patent from 1965 or any other year granted in 2002 or earlier. Therefore, the domain of patents cited by a given cohort contains all patents issued prior to the year of that cohort, going back to 1958, which was the earliest year of patent issuance considered in the study.

For the 2002 patent cohort, fewer than 5% of prior patents received a total of 10 or more total citations from patents in the cohort. The 'hot patents' are ones that not only had 10 or more total citations, but also had a relatively large share of their citations occurring within the selected time period. Specifically, the formula employed by CHI/Breitzman for identifying frequently- and recently-cited 'hot patents' as determined by citations in patents from the 2002 cohort is as follows:

$$\frac{R_i}{C_i} > \frac{(Y_i - 1958)}{K} \quad \text{and} \quad R_i > 9,$$

where R_i denotes the number of citations patent i received from patents published from January 2001 to August 2002; C_i denotes the total number of citations patent i has received; Y_i denotes the publication year of patent i; and K is a calibration constant (in the work reported, $K = 84$).

Just as a 'hot item' in a store is one that is getting a lot of attention from buyers at a certain point in time, we employ the term 'hot patents' to refer to patents that are getting a lot of attention from other inventors at a certain point in time.

Step 3: Identify groups of citing patents that all cite the same frequently- and recently-cited 'hot' patents.   The third and most novel step in the Breitzman *et al.* methodology is to identify subsets of patents within each cohort that cite the same frequently- and recently-cited patent or patents. Where undifferentiated patents in a cohort are a tangled jungle, patents in a cohort sorted using the CHI methodology are something much closer to a tidy orchard, in which trees presenting different pathways of technological discovery are directly identifiable. A particularly large tree represents an emerging technology area. The set of all patents defining all emerging technology areas we refer collectively as the 'emerging technology patents' in the given cohort.

It is important to note that emerging technology branches identified by the way of Breitzman *et al.* methodology are not geographically bounded. They do not necessarily define a local innovation 'cluster'. To the contrary: one potentially interesting aspect of different technology branches is the extent to which the patents of which they are comprised are geographically concentrated or dispersed. Similarly, it is interesting to explore the extent to which the patents comprising a given next-generation technology branch are located in the vicinity of the classic patents from which they collectively originate. We report below on initial investigations along both of these lines of inquiry. In this sense, the concept of an emerging technology branch contrasts both with inter-firm production networks and Porter's spatially situated concept of a 'cluster'.

While the Breitzman *et al.* method described above has distinct advantages over competing approaches, it does not by any means solve all of the problems associated with the measurement of innovation. Two further caveats are particularly warranted: first, at it is based entirely on patent data, the Breitzman *et al.* method does not account for the fact that some innovations are more likely to be protected by patents than others. Second, although intuition and some empirical evidence justify the approach taken, the Breitzman *et al.* method is not yet validated in this context. Additional work (potentially using historical data where ultimate outcomes are known) is required to confirm that the 'emerging technology' citing patents identified by the Breitzman *et al.* methodology are, in fact, more likely than other patents to be of high value and/or to result in commercial innovations. Furthermore, even if additional research is consistent with the claim that the 'emerging technology' patents identified are more likely than others to result in innovations, the question would remain whether the resultant innovations were, on the whole, integrative advancements on existing practice or derivative, incremental improvements. Which of the two turns out to be the case is, clearly, important for the interpretation of results.

2.2   Innovation Correlates

We selected 26 variables to represent four categories of innovation correlates: innovation infrastructure; social capital; creativity and culture; economic context and public policy. Auerswald *et al.* (2007) provides a full list of data sources and of the NAICS definitions relating to variables used.

2.2.1   *Innovation Infrastructure*

Bahrami and Evans (2000) and Kenney and von Burg (2000) are among those to have identified the densely networked set of firms specializing in new firm creation as a form of infrastructure particularly relevant to regional innovation. In a detailed study of Silicon Valley social networks, Castilla *et al.* (2000) note that '[d]ense networks not only within but between sectors of engineers, educators, venture capitalists, lawyers, and accountants are important channels for the diffusion of technical and market information'. These authors argue that innovation today is usually the product of many different types of entities working together. The success of each of these institutional types, the metaphorical equivalents of 'species' in an ecosystem, depends on the presence of others. Institutional species comprising a regional ecology of innovation are conjectured to include not only well-recognized entities such as venture capital firms, large corporations, and universities; but also new forms such as angel networks, angel funds, university and corporate venture capital funds and incubators, experimental R&D programs supported by federal and state governments, fast track regulatory clearance services by state and local governments, and specialized service forms (e.g., in law, real estate, or accounting).[4] Auerswald and Branscomb (2002) refer to the efforts to convert new knowledge into commercial innovations in such a context as 'collective entrepreneurship', addressing the balance, typically required for success, of collaboration between different types of people and of individual visions.

---

[4] Suchman (2000) elaborates on the central role of lawyers in Silicon Valley as brokers of information.

2.2.2 Social Capital

Putnam (1995, 2000) popularized the notion that levels of 'social capital', reflecting the presence of trust and shared values within a community, could be measured via membership to certain institutions including bowling clubs, business associations, and civil social organizations. This work motivates the social capital variables employed in the study. Rather than membership rates, we employ counts of institutions. The institutions selected are intended to reflect the social capital as described by Putnam, rather than later reinterpretations focused more directly on trust and transactions in technology domains (Branscomb, 1996; Fountain, 1998).

2.2.3 Creativity and Culture

A third body of work emphasizes the fundamental role of creative professionals in regional economic development. The conjecture advanced by Florida (2002a, 2002b) is that creative professionals of various types seek to locate near other creative professionals, and that this process of co-location and subsequent interaction is a key driver of economic and innovation outcomes in regions. As a consequence of this dynamic, regions that are more diverse and tolerant will be more innovative (all else equal). As creativity and culture are broad notions, we consider three sub-categories of establishments: arts and craft organizations, professional creative service providers, and religions organizations (hypothesized to be inversely related to the 'new bohemian' variety of creativity suggested by Florida's work).

2.2.4 Economic Context and Public Policy

The domain of policy instruments actually utilized in the USA during the period of study is huge. Within the sub-domain of policy instruments with localized impacts, we selected three as representative of physical and financial infrastructure, respectively:

Business Incubators. In the category of physical infrastructure policies, business incubators are particularly well-defined geographically. While equipment can be moved, buildings cannot.

SBIR Awards. Awards from federal agencies through the small business innovation research (SBIR) program fall in the category of direct financial resources provided to technology entrepreneurs. SBIR awards are of two types: Phase I ($100,000) and Phase II ($750,000). The SBIR program was initiated in 1982. We consider awards from 1992–2002.

ATP Grants. While also a program that awards funds to technology entrepreneurs in a competitive process, the advanced technology program (ATP) differs from the SBIR program in important respects. Two are worth highlighting: (1) ATP awards are considerably larger than SBIR awards; and (2) ATP awards are focused on technology rather than firm development, so large firms are eligible to compete. Data used in this study cover all award years.

SBIR and ATP are, of course, national awards programs. However, as they are competitive programs for which geography is not a consideration in ranking, the actual geographical distribution of awards is highly uneven. (Auerswald *et al.* 2007, Table 3.) It is from this standpoint that we consider impacts of these programs to be localized.

3 RESULTS

3.1 Established Technology Regions

To use patent counts to identify correlates of technological emergence, we emphasize the temporal dimension: 'hot patents' represent a previous generation of invention leading to innovation, 'emerging technology patents' are the new generation. To highlight the shifts that have taken place in one short technological generation (5–10 years) in terms of the geographical dispersion of innovative activity, we compared the top 10% of MSAs ranked in terms of number of inventors of 'hot patents' and 'emerging technology patents', respectively (Auerswald et al. 2007, Table 1). A 100% overlap exists between the two lists of leading technology regions as defined by the frequently- and recently-cited 'hot' patents and by the next generation 'emerging technology patents'. Every MSA present in the list of the top 10% in terms of citing patents is also present in the list of the top 10% of MSAs in terms of emerging technology patents.

Taking this analysis a step further, we can return to the full set of variables introduced earlier characterize the top performing regions. As a baseline, note that the top 10% most innovative MSAs in the mid-1990s (measured in terms of 'hot patent' ranking) account for 44% of the US population. Thus MSAs performing in the top 10% in terms of innovative output are considerably more populous that the average MSA in the US. If, collectively, these regions were to account for exactly 44% of all patents, there would be little left to explain: more people led to more ideas, but per capita patent output was no greater in the top 'hot patent' regions than in other regions. However, as Table I indicates, the top 10% of performing regions accounted for fully 74% of all emerging technology patents – 1.7 times their 'share'[5] if population was the only determinant.

The share of population accounted for by the 10% most innovative MSAs in the mid-1990s (as measured in terms of numbers of cited patents) also helps put results pertaining to other variables into context. As reported in Table I, regions that are disproportionately strong in generating core technology patents also have far greater than the average number per capita[6] of patent lawyers, management consulting firms, theaters featuring live performances, information technology companies, and recipients of awards from the ATP. These variables are identified by superscript 'a' in Table I, and again (to provide an easy comparison) in Table II below.

The strongest technology regions have only slightly more than the average number per capita of SBIR Phase I and Phase II awardees, suggesting that these awards (lower in amounts than the ATP awards) go to firms somewhat more widely distributed throughout the country than the ATP awards. Incubators are also relatively evenly distributed. Like colleges and universities, book stores, business associations, and K-12 schools, incubators are present within the top technology regions at roughly the same rate as they are distributed in other regions.

On a per capita basis, the most innovative regions are home to fewer religious organizations and bowling centers than other regions; in each category, the top 10% of hot patent MSAs have 23% fewer institutions than would be the case if population was the only determinant. The suggestion of a negative correlation with innovative capacity is even stronger when it comes to one particular entertainment category: auto racing. If technology entrepreneurs want to see a NASCAR race, it is likely they will have to travel, as the leading technology regions account for 40% fewer than their population-weighed share of race tracks.

---

[5] Computed as $74\%/44\% = 1.7$.

[6] Specifically: $institutional\ share - population share > 10\%$.

TABLE I   Characteristics of established technology regions.

Variable	Percent accounted for by top 10% most innovative MSAs (2002 cohort)	Divergence from baseline
Innovation infrastructure. Venture capital recipient companies[a]	86%[a]	42%[a]
Innovation infrastructure. Venture capital firms[a]	80%[a]	36%[a]
Emerging technology patents (2002 cohort)[a]	74%[a]	30%[a]
Innovation infrastructure. Patent lawyers[a]	74%[a]	30%[a]
Innovation infrastructure. Hot patents[a]	73%[a]	29%[a]
Policy variable. ATP awards[a]	61%[a]	17%[a]
Creativity and culture – professional. Management consulting[a]	58%[a]	14%[a]
Creativity and culture – art and performance. Live theater[a]	57%[a]	13%[a]
Creativity and culture – professional. Management services[a]	56%[a]	12%[a]
Innovation infrastructure. IT-software companies[a]	55%[a]	11%[a]
Creativity and culture – professional. Architectural services[a]	52%[a]	8%[a]
Policy variable. SBIR Phase I awardees[a]	50%[a]	6%[a]
Creativity and culture – art and performance. Live-band orchestras[a]	50%[a]	6%[a]
Innovation infrastructure. Physical research	49%	5%
Policy variable. SBIR Phase II awardees	48%	4%
Innovation infrastructure. Engineering services	48%	4%
Social capital. Business associations	46%	2%
Innovation infrastructure. Testing labs	46%	2%
Policy variable. Incubators	46%	2%
Creativity and culture – reading, crafts. Book stores	46%	2%
Population 2002	44%	0%
Innovation infrastructure. University R&D funding	44%	0%
Innovation infrastructure. University colleges with more than 1000 employees	42%	−2%
Creativity and culture – reading crafts. Hobby shops	41%	−3%
Social capital. Civic and social associations	38%	−6%
Creativity and culture – art and performance. Museum and art galleries	38%	−6%
Creativity and culture – religion. Religious organizations[b]	35%[b]	−9%[b]
Social capital. Bowling centers[b]	34%[b]	−10%[b]
Creativity and culture – disamenity. Race tracks[b]	27%[b]	−17%[b]
Creativity and culture – disamenity. Correctional facility[b]	25%[b]	−19%[b]

[a]Positive correlates with innovation outcomes (established regions); [b]negative correlates with innovation outcomes (established regions).

With regard to institutions whose presence is negatively correlated with high performance in science-based innovation, the most robust result pertains unsurprisingly to correctional facilities, conjectured to be inversely related to creativity. Compared with their 44% share of the population, the leading hot patents MSAs account for only 25% of correctional facilities in the sample.

3.2 How Technologies Migrate

Advances in fundamental knowledge – basic science on the left hand side of Figure 2 – undergird the innovation system in a modern economy. In the US in 2002, public and private entities invested $50 billion in basic research. Of course, advances in basic science have no impact

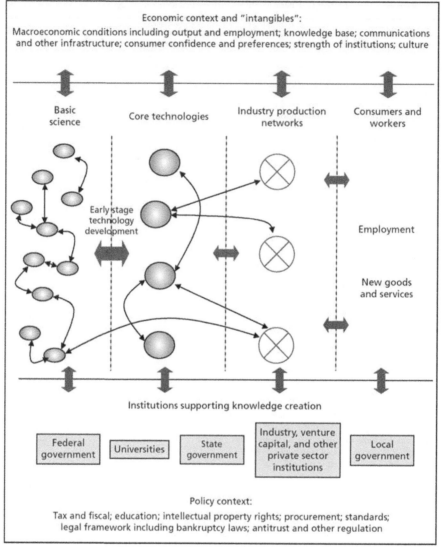

FIGURE 2   Representation of the complex network of resources, capabilities, and institutions that sustain a region's innovative capabilities. Derived in part from Auerswald (2001).

on economic growth or human well-being if they do not translate first into technologies, and ultimately into goods and services. The 'core technologies' represented in the second column of Figure 2 are the direct translation of science into a capability for innovation.[7] A 'core technology space' is a technological sub-domain.

A core technology may be defined by a particular patent or innovation, but then typically branches out in dozens of follow-on patents and innovations (an example is the transistor). Core technologies may link directly to products. However, in most instances, core technologies are employed to improve components of products or processes used to make products.

---

[7] We use 'invention' as shorthand for a commercially promising product or service idea based on new science or technology that is protectable (though not necessarily by patents or copyrights). By 'innovation,' we mean the successful entry of a new science- or technology-based product into a particular market. For further discussion, see Branscomb and Auerswald (2002).

Core technologies cut across conventional industry boundaries. Core technologies may be developed within the university, in an entrepreneurial startup, or, most commonly, in the existing corporation. Developers of core technologies may seek intellectual property protection in different ways, notably including patent protection.

Core technologies typically are combined to create new goods and services. Emergent technology activity refers to a region's developing capability to perform early-stage technology development in one or more core-technology domains. In contrast, when industry production networks are localized, they form 'clusters' of the type described by Porter (1990, 2000), as

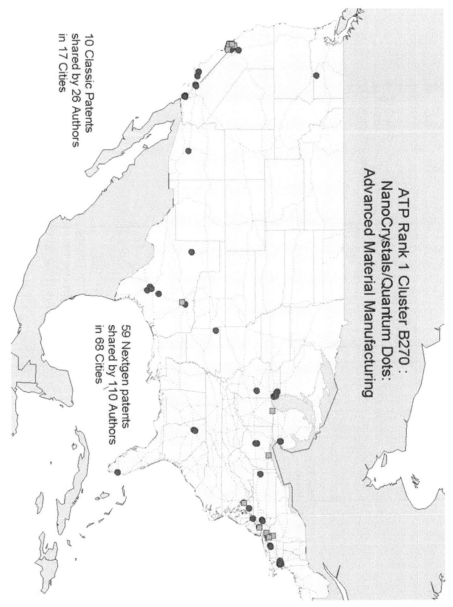

FIGURE 3   The locations of frequently- and recently-cited 'hot patents' (square) and the 'emerging technology patents' (dot) in a core technology space: advanced materials manufacturing – nano crystals/quantum dots (CHI technology category No. B270).

represented in the third column from the left in Figure 2. It is important to emphasize that clusters in this sense are defined in terms of goods and services, not in terms of technologies. A given regional cluster may or may not be intensively engaged in early-stage technology development; however, all clusters attract specialized services, have open membership, and require both cooperation and competition.

We argued in the foregoing that 'hot patents' and 'emerging technology patents' are indicators pertaining to two different generations in the development of core technologies. This point is made more clearly in Figures 3–6, in which plot hot patents and subsequent emerging technology patents for four technology areas prominent in the 2002 patent cohort: advanced

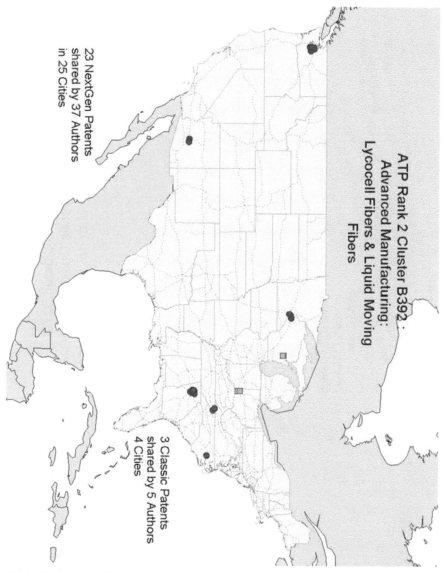

FIGURE 4   The locations of frequently- and recently-cited 'hot patents' (square) and the 'emerging technology patents' (dot) in a core technology space: advanced manufacturing – lycocell fibers and liquid moving fibers (CHI technology category No. B392).

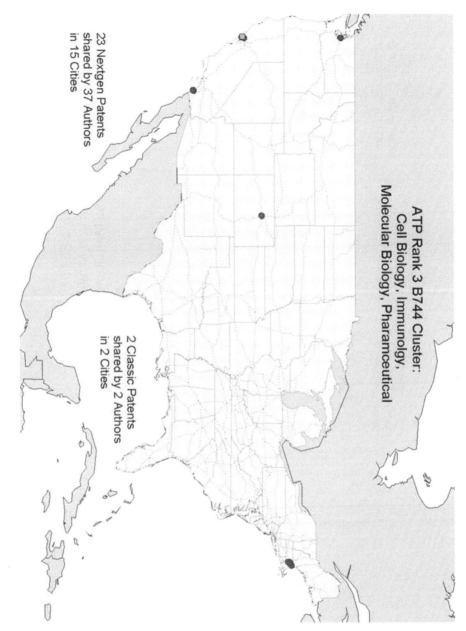

FIGURE 5 The locations of frequently- and recently-cited 'hot patents' (square) and the 'emerging technol-ogy patents' (dot) in a core technology space: intersection of cell biology, immunology, and molecular biology (biotechnology sub-category, CHI technology category No. B544).

materials manufacturing—nano crystals/quantum dots (Fig. 3); advanced manufacturing—lycocell fibers and liquid moving fibers (Fig. 4); cell biology, immunology, molecular biology, pharmaceutical (Fig. 5); and microfluidic and miniaturized systems manufacturing (Fig. 6).

It is clear from these maps that technologies migrate. The 26 inventors responsible for the 10 frequently- and recently-cited hot patents in nano crystals/quantum dots, for example, are concentrated in the four top technology MSAs: San Jose, CA (Silicon Valley); San Francisco, CA; Boston, MA; and New York, NY. The further development of these technologies has taken

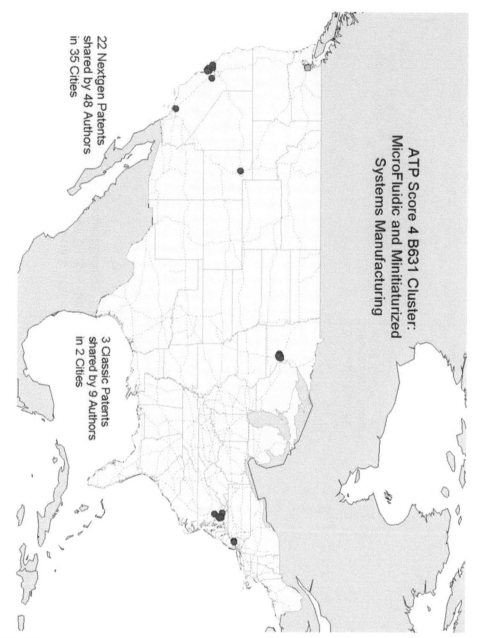

FIGURE 6   The locations of frequently- and recently-cited 'hot patents' (square) and the 'emerging technology patents' (dot) in a core technology space: microfluidic and miniaturized systems manufacturing (CHI technology category No. B631).

place in diverse MSAs from the State of Washington to the bottom of the Florida peninsula. Patents for the lycocell fibers and liquid moving fibers (core technologies in diapers, among other products) have similarly migrated from a pair of Midwest MSAs to a variety of locations, none of which are in the top 10% of hot patent MSAs (Fig. 4). In contrast, the cell biology, immunology, and molecular biology core technology area (Fig. 5) and the microfluidic and miniaturized systems manufacturing core technology area (Fig. 6) both show a concentration

TABLE II Characteristics of emerging technology regions.

Variable	Percent accounted for by highest 10% of MSAs in terms of citing-to-cited ratio (emerging technology regions)	Divergence from baseline
Emerging technology patents (2002 cohort)[a]	16.9%[a]	6.9%[a]
Innovation Infrastructure. Hot patents[a]	13.2%[a]	3.2%[a]
Policy variable. Incubators	12.8%	2.8%
Innovation infrastructure. University Colleges with more than 1000 employees	12.5%	2.5%
Social capital. Civic and social associations	11.9%	1.9%
Innovation infrastructure. Testing labs	11.7%	1.7%
Social capital. Bowling centers[b]	11.4%[b]	1.4%[b]
Social capital. Business associations	11.0%	1.0%
Creativity and culture – professional. Architectural services	10.7%	0.7%
Creativity and culture – religion. Religious organizations[b]	10.6%[b]	0.6%[b]
Creativity and culture – art and performance. Museums and art galleries[b]	10.4%[b]	0.4%[b]
Creativity and culture – disamenity. Race tracks[b]	10.3%[b]	0.3%[b]
Creativity and culture – reading, crafts. Hobby shops	10.3%	0.3%
Innovation infrastructure. Physical research	10.3%	0.3%
Creativity and culture – art and performance. Live-band orchestras	10.3%	0.3%
Creativity and culture – disamenity. Correctional facility[b]	10.3%[b]	0.3%[b]
Creativity and culture — reading, crafts. Book stores	10.1%	0.1%
Innovation infrastructure. University R&D funding	10.1%	0.1%
Innovation infrastructure. Engineering services	10.0%	0.0%
Creativity and culture — professional. Management consulting[a]	9.8%[a]	−0.2%[a]
Innovation infrastructure. IT-software companies[a]	9.5%[a]	−0.5%[a]
Creativity and culture — professional. Management services	9.4%	−0.6%
Creativity and culture – art and performance. Live theater[a]	9.2%[a]	−0.8%[a]
Policy variable. ATP awards[a]	8.9%[a]	−1.1%[a]
Innovation infrastructure. Patent lawyers[a]	8.4%[a]	−1.6%[a]
Population 2002	8.1%	−1.9%
Policy variable. SBIR Phase I awardees	5.4%	−4.6%
Policy variable. SBIR Phase II awardees	4.1%	−5.9%
Innovation infrastructure. Venture capital firms[a]	3.2%[a]	−4.9%[a]
Innovation infrastructure. Venture capital recipient companies[a]	1.8%[a]	−6.3%[a]

[a]Positive correlates with innovation outcomes (established regions); [b]negative correlates with innovation outcomes (established regions).

of inventive activity in a few of the top ten technology MSAs for both generations of technology development.

3.3 Emerging Technology Regions

Given the dynamic of technology development illustrated by Figures 3–6, the relationship between cited patents and citing patents would seem to provide an indication of emerging technology activity. In particular, a simple ratio of citing patents to cited patents provides a measure of the extent to which a region contains people capable of deriving new inventions

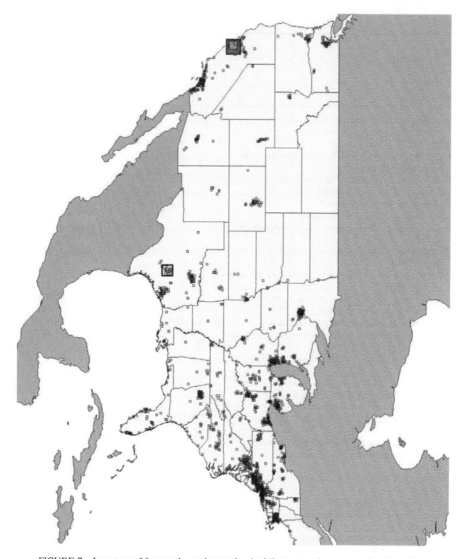

FIGURE 7   Inventors of frequently- and recently-cited 'hot patents', concentrations by cities.

(possibly integrative, possibly derivative) from past inventions.[8] This ratio is the measure we use as a first approximation for emergent technological capability. The cited patents used are the ones we have so far referred to as frequently- and recently-cited 'hot patents'; the citing patents used are the ones we have so far referred to as 'emerging technology patents.'

Ordering MSAs in terms of a citing-to-cited patent ratio (omitting MSAs with no cited patents, to avoid division by zero) yields a very different list of top performers than a ranking based on numbers of hot patents. We will refer to the top 10% of MSAs in terms of a citing-to-

---

[8] An obvious alternative is the difference between the number of emerging technology patents and the number of hot patents. This indicator is highly sensitive to the scale of the overall regional innovation system. For this reason, it tends to rank large MSAs systematically above small ones. Calculating the difference in terms per capita output is a slight improvement, but at the cost of reduced simplicity. The ratio was chosen because it captures the desired phenomenon most directly.

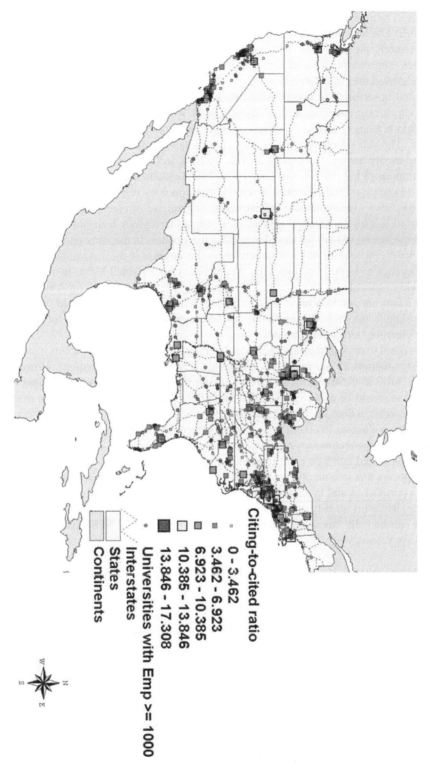

FIGURE 8   Emerging technology regions (cities) identified by the ratio of citing to-cited patents.

cited patent ratio as the 'emerging technology regions.[9]' Their characteristics are summarized in Table II. The indicators are the same as those used in Table I to characterize leading technology regions; the indication of the variables used in that figure to identify apparent positive correlates (superscript 'a') and negative correlates (superscript 'b') of leading technology status is carried over into Table II.

The first observation to make is that, where leading technology regions are substantially larger than average, emerging technology regions are smaller: the average population of leading technology regions is 3,275,179; of emerging technology regions, 569,632; and of all MSAs, 731,062. The second observation is that the emerging technology regions are distributed far more evenly across the country than the leading technology regions: Figure 7 displays concentrations of hot patents, associated with leading technology regions; Figure 8 displays citing-to-cited patent ratios, indicating emerging technology regions.

The data also suggest that the infrastructure and culture of emerging technology regions differ from leading technology regions. The emerging regions lead not only in emerging technology patents (which we would expect, as this count is in the numerator of the ratio) but also in hot patent counts (which is surprising, as this count is in the denominator of the ratio). Emerging regions started out somewhat ahead of comparable small MSAs in the country, and are moving forward at a faster pace. This 'increasing returns to scale' (or 'rich get richer') story is a familiar one in economic geography. While the story does not hold for most of the large leading technology regions, initial evidence indicates that it may hold for the relatively smaller emerging technology regions.

With regard to most of the variables examined in our study other than patents, the emerging technology regions do not appear to differ significantly from other regions. However, surprisingly, firms in these regions have received significantly fewer SBIR Phase I and Phase II awards than would be expected overall. This striking finding requires additional research to clarify. However, it does seem to support the notion that SBIR awards are sought by companies that do not have access to other forms of early stage finance that predominate in leading and, possibly, emerging technology regions.

If citing-to-cited ratios do turn out to indicate technological emergence as we hypothesize, then it appears that in a number of large MSAs, emergent innovative activity is taking place in urban peripheries and in small- to mid-sized cities rather than in established locales. Furthermore, while (as already noted) emergent regions are much smaller than leading regions, they are substantially larger, on average, than MSAs that received no hot patents or emerging technology patents.

4   CONCLUSION

This paper utilizes a novel approach to measuring innovation in order to identify emergent technology clusters. The methodology presented allows for study of the flow of technology from region to region over time. In the twenty-first century, these flows are more likely to cross national boundaries than they are to stay within them. Considerable policy-relevant information could be produced by applying the methodology presented in this report beyond the US to a set of regions distributed globally.

In general, new methods, particularly the tools of geographical information systems (GIS), permit the creation of different and better quality datasets pertaining to regional innovation than have existed in the past. We can expect that further insights on the relationship between infrastructure and regional development will follow as hypotheses regarding the determinants of

---

[9] See Auerswald *et al.* (2007, Table 4), for a list of emerging technology regions.

regional innovation are tested using such datasets in combination with new spatial econometric techniques and other advanced inferential approaches.

Acknowledgements

The work in this paper was supported in part by the US Department of Commerce, National Institute for Standards and Technology (Contract No. SB1341-03-W-1235). The authors thank Lewis Branscomb, Laurie Schintler, and Sean Gorman for their contributions to the broader project of which this paper represents a part; we also thank Connie Chang, Stephanie Shipp and Prasad Gupte for helpful comments provided in the course of the project.

References

Acs, Z.J., Anselin, L. and Varga, A. (2002) Patents and Innovation Counts as Measures of Regional Production of New Knowledge. *Research Policy*, **31**, 1069–1085.

Allison, J.R., Lemley, M.A., Moore, K.A. and Trunkey, R.D. (2003) Valuable Patents. George Mason Law and Economics Research Paper No. 03-31.

Auerswald, P.E. (2001) Competitive Imperatives for the Commonwealth: A Conceptual Framework to Guide the Design of State Economic Strategy. Commonwealth of Massachusetts: Department of Economic Development.

Auerswald, P.E. and Branscomb, L.M. (2002) Spin-offs and Start-ups: The Role of the Entrepreneur in Technology-based Innovation. In Hart, D. (ed.) *The Emergence of Entrepreneurship Policy: Governance, Start-Ups, and Growth in the Knowledge Economy.* Cambridge University Press.

Auerswald, P., Branscomb, L., Gorman, S., Kulkarni, R. and Schintler, L. (2007) Placing Innovation: A Geographical Information Systems (GIS) Approach to Identifying Emergent Technological Activity. Report No. NIST GCR 06–902. Advanced Technology Program, US Department of Commerce, May.

Bahrami, H. and Evans, S. (2000) Flexible Recycling and High-technology Entrepreneurship. In Kenney, M. (ed.) *Understanding Silicon Valley: The Anatomy of an Entrepreneurial Region.* Stanford University Press.

Branscomb, L.M. (1996) Social Capital: The Key Element in Science-based Development. *Annals of the N.Y. Academy of Science*, **798**, 1–8.

Branscomb, L.M. and Auerswald, P.E. (2002) Between Invention and Innovation: A Analysis of Funding for Early Stage Technology Development. Report No. NIST GCR 02–841. Advanced Technology Program, National Institute for Standards and Technology NIST, US Department of Commerce, November.

Breitzman, A. (2005) Automated Identification of Technologically Similar Organizations, *Journal of the American Society for Information Science*, **56**(10), 1015–1023.

Castilla, E.J., Hwang, H., Granovetter, E. and Granovetter, M. (2000) Social Networks in Silicon Valley. In Lee, C.-M., Miller, W.F., Hancock, M.G. and Rowen, H.S. (eds.) *The Silicon Valley Edge.* Stanford University Press.

Florida, R. (2002a) *The Rise of the Creative Class.* New York, NY: Basic Books.

Florida, R. (2002b) The Economic Geography of Talent. *Annals of the Association of American Geographers*, **92**, 743–755.

Fountain, J. (1998) Social Capital: A Key Enabler of Innovation. In Branscomb, L. M. and Keller, J. (eds.) *Investing in Innovation: Creating a Research and Innovation Policy that Works.* Cambridge, MA: MIT Press.

Griliches, Z. (1979) Issues in Assessing the Contribution of R&D to Productivity Growth. *Bell Journal of Economics*, **10**, 92–116.

Griliches, Z. (1990) Patent Statistics as Economic Indicators: A Survey. *Journal of Economic Literature*, **28**, 1661–1707.

Hall, B., Jaffe, A. and Trajtenberg, M. (2001) The NBER Patent Citations Data File: Lessons, Insights and Methodological Tools. WP 8498. National Bureau of Economic Research.

Kenney, M. and von Burg, U. (2000) Institutions and Economies: Creating Silicon Valley. In Kenney, M. (ed.) *Understanding Silicon Valley: The Anatomy of an Entrepreneurial Region.* Stanford University Press.

Lanjouw, J. and Shankerman, M. (1999) The Quality of Ideas: Measuring Innovation with Multiple Indicators. NBER Working Paper No. 7345. National Bureau of Economic Research, September. Available Online at: www.nber.org/papers/w7345.

Pakes, A. and Griliches, Z. (1980) Patents and R&D at the Firm Level: A First Report. *Economic Letters*, **5**, 377–381.

Porter, M.B. (1990) *The Competitive Advantage of Nations.* New York: The Free Press.

Porter, M.B. (2000) Location, Competition, and Economic Development: Local Clusters in a Global Economy. *Economic Development Quarterly*, **14**(1), 15–34.

Putnam, R.D. (1995) Bowling Alone: America's Declining Social Capital. *The Journal of Democracy*, **6**(1), 65–78.

Putnam, R.D. (2000) *Bowling Alone.* New York, NY: Simon & Schuster.

Suchman, M. (2000) Dealmakers and Counselors: Law Firms as Intermediaries in the Development of Silicon Valley. In Kenney, M. (ed.) *Understanding Silicon Valley: The Anatomy of an Entrepreneurial Region.* Stanford University Press.

Thomas, P. and Breitzman, A. (2006) A Method for Identifying Hot Patents and Linking Them to Government-Funded Research. *Research Evaluation*, **15**(2), 142–152.

BARRIERS TO THE DIFFUSION
OF NANOTECHNOLOGY

BARRY BOZEMAN[a], JOHN HARDIN[b,c] and ALBERT N. LINK[d]

[a]*Department of Public Administration and Policy, University of Georgia, Athens, GA, USA*
[b]*Department of Public Policy, University of North Carolina at Chapel Hill, Chapel Hill, NC, USA*
[c]*North Carolina Department of Commerce, Raleigh, NC, USA*
[d]*Department of Economics, University of North Carolina at Greensboro, Greensboro, NC, USA*

1 INTRODUCTION

The 21st Century Nanotechnology Research and Development Act (PL 108-153; hereafter, the Act) was signed into law in December 2003 by US President George W. Bush. It authorized $3.7 billion in federal nanotechnology-related R&D spending over four years, starting in fiscal year 2005. Receiving broad bipartisan support in Congress, the Act put into law the programs and activities supported by the National Nanotechnology Initiative (NNI), one of the President's highest multi-agency R&D priorities.[1] The Act formally made nanotechnology the highest priority funded science and technology effort since the efforts of the United States to win the 'space race' (Choi, 2003).

---

[1] The NNI was promulgated in FY 2001 as part of the Clinton administration's efforts to raise nanoscale science and technology to the level of a federal initiative.

Although there is not a uniformly agreed upon definition of nanotechnology, the widely accepted NNI definition states that:

[Nanotechnology refers to] the understanding and control of matter at dimensions of roughly 1 to 100 nanometers, where unique phenomena enable novel applications.[2]

The US government fostered the NNI, and hence the Act, in part because of the expected economic impact associated with nanoscale science and technology. While estimates of nanotechnology's economic impact vary widely across academic, government, and business experts – ranging from $1 trillion to $2 trillion in 2015[3] – most agree that its future potential is enormous.[4] According to the National Research Council (2002, p. 2):

With potential applications in virtually every existing industry and new applications yet to be discovered, nanoscale science and technology will no doubt emerge as one of the major drivers of economic growth in the first part of the new millennium.

Widespread commercial adoption of nanotechnology is already growing rapidly, and early-commercial applications of nanotechnology have focused on improving existing products in such varied markets as cosmetics, coatings, textiles, and displays. Examples of areas in which nanotechnology is expected to have a high commercial impact in the future include improved chemical and biological sensors (within 1–5 years), new targeted drug therapies (within 5–10 years), and new molecular electronics (in 20+ years) (PCAST, 2005). The extent to which commercial potential in these areas is achieved, however, and the speed with which the United States achieves it, will depend in large part on the extent to which barriers to companies' adoption and integration of nanotechnology can be identified and then lessened.

Perhaps not surprising, given the recent origins of nanotechnology research, there is heretofore no systematic research on barriers inhibiting the diffusion of nanotechnology from the laboratory to commercial application. This void of information is troubling, especially from the perspective of economic growth. Nanotechnology, a general purpose technology as discussed below, is also a key element of technology infrastructure in that it is the foundation to the design, development, deployment, and use of other technologies and technology-based products and processes that are or could be central to the innovation process. This paper provides the first such information.

Based on data collected from a survey of the population of North Carolina companies already using nanotechnology, the paper identifies existing barriers and the extent to which they are perceived by survey respondents as inhibiting the future growth and competitiveness of their companies. North Carolina is one of the states in the United States long recognized as being among the leaders in high-technology research, development and commercialization and, thus, seems a good leading indicator of early prerequisites to the rapid diffusion of nanotechnology research (Luger and Goldstein, 1991; Link, 1995, 2002; Link and Scott, 2003; Fesler et al., 2005).

Section 2 presents a brief historical overview of US efforts to advance nanotechnology.[5] We discuss in Section 3 the population of nanotechnology companies in North Carolina and the methodology used to collect our survey information. Our statistical analysis is presented in Section 4. In Section 5, we provide preliminary policy recommendations for ways to address diffusion barriers and enhance the adoption of nanotechnology.

---

[2] 'Encompassing nanoscale science, engineering and technology, nanotechnology involves imaging, measuring, modeling, and manipulating matter at this length scale' (http://www.nano.gov/).

[3] The $1 trillion estimate is from the National Science Foundation; the $2 trillion estimate is from Lux Research.

[4] Zucker and Darby (forthcoming) provide technology-based information (e.g., patent activity) to support indirectly this conjecture.

[5] The section was prepared with the assistance of Craig Boardman (Bozeman and Boardman, 2004).

2   US EFFORTS TO ADVANCE NANOTECHNOLOGY

The NNI serves as the US government's primary mechanism for supporting nanoscience research and nanotechnology development. Since its inception, the NNI's focus has been to develop an understanding of the novel properties that occur at the nanoscale and to harness the ability to control matter at the atomic and molecular level (PCAST, 2005).

2.1   Activities Setting the Stage for the Nanotechnology Act

Two motivations gave rise to the NNI. First, as mentioned above, nanoscale science and technology are predicted to have an enormous impact on the quality of life throughout the world. Second, at the time the NNI began there were no established major industrial markets for nanotechnology products. Government leadership and funds were deemed necessary to promote technology transfer activities to private industry by accelerating the time required for developing the infrastructure and technologies industry needs to exploit nanotechnology innovations and discoveries.

The NNI began long before the Act was passed. In early 1996, representatives from industry, government, and university laboratories convened to discuss the prospects for nanoscale science and technology. The attempt to coordinate at the federal-level scientific and technical work at the nanoscale began in November of that same year when staff members from six agencies decided to meet regularly to discuss their respective plans for programs in nanoscale science and technology. This group met informally until September 1998, when the National Science and Technology Council (NSTC) designated the group the Interagency Working Group on Nanotechnology (IWGN) under the White House Office of Science and Technology Policy (OSTP).

The IWGN laid the groundwork for the NNI by sponsoring numerous workshops and studies to help to define the state of the art in nanoscale science and technology and to forecast potential future developments in the field. Moreover, the group published reports on the state of the science between July and September 1999, including:

- *Nanostructure Science and Technology: A Worldwide Study*, a report based on the findings of an expert panel that visited nanoscale science and technology laboratories around the world.
- *Nanotechnology Research Directions*, a workshop report with input from academic, private, and government participants.

These two documents supported the IWGN efforts to raise nanoscale science and technology to the level of a national initiative by pointing up the current and potential future impacts of nanotechnology innovations and discoveries, respectively. According to Mihail Roco, Senior Advisor for Nanotechnology at the National Science Foundation (NSF) and primary author of the above reports, this was a crucial time for nanoscale science and technology (Bozeman and Boardman, 2004, p. 17):

> At that moment many looked at nanotechnology as science fiction. So we developed [the NNI] like a science project, from the bottom up. We started first of all to look at the fundamentals that would justify investment and not just to the smallness. We emphasized the new properties, the new phenomena where you have only a few mechanisms that could potentially revolutionize fields from medicine to electronics, as well as benefit society. It was a process to convince people. The NNI was not a decision at the political level.

In August 1999, IWGN drafted its first plan for a national-scale initiative in nanoscale science and technology. Both the President's Council of Advisors on Science and Technology (PCAST) and OSTP were involved in approving the plan.[6] In January 2000, the White House officially announced its endorsement of the NNI and included the initiative in its 2001 budget submission to Congress.

To assist the Clinton administration convince Congress that the NNI should be a top priority, in February 2000 the IWGN prepared another report, *National Nanotechnology Initiative: Leading to the Next Industrial Revolution*, this time to supplement the President's budget request. The report highlighted the nanotechnology funding mechanisms developed for the initiative as well as the funding allocations by each participating federal agency. Moreover, it outlined nanotechnology goals and benchmarks, infrastructure requirements, and it contained examples of already-existing nanotechnology applications and partnerships that would become key components of the NNI.

After the February report, IWGN disbanded and the NSTC's Committee on Technology established the Nanoscale Science, Engineering, and Technology subcommittee (NSET) to fill IWGN's shoes.[7] This 'new' group, which was chaired by Roco and comprised of the same people who staffed IWGN, drafted the NNI implementation plan, *National Nanotechnology Initiative: The Initiative and Its Implementation Plan*. NSET submitted this plan to Congress in July 2000, which was identical to the February report save new sections on interagency management objectives and coordination.

In November 2000, Congress appropriated $422 million for the NNI for fiscal year 2001, raising nanoscale science and technology to the level of a federal initiative. The subsequent activities paved the way to the formalized policies of the Nanotechnology Research and Development Act.

2.2 Events Subsequent to the Passage of the Act

Consistent with that focus, approximately 95% of the funding authorized by the Act was targeted to scientific R&D – roughly 60% for academia and 35% for government laboratories. Thus, by design, and consistent with similar national programs of this type, the NNI's primary purpose is to provide a strong R&D foundation from which industry can select technologies to exploit for commercial purposes.

Even with this strong focus on R&D, advancing nanotechnology commercialization remains a critical component of the NNI. Two examples clearly illustrate this point. First, The 2004 National Nanotechnology Initiative Strategic Plan (hereafter, the Strategic Plan), mandated by the Act, outlined the following four national goals:

1. Maintain a world-class research and development program aimed at realizing the full potential of nanotechnology.

---

[6] PCAST was originally established by President George Bush in 1990 to enable the President to receive advice from the private sector and academic community on technology, scientific research priorities, and math and science education. The organization follows a tradition of Presidential advisory panels on science and technology dating back to Presidents Eisenhower and Truman. Since its creation, PCAST has been expanded and currently consists of 23 members plus the Director of the Office of Science and Technology Policy who serves as the Council's Co-Chair. The council members, distinguished individuals appointed by the President, are drawn from industry, education, and research institutions, and other nongovernmental organizations.

[7] The purpose of the Committee on Technology is to advise and assist the NSTC in improving the overall effectiveness and productivity of federal research and development (R&D) efforts. The Committee will address significant national policy matters that cut across agency boundaries and shall provide a formal mechanism for interagency policy coordination and the development of federal technology activities. The Committee will act to improve the coordination of all federal efforts in technology. This includes creating balanced and comprehensive R&D programs, establishing structures to improve the way the federal government plans and coordinates R&D, and advising the Director, Office of Science and Technology Policy, and the Director, Office of Management and Budget, on R&D budget crosscuts and priorities.

2. Facilitate transfer of new technologies into products for economic growth, jobs, and other public benefit.
3. Develop educational resources, as skilled workforce, and the supporting infrastructure and tools to advance nanotechnology.
4. Support responsible development of nanotechnology.

Underlying the first three goals, particularly the second one, is a fundamental appreciation of nanotechnology's importance to the economy and the need to harness nanotechnology for commercial purposes.

Second, the Act charged the NSTC with developing a plan to utilize federal programs, such as the Small Business Innovation Research (SBIR) program and the Small Business Technology Transfer (STTR) program, to support commercialization of nanotechnology.[8] Consistent with that charge, the Strategic Plan:[9]

> Encourage[s] agencies participating in the NNI to have components of their SBIR and STTR programs focused on nanotechnology topics, and in particular on nanomanufacturing. . .[and to]. . .Facilitate use of NNI-supported user facilities by small businesses that seek and receive SBIR and STTR grants and contracts.

In addition to these two examples, the Strategic Plan documented a number of current activities and plans to support the transfer of nanotechnology discoveries from the laboratory to commercial use. Among these are establishing industry liaison groups; supporting meetings involving industry, government, and industry; establishing and supporting user facilities available to researchers from all sectors; funding multidisciplinary research teams that include industry and university researchers; encouraging the exchange of researchers between universities and industry; establishing centers focused on nanomanufacturing research; and engaging with regional, state, and local nanotechnology initiatives.

Due to the brevity of the NNI's existence, efforts to assess how well it is meeting its goals have only recently begun (e.g. Bozeman and Boardman, 2004). In 2005, the PCAST undertook the first formal US federal government assessment of the NNI: *The National Nanotechnology Initiative at Five Years: Assessment and Recommendations of the National Nanotechnology Advisory Panel* (hereafter, the Assessment). The Assessment's executive summary stresses that (PCAST, 2005, p. 1):

> [The federal government's] substantial and sustained investment in nanotechnology has been largely based on the expectation that that advances in understanding and harnessing novel nanoscale properties will generate broad-ranging economic benefits for our Nation.

With respect to the NNI's progress on issues related to nanotechnology's economic impact, the Assessment found that several industrial sectors have a high and growing level of interest and investment in nanotechnology and are likely to outpace levels of national investment in the near future.

Nanotechnology is, or perhaps more correctly is expected to be, a general purpose technology (Youtie *et al.*, forthcoming). A general purpose technology is an enabling technology, one that when adopted and used is expected to change production and consumption activity and behavior. Bresnahan and Trajtenberg (1995) argue that a general purpose technology has the following three characteristics: pervasiveness, an inherent potential for technological improvements, and innovational complexities that give rise to increasing returns to scale; thus, in a broad sense, general purpose technologies are part of technology infrastructure.[10] And, over

---

[8] The National Science and Technology Council (NSTC) was established by an Executive Order on November 23, 1993. This Cabinet-level Council is the principal means for the President of the United States to coordinate science, space, and technology to coordinate the diverse parts of the federal research and development enterprise. See, http://www.ostp.gov/NSTC/html/NSTC_Home.html.

[9] Here, too, the NNI's recognition of nanotechnology's potential importance to the economy is clear.

[10] Javanovic (1982) and Javanovic and Rousseau (2005) refer to the latter characteristic as 'innovation spawning.'

time, nanotechnology is expected to possess these characteristics.[11] We argue that nanotechnology represents, in the form of a general purpose technology, a technology infrastructure, supporting the conduct of R&D and the application of innovations in production and in other technology-based activities. According to Davey (2003, p. 2):

> All natural materials and systems establish their fundamental properties at the atomic and molecular scale. Consequently, the ability to control matter at the shoes [nano] levels provides the means for tailoring the fundamental properties, phenomena, and processes exactly at the scale where the basic properties are determined.

In an effort to facilitate further nanotechnology transfer from the laboratory (company as well as federal) to the marketplace, the *Assessment* recommended two action steps beyond those outlined in the 2004 Strategic Plan (PCAST, 2005, p. 3):

(1) The NNI's outreach to, and coordination with, the States should be increased.
(2) The NNI should examine how to improve knowledge management of NNI assets.

These recommendations stem from PCAST's position that, while the federal government can take steps to help promote technology transfer, the primary responsibility for funding product manufacturing should be left to the private sector with appropriate assistance from state and local governments.

3   DATA COLLECTION METHODOLOGY AND SURVEY FINDINGS

At the end of 2005, the population of nanotechnology-based or nanotechnology-related companies in North Carolina totaled 40.[12] With the assistance of the North Carolina Board of Science and Technology,[13] the president (or his/her counterpart) of each company within this population of nanotechnology companies was asked to complete a pre-tested survey instrument related to, among other things, barriers to the diffusion of nanotechnology.[14]

Twenty-five of the 40 companies responded to the survey. This represents a 62.5% response. Figure 1 shows the location of each of the 40 companies in North Carolina in relationship to many of the state's universities with nanotechnology research centers. All but two of the companies in the population, one of which did not respond to the survey, are within 30 miles of at least one university-based nanotechnology research center.[15]

Although not the focus of this paper, and thus not an issue in the empirics that follow, it is probably not coincidental that the vast majority of the nanotechnology companies shown in Figure 1 are juxtaposed to the state's research universities. Such location provides the opportunity for the acquisition of new knowledge – tacit knowledge in particular – and easier access

---

[11] David (1990) emphasizes that general purpose technology does not deliver productivity gains on arrival, hence our emphasis on expectations over time.

[12] The 40 companies represent those for which the staff of the North Carolina Board of Science and Technology had a high degree of certainty regarding whether or not they were using nanotechnology. The staff constructed the list by searching the nanotechnology company directories of reputable organizations such as *Small Times Media* and *NanoVIP.com*; soliciting input from academic, corporate, and nonprofit researchers and staff in the state; conducting extensive Internet searches using a variety of relevant search terms; and drawing upon their first-hand knowledge of R&D and commercial activities in the state.

[13] The Board is the state's leading government advisory body on issues related to science- and technology-based economic development. Established in 1963 by the state's legislature and currently housed in the state's Department of Commerce, its mission is to encourage, promote, and support scientific, engineering, and industrial research applications in North Carolina.

[14] This data collection effort by the North Carolina Board of Science and Technology was also part of the state's overall Nanotechnology Initiative. See, http://www.ncscienceandtechnology.com.

[15] Regarding the two companies that are not within the 30-mile radius shown in Figure 1, neither is within 30 miles of a university-based nanotechnology research center nor in another state.

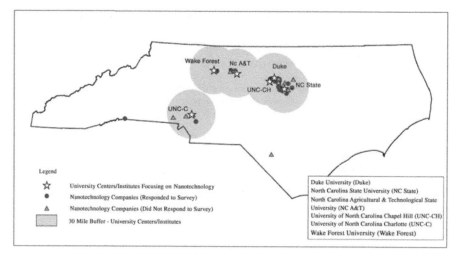

FIGURE 1   Population of nanotechnology companies in North Carolina.

TABLE I   Survey questions related to barriers to the diffusion of nanotechnology.

Regarding the following selected factors for promoting your company's nanotechnology-based growth and
  competitiveness, please respond to the following statements using the response codes -3 = completely
  disagree, -2 = mostly disagree, -1 = somewhat disagree, 0 = neutral, $+1$ = somewhat agree, $+2$ =
  mostly agree, and $+3$ = completely agree:
'My company could grow faster and be more competitive if it:

1. ... had significantly greater access to university faculty who were doing research related to nanotechnology.'
2. ... had significantly greater access to university nanotechnology-related facilities and equipment.'
3. ... had significantly greater access to early-stage capital.'
4. ... had access to a significantly more qualified – in terms of nanotechnology skills – labor force in North
   Carolina.'

to new innovations. The theory of agglomeration economics emphasizes such knowledge
spillovers (Swann, 1998).[16]

The four survey statements that are the focus of this paper are in Table I and the mean
responses ($n = 25$) to each question are in column (2) of Table II. Overall, there was, on
average, 'agreement' to each of the statements, but the greatest agreement was to the statement
about access to early-stage capital. Access to early-stage capital being the greatest barrier is
not surprising because nanoscience is not yet fully understood either in terms of its properties
or capabilities for leveraging the commercialization potential of nanotechnology. As such,
there are aspects of market failure in the capital market because of asymmetry of information
regarding risk and return between a company and a financial institution.[17]

From previous research (e.g. Feller and Roessner, 1995; Lee, 1996), we expected companies
to perceive benefits from an association with a university – its faculty and especially its
facilities (Santoro and Chakrabarti, 2001). Also, because nanoscience and nanotechnology
are only in their infancy, qualified labor is an issue for at least some companies, especially
small companies.

In the following section, we posit an econometric model to explain inter-company differences in the importance of access to the resources listed in Table I. We view a stated company's

---

[16] Scholars have not yet formally tied the geographic nexus among nanotechnology companies and universities to
cluster theory, but we believe that is only a matter of time because the pattern in Figure 1 is certainly not atypical.

[17] For an in-depth discussion of technology-related market failure, see Link and Scott (2005) and Link (2006).

TABLE II Descriptive statistics on the variables.

Variable	Mean (n = 25)	Mean (n = 19)	Standard deviation (n = 19)	Range (n = 19)
Barrier to Growth				
Access to faculty	0.88	1.06	1.59	−2 to +3
Access to equipment	1.20	1.22	1.52	−2 to +3
Access to early-stage capital	1.68	1.61	1.65	−2 to +3
Access to more qualified labor force	1.16	1.39	1.29	−2 to +3
RD	Na	0.67	0.49	0/1
Years	Na	3.94	4.12	1–15
NanoPct	Na	58.03	44.56	0–100
Emp (1000s)	Na	0.18	0.38	0.005–1
Rev ($M)	Na	3.89	0.46	0.025–20

need for greater access to a resource as evidence that there is an existing barrier inhibiting an efficient diffusion of nanotechnology. Thus, the policy question raised by our findings is how to assist companies acquire these needed resources assuming that the existence of the identified barriers represents a market failure.

4 THE STATISTICAL ANALYSIS

To explain inter-company differences in the need for greater access to complementary resources to enhance the diffusion of nanotechnology and thereby facilitate greater nanotechnology-based growth and competitiveness, we posit the following model:

$$\text{ResourceNeed}_i = f(\text{RD, Years, NanoPct, Size}) \qquad (1)$$

where the variable (ResourceNeed_i) represents the ith resource barrier that is inhibiting a greater diffusion of nanotechnology, $i = 1, 2, 3,$ and 4 based on the -3 to $+3$ Likert scale response to each of the four statements in Table I. The greater the value of (ResourceNeed_i), the greater the relative importance of a company needing access to that ith resource.

The four independent variables in Eq. (1) represent selected company characteristics. Emphasizing these variables follows from various niches of economic and innovation theory, but their inclusion in the model in Eq. (1) is also driven by the availability of company-specific information. Estimating Eq. (1) will allow a description of the type of company that is facing a particular resource barrier, and thus substantiate policy recommendations to lessen barriers to the diffusion of nanotechnology.

RD is a dummy variable equalling 1 if the responding company's role in the value chain for nanotechnology is in research and development (as opposed to production of a product or service), and 0 otherwise.[18] All else equal, R&D-based nanotechnology companies may have a differentiated need for resources than other companies farther down the supply chain, and thus may face skilled knowledge and specialized equipment barriers more so than general labor market barriers. To the extent that R&D-based nanotechnology companies have a greater absorptive capacity to utilize efficiently skilled knowledge and specialized equipment, they may have a greater demand for such internally lacking resources. The presence of skilled knowledge and specialized equipment barriers could imply a related need for early-stage

---

[18] Data on company R&D expenditures, in total or as a ratio to a measure of size, were not available.

capital. *Thus, we hypothesize that the estimated coefficient on RD in the university faculty, the university equipment, and early-state capital equations to be positive.*

Years is the number of years the company has been incorporating nanotechnology materials and/or methods into its activities, and thus it measures accumulated experience of the company with the technology and its underlying science base. Holding constant the stage of the company in the supply chain, experience could dampen the company's need for greater access to early-stage capital, but it could also enhance the company's need for each of the other complementary resources. *Thus, we hypothesize that the estimated coefficient on Years to be negative in the early-stage capital equation but positive in the other three equations.*

Finally, companies differ in the extent to which they are involved with nanotechnology. NanoPct is the percent of each company's R&D activities that incorporate or involve the use of nanotechnology-based materials and/or methods. Antonelli (2006, p. 211) noted:

> Localized technological change consists of creative adoption where external knowledge and embodied technologies are implemented with *internal competence* [emphasis added] and idiosyncratic knowledge acquired by means of learning processes.

Internal competence reflects, in part, the pervasiveness of a company's ability to adopt and effectively use nanotechnology. Thus, to the extent that NanoPct reflects such internal competence, *we hypothesize a negative relationship between it and university faculty, university equipment, and labor resources.* To the extent that such experience also dampens a company's need for early-stage capital, *we hypothesize that the estimated coefficient on NanoPct in the early-stage capital to be negative.*

A scale variable is also held constant in alternative specifications of Eq. (1).[19] Size represents the size of the company, and it is measured alternatively as the number of employees (Emp) or total revenue (Rev) in year 2004.[20] We offer no hypothesis about the impact of size on the existence of diffusion barriers.

Data on the four independent variables came from the company survey. Observations on some independent variables, such as Emp and Rev, are missing which reduces the sample size from 25 to 19. Descriptive statistics ($n = 19$) on all of the variables relevant to the estimation of Eq. (1) are in Table II. And, the distribution of responses to the survey questions for the barriers to growth variables are in Table III.

The ordered probit regression results from question (1) are in Table IV. We did not control for response bias to the survey for three related reasons. First, the only data that were available about the non-respondents was distance – miles to the nearest university. The mean distance for the sample of 19 responding companies was not statistically different from the mean distance for the sample of 6 non-responding companies. Second, there was no *a priori* argument to hypothesize why a company would respond or would not respond. And third, Figure 1 shows clearly that all but two of the population companies are within 30 miles of a university nanotechnology research center. We did test for non-linear effects in Eq. (1) but none were present; we also considered Emp and Rev entering logarithmically in Eq. (1), but while the sign pattern on these variables was the same as reported in Table IV, the level of significance was lower.[21] Finally, Emp and Rev are highly co-linear – the correlation coefficient is 0.859 and highly significant – so each was considered separately in the estimation.

Not all of our hypotheses are confirmed, but the results are nevertheless informative. R&D-based companies have a greater probability of completely agreeing (see the response scale in

---

[19] *Size* also allows for an indirect test of Gilbrat's Law. Gilbrat's Law states that the size of a company and its growth rate are independent, although the empirical evidence is mixed (Sutton, 1997). We hypothesize that it follows that the size of a company and its need for resources that generate growth are also independent.

[20] When either employment (1000s) or revenues ($M) were reported on the survey as a range of values, the mid-point of the range was used.

[21] These results are available upon request from the authors.

TABLE III   Discrete response profiles of the barriers to growth variables.

Variable	Distribution of responses						
Access to:	−3	−2	−1	0	+1	+2	+3
Faculty (%)	0	5.6	16.7	11.1	22.2	22.2	22.2
Equipment (%)	0	11.1	0	33.3	22.2	22.2	22.2
Early-stage capital (%)	0	5.6	5.6	16.7	16.7	5.6	50
More qualified labor force (%)	0	5.6	0	11.1	38.9	22.2	22.2

Note: Percentages may not sum to 100 due to rounding.

TABLE IV   Ordered probit regression results from Eq. (1) (standard errors in parentheses; $n = 19$).

Variable	Access to University faculty		Access to University equipment		Access to early-stage capital		Access to more qualified labor force	
RD	0.0004	−0.170	3.184*	2.249**	3.258*	2.978*	0.569	0.715
	(0.943)	(0.899)	(1.222)	(1.014)	(1.230)	(1.146)	(0.938)	(0.899)
Years	0.271**	0.279**	0.004	−0.053	0.019	−0.063	0.037	0.038
	(0.124)	(0.118)	(0.083)	(0.070)	(0.089)	(0.72)	(0.86)	(0.073)
NanoPct	−0.003	0.0005	−0.028***	−0.015	−0.035**	−0.032**	0.0006	−0.002
	(0.012)	(0.012)	(0.014)	(0.012)	(0.015)	(0.014)	(0.012)	(0.012)
Emp	−	0.719	−	−0.019	−	−1.923***	−	−0.446
		(1.061)		(1.063)		(1.149)		(1.051)
Rev	0.016	−	−0.100	−	−0.162***	−	−0.008	−
	(0.073)		(0.081)		(0.089)		(0.074)	
Intercept	1.165	1.016	1.471**	1.109***	2.696*	2.682*	1.115	1.207
	(0.823)	(0.838)	(0.689)	(0.666)	(1.043)	(1.009)	(0.691)	(0.711)
Threshold parameters								
μ_1	1.009***	0.992***	0.637	0.578	0.744	0.678	0.649	0.634
	(0.531)	(0.525)	(0.412)	(0.374)	(0.736)	(0.660)	(0.438)	(0.427)
μ_2	1.395**	1.379**	1.855*	1.789*	1.658**	1.574**	1.763*	1.758*
	(0.565)	(0.561)	(0.547)	(0.530)	(0.841)	(0.775)	(0.528)	(0.522)
μ_3	2.125*	2.145*	2.649*	2.567*	2.224**	2.134*	2.438*	2.444*
	(0.617)	(0.619)	(0.615)	(0.597)	(0.867)	(0.802)	(0.573)	(0.567)
μ_4	3.084*	3.126*			2.382*	2.295*		
	(0.697)	(0.700)			(0.870)	(0.806)		
μ_5								
Log-likelihood	−25.45	−25.24	−23.05	−23.85	−21.50	−21.71	−25.10	−25.02

Key: *significant at the 0.01-level or greater; **significant at the 0.05-level; ***significant at the 0.10-level.
Note: The pattern of significant variables mirrors OLS results, which are available upon request from the authors.

Table I) that access to university equipment and early-stage capital is a barrier to the diffusion of nanotechnology. The case studies of emerging technologies by Link (1996) and Link and Scott (1998) demonstrate that even the most experienced R&D companies rarely have sufficient equipment or complementary facilities to keep pace with the technology, and rarely are they willing to invest in such equipment or facilities until the technology becomes more mature.

Companies with greater nanotechnology experience have a higher probability of completely agreeing that greater access to university faculty is a barrier to the diffusion of nanotechnology, perhaps suggesting a minimum efficient level of internal knowledge is needed before accessing faculty expertise. If so, this would conform to evidence from previous studies of need and use of technical expertise.[22] Hall *et al.*,'s (2003, p. 491) analysis concludes that university faculty are included in:

> ...research projects that involve what we have called *new* science. Industrial research participants perceive that the university could provide research insight that is anticipatory of future research problems and could be an ombudsman anticipating and translating to all the complex nature of the research being undertaken.

Some internal resource base or experience base is thus needed for such university insights to be useful.

The more pervasive nanotechnology is within a company's operations the greater the probability of completely disagreeing that a barrier to the diffusion of nanotechnology is greater access to university equipment or early-stage capital. The latter finding is almost definitional because a company would not be in an early stage of technology development if the technology was pervasive. That the need for university equipment is not a barrier to the diffusion of nanotechnology in companies in which nanotechnology is more broadly utilized could be interpreted to mean that relevant scientific equipment is already in-house otherwise nanotechnology would not be so broadly utilized.

Finally, there is only very weak evidence that, in smaller companies, the probability of completely disagreeing that access to early-stage capital is a barrier to the diffusion of nanotechnology. And, regardless of the size of the company, access to a qualified labor force is not systematically a barrier to the diffusion of nanotechnology.

5   CONCLUSIONS

Although the empirical findings in Table IV represent the only quantitative information about barriers to the diffusion of nanotechnology, they must nevertheless be interpreted very cautiously. Mitigating the fact that we surveyed the population of nanotechnology companies in North Carolina, we have no way to determine if the population of nanotechnology companies in North Carolina is representative of the national population.[23] And, we lack information about the non-responding companies in the population of North Carolina nanotechnology companies

In fact, what we do not know about each company may be more important than what we do know. For example, we do not know if a company is a university spin-off (Libaers *et al.*, 2006). If it is, it could view access to university faculty and equipment differently than a company that is not (Steffensen *et al.*, 2000). Also, we have no information about how effectively a company utilized its existing nanotechnology intellectual property and process technology. A company that is more efficient in its use of the extant technology could also view access to university faculty and equipment differently especially if the company utilizes university faculty to help it overcome technology-based research problems and especially at the basic end of the R&D spectrum (Hall *et al.*, 2003).

With these caveats in mind, we offer two specific recommendations to ameliorate barriers to the diffusion of nanotechnology that follow from the findings in Table IV. First, there is a market failure in the capital market because of asymmetry of information about the risk and return associated with the adoption of nanotechnology and its impact on commercialization. While policy makers cannot solve this problem, state governments could act as venture capitalists in this regard in much the same way as the SBIR program acts as venture capitalist for

---

[22] See Bozeman (2000) for a review of this literature.

[23] In fact, there is uncertainly about the present size of the national population of US nanotechnology companies. One estimate places the total at 391. See, www.nanotech-now.com/business.htm. Another estimate is 860. See, www.nanovip.com/directory/International/index.php. Lux Research estimates the US population of nanotechnology companies at 1100. These differences are, in all likelihood, due to differences in the definition of nanotechnology.

agency-needed technologies. The step would not be unprecedented inasmuch as some states, most recently the State of Ohio (2005), have already developed legislation to permit state government venture capital funding. Second, states could provide incentives to universities for sharing capital equipment and facilities with nanotechnology companies. Such a policy effort would likely raise issues as to why nanotechnology and not some other burgeoning technology. One way to counter that argument is, say, for states to establish at public universities public/private partnership centers of excellence whereby new equipment is provided by the state with an understanding that its use is to foster partnerships with the private sector. Such activity would be in line with existing state policies in the many centers of excellence programs (Plosila, 2004).

Additional policy prescriptions await the emergence of more quantitative information about the economic impact potential of nanotechnology, in general, and the diffusion of nanotechnology, in particular. In the United States, early activities seem to indicate a continuing strong role not only for the federal government but also many state governments.

References

Antonelli, C. (2006) Diffusion as a Process of Creative Adoption. *Journal of Technology Transfer*, **31**, 211–226.

Bozeman, B. (2000) Technology Transfer and Public Policy: A Review of Research and Theory. *Research Policy*, **29**, 627–655.

Bozeman, B. and Boardman, C. (2004) Research and Technology Collaboration and Linkages: The Case of the National Nanotechnology Initiative. Report to the Council of Science and Technology Advisors. Ottawa, Canada: Study of Federal Science and Technology Linkages, July 2004.

Bresnahan, T.F. and Trajtenberg, M. (1995) General Purpose Technologies: Engines of Growth? *Journal of Econometrics*, **65**, 83–108.

Choi, C. (2003) Analysis: Nano Bill Not Just a Grand Gesture; It Promises Real Results. *Small Times Media*, December 5, 2003. Available online at: www.smalltimes.com/document_display.cfm?document_id=7049. Accessed on October 18, 2006.

Davey, M.E. (2003) Manipulating Molecules: The National Nanotechnology Initiative. CRS Report for Congress, May 23.

David, P.A. (1990) The Dynamo and the Computer: An Historical Perspective on the Modern Productivity Paradox. *American Economic Review*, **80**, 355–361.

Fesler, E., Sweeney, S. and Renski, H. (2005) A Descriptive Analysis of Discrete U.S. Industrial Complexes. *Journal of Regional Science*, **45**, 395–419.

Feller, I. and Roessner, D. (1995). What Does Industry Expect from University Partnerships? *Issues in Science and Technology, Fall*, 80–84.

Hall, B.H., Link, A.N. and Scott, J.T. (2003) Universities as Research Partners. *Review of Economics and Statistics*, **85**, 485–491.

Jovanovic, B. (1982) Selection and the Evolution of Industry. *Econometrica*, **50**, 649–670.

Jovanovic, B. and Rousseau, P.L. (2005) General Purpose Technologies. NBER Working Paper 11093, January

Lee, Y. (1996) Technology Transfer and the Research University: A Search for the Boundaries of University–Industry Collaboration. *Research Policy*, **25**, 843–863.

Libaers, D., Meyer, M. and Guena, A. (2006) The Role of University Spinout Companies in an Emerging Technology: The Case of Nanotechnology. *Journal of Technology Transfer*, **31**, 443–450.

Link, A.N. (1995) *A Generosity of Spirit: The Early History of Research Triangle Park*, Research Triangle Park: The Research Triangle Foundation of North Carolina.

Link, A.N. (1996) *Evaluating Public Sector Research and Development*. New York: Praeger.

Link, A.N. (2002) *From Seed to Harvest: The Growth of Research Triangle Park*. Research Triangle Park: The Research Triangle Foundation of North Carolina.

Link, A.N. (2006) *Public/Private Partnerships: Innovation Strategies and Policy Alternatives*. New York: Springer.

Link, A.N. and Scott, J.T. (1998) *Public Accountability: Evaluating Technology-Based Institutions*. Norwell, Mass.: Kluwer Academic Publishers.

Link, A.N. and Scott, J.T. (2003) The Growth of Research Triangle Park. *Small Business Economics*, **20**, 167–175.

Link, A.N. and Scott, J.T. (2005) *Evaluating Public Research Institutions: The U.S. Advanced Technology Program's Intramural Research Initiative*. London: Routledge.

Luger, M. and Goldstein, H. (1991) *Technology in the Garden*. Chapel Hill: University of North Carolina Press.

Lux Research. Available online at: www.luxresearchinc.com. Accessed on October 18, 2006.

National Nanotechnology Initiative. Available online at: www.nano.gov. Accessed on October 18, 2006.

National Research Council (NRC) (2002) Small Wonders, Endless Frontiers: A Review of the National Nanotechnology Initiative, Washington, D.C.: National Academy Press. Available online at: www.nap.edu/ books/0309084547/html. Accessed on October 18, 2006.

National Science and Technology Council (NSTC), Nanoscale Science, Engineering and Technology Subcommittee (NSET) (2004) The National Nanotechnology Initiative: Strategic Plan, Washington, D.C.: The Council. Available online at: www.nano.gov/NNI_Strategic_Plan_2004.pdf. Accessed on October 18, 2006.

National Science Foundation. Available online at: www.nsf.gov. Accessed on October 18, 2006.

Plosila, W. (2004) State Science- and Technology-Based Economic Development Policy: History, Trends and Developments, and Future Directions. *Economic Development Quarterly*, **18**, 113–126.

President's Council of Advisors on Science and Technology (PCAST) (2005) The National Nanotechnology Initiative at Five Years: Assessments and Recommendations of the National Nanotechnology Advisory Panel. Washington, DC: Executive Office of the President. Available online at: www.nano.gov/html/res/ Final_PCAST_Nano_report.pdf. Accessed on October 18, 2006.

Santoro, M. and Chakrabarti, A. (2001) Corporate Strategic Objectives for Establishing Relationships with University Research Centers. *IEEE Transactions on Engineering Management*, **48**, 157–163.

Steffensen, M., Rogers, E.M. and Speakman, K. (2000) Spin-offs from Research Centers at a Research University. Journal of Business Venturing, **15**, 93–111.

State of Ohio (2005) *Ohio Revised Code* Title 1. State Government Chapter 150. Venture Capital Program. http://codes.ohio.gov/orc/1. Accessed on October 18, 2006.

Swann, G.M.P. (1998) 'Towards a Model of Clustering in High-Technology Industries.' In Swann, G.M.P., Prevezer, M. and Stout, D. (eds.) *The Dynamics of Industrial Clustering*. Oxford: Oxford University Press.

Sutton, J. (1997) Gilbrat's Legacy. *Journal of Economic Literature*, **35**, 40–59.

Youtie, J., Iacopetta, M. and Graham, S. (2007) Assessing the Nature of Nanotechnology: Can We Uncover an Emerging General Purpose Technology? *Journal of Technology Transfer*, **32**(6), 123–130.

Zucker, L.G. and Darby, M.R. (forthcoming) Evolution of Nanotechnology from Science to Firm. *Journal of Technology Transfer*.

Index

Page numbers in *Italics* represent tables.
Page numbers in **Bold** represent figures.

Printed and bound by CPI Group (UK) Ltd, Croydon, CR0 4YY
01/05/2025
01858365-0003